All That Changes From My Front Porch

Downsizing wants and having more life

By Kate Singh

Author of Dirt Poor And Lovin' It!

Table Of Contents

Chapter 1

Winter going into Spring

This book is a collection of daily writings. At the beginning of January 2022, I felt the best thing to do for my family was to remove the internet from our house and for me to stop doing all the hustles of working online. It was time to slow down, unplug, and go into the wilderness, figuratively. I called Xfinity, shut off the internet, and stripped our budget down to the shelter, food, water, heat, solar, two cell phones, and gas for the vehicles. It took me about three days to sort through the extras with my bank statements and discontinue all the little services until we were bare bones.

I have been stripping down and stocking up for a year, preparing for an easier life. I was addicted to working too much. I always tried to make more money, build up my YouTube channel, and sell more books. It was never enough. Many of us are like this. We are like Gollum with the Ring in Lord Of The Rings. Gollum was obsessed with the Ring, which turned him into a soulless, ugly creature. We get our sights on a shiny object and work like crazy with such focus that we forget about our lives. We remove the shiny Ring, and the focus returns to our lives and sanity. Like many of us, the Ring represented my hustles and constant work.

I love watching documentaries about Zen monks. I have no desire to be one, but I want our life to feel like their lives look. I began to have a vision and a robust emotional push to do some major weeding out of what was not life-sustaining for the family. Chasing money and popularity is life-draining. Finding that contented bliss from doing things from the heart is life-giving. A decluttered house is life-giving. A crowded place is energy-draining.

Homemaking can become tiring. It is a formula that we do daily. I get up each morning and cook and clean every day. It gets old. Naturally, all jobs get old at some point if we don't make them exciting and use our imaginations. That is the journey. We are finding that perfect balance between enjoying life and prioritizing our goals. How do we create a productive life that nourishes our souls?

I want to work less. I need more rest to heal from years of burnout that have occurred throughout my life. I needed a long, deep year of peace and rest. We needed to stop spending extra money and get back to living under one paycheck. However, we had been living on much more than that for the last couple of years. My husband made very little, but we were comfortable with my royalties from books and YouTube, all the stimulus checks during the quarantine, advanced child credits, and tax returns.

At the beginning of 2022, I stopped working for a few months. No more stimulus checks or advanced tax credits were coming. Bali was only bringing home around $2600 a month. We had some debt from renovating the house, mainly a giant Home Depot credit card bill. Then the car broke down, the dog needed teeth pulled, and you know how it goes. There will always be something that will need care. "I'll take time off once we pay off this...or take care of that...or get this one thing done..." It will go on forever. You just jump in and have faith that the Universe will meet you on the path with support and help when needed.

I quit at an inconvenient time. We were overdrawn at the bank weekly and had debt, car repairs, and vet bills happening in rapid fire.

But I shut it all down and fled to a safe oasis.

My boys will only be boys for a short time. They will be confused young men one day, and that is another drama. But pure childhood is a flash in the pan. So I made my family my priority and home management my daily job. I have never been more content overall. Some moments are almost too small and infrequent to mention.

Our money situation did straighten out within five months. It was partly due to the new budget and all that "discontinuing" of small money drains. It came from having bare-bones bills, and some incredible money windfalls occurred, such as a tax return and a refund check from our previous house insurance.

I'm still working on balancing living on a small budget without hustling all the time. We like to go out and eat sometimes. We love shopping at fancy health food stores and buying quality ingredients. I love the movie theater, which costs half an arm and leg. So, we do those things now and then and enjoy life, but at least 90% of the time, if not more, we do things at home. We do things in a frugal and thrifty way.

We have a vast movie library at home because we only have the DVD player in our unplugged lives. We have stacks of novels and more movies from the library scattered and stacked about our humble abode. We are preparing to set up a large above-ground pool for this summer. Sam and I have been planning our little Oasis in the pool area of the yard. We have big ideas; the fun part is figuring out how to do them without spending much. You find what you already own and work with it as much as possible to save expenses. I've had to find cheap alternatives for our big ideas and wants.

Instead of a **$60,000** in-ground pool, we purchased a **$350** above-ground pool from Habitat For Humanity. I don't know how well it's going to work, but it looks fun, and I saw a news clip of a frugal mother who bought an above-ground pool for her kids off Craigslist. It looked great with kids splashing about during a heat wave. So, I see it as we will enjoy this pool just as much as a big, inground pool, but we saved ourselves **$59,650**.

This book is my journey of creating a Zen-like but modern life with a rich mix of old-fashioned and homemade. We enjoy lovely life luxuries like good coffee or a night at the movies without breaking the bank, finding contentment at home, and finding ways to make it more creative and nurturing to our souls. And to see that without the outside world's distractions, do we heighten our other senses and find a world of more meaning and happiness?

So far, I have enjoyed slowing down and clearing my schedule book. I only have to get up, appreciate that first mug of coffee, and decide what might interest me each day. Is it my laundry or my garden today? Is it organizing my pantry or rearranging and deep cleaning the living room? Or maybe I just want to walk into town with the boys and Molly, then come home and watch movies we chose from the library and popcorn we pop in a big pot on the stove.

So far, life keeps getting more straightforward, and I'm observing such delightful side effects for myself and my family. I don't know if I'll ever want to bring the internet back into the house. I just might cry the day I receive the Xfinity modem.

I'm keeping a journal. I share movies, books, and some ideas or tips for saving money, shopping, living, and working.

I started journaling our experience, and if you are reading this now, I decided it was worth publishing. Perhaps it will comfort you or inspire you to change your lifestyle. Many things in this book may resonate with you and cause shifts and growth. Who knows, but I hope this book has a positive effect on whom ever picks it up.

One last thing. I started changing our lifestyle over a period of more than two years. Part of it was large-scale, such as moving to another town. We moved from a struggling little town on flat farmland to a thriving old town in the forest. We went from living across the street from a slum apartment with cops making grand entrances there weekly to being surrounded by natural beauty and peace. Once we moved to this town and into a charming, old 121-year-old house, I began to nest, and that involved a lot of decluttering and changing everything from the home to my mind. I have become so interested in simplifying our lives so we can enjoy more natural living. I didn't realize until reading this writing that I was self-soothing. I was stripping things down to focus on only what is precious and vital to me. My beautiful boys and family are precious to me. My family is my world. I love who I've become as a mother and homemaker. Unfortunately, over the years, I became so busy writing books and blogs and making content for a YouTube channel. I became focused on working and making money and lost that calm, loving internal state of being. I was waking up with guilt and stress. The book *Essentialism* by Greg McKeown was suggested, and after reading it several times, I began weeding our life of nonessentials. One thing led to another, and it became about how could I make our life slow, sweet, calm, and natural. Could we go back in time somewhat and create a life before internet and social media became front and center in our lives? And could we work less and still live comfortably?

I started making serious changes a few months before I started this book. I was unplugging the modem during the day and journaling my feelings. I found three composition books filled with my writing just the other day. I started writing in September 2021. We were so addicted to the internet and video games at that point that I had to remove the internet slowly, and it caused a lot of drama. I wrote about the boy's mood swinging and wandering around, lost and confused as if they had been unplugged directly from some source. I would hide in the bathroom to check my channel on my cell phone. It was pathetic. By January, I eradicated the internet and started reducing bills so I wouldn't have to work so much.

A journey may start with one step, but when you get a few miles into the path, it becomes a many-layered adventure. One thing leads to another and another. One path leads to another and different people and valleys and villages. So, this book will end, but our journey will go on and become more interesting each season because making a few little changes opens up the eyes and mind to change more and more things.

Chapter 2

A New Year, New Lifestyle

Monday

Today we are switching out the cell plans to Mint Mobil. This is one part of many parts to reduce our monthly bills. Thus far, I have cut $700 from the budget.

I'm trying to work with a $300 monthly grocery bill, which is not easy. I ambitiously thought I could do our groceries, dog food, bird feed, toiletries, and extras on this paltry sum. Fortunately, I stocked up on homemade cleaning ingredients such as Dawn, baking soda, and white vinegar by the gallon. I stocked up on laundry soap and toiletries. However, dog food is dwindling. I've been stretching out the canned dog food that I add into the dry kibble by adding bacon grease I save from cooking. I even found a can of pumpkin and used that as well.

The days are slowing down, I have more time, and I enjoy each day more than the last.

I made handmade perogies the other day. The perogies require some work, and it was a big batch. They took me three hours. They were delicious little sleep bombs. I boiled then fried them in a bit of butter. I ate two (I made them twice the average size. They were like small calzones) and was full and ready for a nap. I found this recipe in **Good And Cheap** by Leanne Brown. She put together this book for people on food stamps. You can download a free copy from her website if you have internet.

I've been enjoying my day's homemaking. I've been planting clay pots of herbs and saving cans from canned foods to plant tomato and cucumber seeds. I have the pots and cans on my kitchen table under the windows, one in the living room window, and one outside on the porch.

I rearranged the living room for the first time in ages, and it feels a little roomier. I did some purging, but I did so much decluttering last year that it's just small items and clothes. I put a box out on the street, and I have one started with odds and ends. I set up the whiteboard in the kitchen, and on it, I have menu ideas, a grocery list I add to as I think of things, and my planting guide.

I've been cooking from scratch and baking all our bread faithfully. I need to bake two loaves of wheat, two loaves of white Amish, and one loaf in the bread machine. We eat it for sandwiches and toast, cinnamon toast, and nighttime snacks of toast with butter and honey. Everybody loves bread! Even the dogs.

The Amish bread makes decent sandwiches, but the slices are thick. We had the best tuna sandwiches yesterday. We ate the bread straight out of the oven greedily, and I had to slice it thick so it wouldn't fall apart. We had open-faced with extra lettuce and cheese and pickles. It was so good and messy!

My love for reading has returned. I may take my novel and read in the hammock on the porch or a gardening book and my afternoon espresso and read about container gardening.

Bali will be changing jobs soon. Until then, we make it work on $2450 monthly. I have been working from our pantry supplies, and the other day I found perfectly good canned food on one of the neighborhood streets. There were two big boxes of brand-new canned foods without dents, and nothing expired. I gingerly took a few cans; however, when the boys and I returned from a hike a week later and saw the boxes still there, we hauled it all home. I've been cooking canned meats and vegetables with gratitude.

We watch the birds outside the living room window for entertainment. We set up a bird hangout with all sorts of feeders and a bird bath. Arjan hauls home sticks from the forest to make perches and bird hangouts. We spend a lot of time outside in our yard. I drink coffee and talk on the phone, and Arjan and Sam play, fight, build things, ride their bikes, and set up landscapes for dinosaurs.

I think about Miss B and how she passed her time. She didn't work in the last few years. She stayed home, kept her house clean and tidy, and was home for her two kids. She cooked but loved using those cheap mixes. She did the "just add water" mixes and minute rice. It's how her mother cooked. She had old furniture and older carpets and couldn't afford to replace them, but she made things look nice. Her carpet was threadbare but vacuumed to perfection.

She drank a lot of iced tea she brewed in the sun in a big jar and loved Maxwell House coffee in her old coffee pot. Even as her health deteriorated, she kept up her appearance, always a full face of makeup and always had her toenails painted. It was a simple life, and now, looking back, it seems charming. I don't think she was so happy. She always thought her married friends had it better, and maybe they did, but if she could have just loved where she was in her life, it was not a bad life.

I used to be envious of those that could stay home. The lucky souls didn't have to commute in traffic and worked long weeks in unfulfilling jobs. I wanted to stay home, nest, cook, and have slow days where I could read on the porch in the middle of the day. I would answer to know one and tend my home.

It's strange not to write, blog, film, and edit all day. Not to feel urgent about getting content on the channel or a book published. It's strange to make a few pizzas and wash dishes, sweep a little, tidy up, and call it a day. I sit here now drinking my afternoon coffee with this delicious, flavored plant-based creamer, and I have on a documentary just for background noise. I'm working on crocheting a scarf in blue after finalizing a thick one in brown. I'm making crocheted scarves like hotcakes. Crocheting is calming therapy.

We may have a poor man's budget, yet life has never felt richer. It feels like the old technicolor films. That is how I would describe life right now—a technicolor film about a family living a humble life. It's no **Meet Me In St. Louis**, but close.

I use all the technics I read about in Connie Hultquist's books and the Depression Era stories. The more uplifting ones. I make do with everything. If I need kitchen tools or we want more movies for our library, I go to a hospice thrift store down the street and get things for .50 cents or a dollar.

I've never loved the library more. We bring home bags full of novels and enjoy these Ghibli Studio movies! That feels like abundance. I feel luxurious watching good movies at night with the family and losing myself in a mystery novel in the middle of the day. I feel spoiled drinking coffee with a flavored creamer.

I would feel luxurious having a nice bathtub. Our bathtub is small and too weird for me to relax in. One day we will replace it. Or do the cheap repainting kits from the hardware store.

I love having two fully paid cars that are reliable. They are solid and take us safely from home to many destinations and back home again. I could care less if the paint is peeling and they look old and banged up (mostly from my getting in or out of the driveway and usually engaging parts of the fence). And we don't need much gas because we can walk everywhere. We live in a beautiful forest area, so walking everywhere is lovely.

I feel rich living in this area. We made it just before the housing market soared to unreasonable heights. We negotiated a deal and won! We couldn't sell our other house at first, so we rented it out, making it possible to afford it here with the extra rental income. We sold the rental at the perfect time a year later and made a nice profit. With the profit from the rental sale, we paid off almost half of this house.

The stimulus checks were such a gift. We used most of them for building our orchard and garden. The rest was for stocking up everything in the house. We traveled to Savers Thrift for a 50% off sale and stocked up on clothes for the boys. I stocked cleaning supplies and toiletries, seeds, tools, and food.

I have two years of clothes for the boys. There is enough laundry detergent for maybe a year. I don't know why I bought so much conditioner, but I have enough for the end of time. I'll run out of shampoo in a year or so.

I water down detergents and fill our plates with brown rice and pinto beans. We are finally harvesting some greens. I craved Mustard greens so much this winter and couldn't find any in the stores, and now I pick huge pots of greens each night. I have four rows of greens growing bigger each day. I've frozen bags of ripened bananas, and we'll have kale smoothies soon for breakfast.

I have more hope for gardening this year, but I intend to keep it simple and small—one slight improvement at a time. Gardening can turn on you. It can be therapeutic or overwhelming.

Even the fence has taken on a more straightforward and cheaper path. The carpenter didn't show up, so we built the fence ourselves with the neighbor's help. This will save us $2000.

Bali's car needed a lot of work, but he found all the parts online for a low cost and hired a street mechanic with a good reputation to do the work. Initially, we went to a shop up the street and paid a small fortune for some work. They failed us with the filter; the car leaked oil for days and almost burnt the engine. The street mechanic was a quarter of the price and did a better job than the auto shop we took the car to for the initial work.

We have over 200,000 miles on both cars. The Toyota Carola has 273,000 miles, and the Toyota Tacoma has 250,000. And they run great.

Bali has decided to leave his managerial position at the little gas station in the valley and take a job a few miles from our house. He used to work for this boss part-time before we moved up here. Bali will make a dollar more and have no commute. He will be a cashier without the stress of being a manager and watching over a small staff. The hours will be regular, but that extra dollar will make a big difference.

I believe I've gotten the bills down as low as I can. I can't think of much more to do. Now my job is to find the sales and deals, forage, hunt for things free on Craigslist, and make do with what we have.

It takes some thinking and planning to have such a small grocery budget. It takes searching and waiting for small things we may need for the home. I can't afford everything organic, so I buy from the clean fifteen list and non-GMOs.

Learning to cook vegetarian is very helpful right now. I'm waiting on a vegan cookbook from the library. I used to make delicious cheese and tasty baloney from cashews, gluten, and tofu. It is cheaper to make the phony baloney than to buy lunch meat. Sam and I love carrot dogs, which are much more affordable and healthier than packaged hot dogs.

Growing food, cooking from scratch, and supplementing vegan homemade meat and cheese or milk alternatives are great ways to save a bundle. The vegan cheese for mac and cheese is pretty good and made with carrots and potatoes.

The dogs still eat well; we buy All-Natural Diamond now instead of Taste Of The Wild. It saves us $5 to $10. We buy cheap canned dog food, and I put a few spoons full in each dish of dry food to stretch it. The dogs are so picky they won't eat unless there is at least a hint of something special. I cook up bacon ends I got for $8 a big package and use them to flavor beans and save the oil for drizzling on the dog food to stretch the canned even more.

We don't have much else going on. We wake up, enjoy the sunrise and the coffee, and set about cleaning, baking, cooking, or gardening each day. Between the chores, we hang out, play, read, watch the birds, and fill the bird feeders and baths. We aren't running here and there. We are present with our little life on a quarter-acre yard and a small 120-year-old house, and we love our days. I wake up grateful every day.

I would be sad to leave this paradise and work for someone else. I love waking up when I'm ready and planning a day that serves our family. I enjoy finding ways to save as much as possible. The more I save, and the less I use, the more stable our life is without me having to find work outside the home.

So, I'm careful with the paychecks and deliberate with every dollar.

Wednesday

The other day I made four pizzas. I wanted to try different toppings. We only had a few items, and I learned a big cooking lesson. Defrost your real meat or plant-based meats thoroughly and naturally. I took things out of the freezer and tried to defrost them quickly in the microwave, thus cooking them partially and then sauteed too fast and hot. Defrost naturally by taking meat out of the freezer and letting it sit in the fridge for a couple of days, then cook slowly on low heat.

I did an onion, and ginger pizza for Bali, a taco-seasoned turkey pizza, but the turkey got burnt and funky. Then I tried cooking up Italian plant-based sausage, which turned out burnt and weird. I did plain cheese for half of those. I saved one ball of dough and sauce for another pizza later this week.

Yesterday I made chicken enchiladas. They were delicious. The day before, I tried baking a whole chicken straight from the freezer, but it turned out dry, so I recovered the chicken by making two big batches of enchiladas with leftover pintos, fresh rice, and some cheese I had set aside. We ate well, and the next day, we fed another family.

We planned a playdate, so the boys and I cleaned and tidied up the day before. The playdate was fun for us all, and I attribute that to not having computers. We enjoy hanging out with others more since that is our big entertainment now. We took Molly for a walk through the neighborhoods and the school field, where the boys ran and wrestled. We cooked and ate and played all day. The only cost was the time it took to make enchiladas; that one big casserole dish fed everyone.

Today, I had a two-hour conversation with Dawn while doing chores and putting a Pork Loin roast in the oven with Idaho potatoes and carrots. We buy big bags of organic carrots and Idaho potatoes because they are the cheapest vegetables, and we like them. It's hearty food that fills you nicely and is loaded with nutrition.

Because of the earphones with the phone in my apron pocket, I was able to chat on the phone while doing two loads of laundry, shaking out the pantry rug, sweeping the pantry out, putting on a roast, and throwing ingredients into the bread machine, which has become my right-hand man.

I rested with a homemade latte and did some drawing. Drawing is my new thing. I haven't drawn anything since I was a girl, but I have wanted to draw lately. I have been working with grown-up coloring books, but I wanted to draw a whole picture. Arjan gave me one of his big sketch pads, and I have nice pens I bought myself for Christmas. I stocked up on those and notepads from Dollar Tree last year.

I have been drawing pictures of cozy homes in a forest with gardens, showing night and day or the seasons. I spend hours just having all kinds of fun doing this. I was inspired by someone's thumbnail of a farm scene.

I spent last night rereading **Possum Living** and finished it today. Learning to skim a book has been liberating. Books have so much filler and fluff; if you slide through that, it makes the book more enjoyable.

I've been reading a book every few days. My goal was a book a week, but I'm up to two books a week.

It's unbelievable how much time has opened up just by removing the internet. I had no idea how many hours we wasted daily.

Today I received the last decent payment from Google AdSense from the channel. I used it to pay off the Amazon credit card and close that account. We have one bank account, which is our checking account. We used to have checking and saving and a credit card. Now it's downsized to one checking account. That will make it easy to keep an eye on things.

We have stopped the bleeding of funds that all the small bills were causing. With just essential bills such as a mortgage, water, gas, garbage, and solar, the account stays simple, and money isn't vanishing daily.

We drink coffee and eat fresh wheat bread with butter and honey in the mornings—popcorn with nutritional yeast, apples, and carrots for snacks. We drink gallons of filtered water from the Berkey. I fill an old quart-sized peanut butter jar with ice and water several times daily.

Today Arjan made homemade barbecue sauce, and when my friend comes with her child, I'll make homemade sweetened condensed milk since I'm out of creamer but have plenty of powdered milk and sugar. I run out of things, but I can quickly whip up sauces, salad dressings, and even creamer with the dried goods I've stocked up.

My tomatoes and herbs are sprouted and doing well. I thinned out the tomatoes, waiting on the cucumbers to show themselves, and then I fed everything with watered-down fish emulsion. I got the idea to attempt this in the house after someone threw pinto beans into a house plant, and they all sprouted despite my not watering much or having much sun in the bathroom window. I realized it doesn't have to be that hard (I would learn otherwise later).

Thursday

The smallest things are enjoyable *and* beneficial, such as the minty smell of toothpaste after the boys have brushed their teeth. We are working on the habit of brushing our teeth after breakfast. I love brushing my teeth and having that fresh mouth. The boys need to build more of a habit. Thankfully, the boys haven't had any cavities in two years, so we are doing well. We floss, brush, drink lots of water, and eat fewer sweets.

I'm cleaning the house in preparation for tomorrow's playdate. It's with a new mother and her daughter. They are both cheerful and fun people, so I look forward to their visit. I am cleaning the home a bit deeper than usual. Having guests is a great motivator. I drag my feet on steam mopping the kitchen and bathroom. It's the picking things up that gets me. I have smartened up, and now the boys pick up and haul items. It saves my back and my time.

I want to simplify the house even more without losing the coziness and charm. If there was less to move around or pick up, I could do a daily house cleaning that would take only an hour. Deep cleaning can happen every few months. I give myself a few days to pull everything out, sweep, vacuum, and wash under and behind the furniture and appliances.

I've been making organic honey wheat bread in the bread machine daily. We devour a small loaf quickly.

I was steaming the floor a bit ago and thinking about a book I'm reading. I am not impressed with the writing or the story, and I find all the characters creepy. The book is supposed to be a mystery, and I'm only following through because Dawn said the ending was nothing you would ever guess.

I was thinking critically about how it's written and the character development. After seven years of writing and reading copious amounts of books, I look at a story with a dissecting eye.

I remember when I first started writing books. I had no clue how to get published, I would later figure out how to self-publish, but I felt driven to sit down and write. Bali bought me a new laptop at Costco for $300, and I wrote like crazy. I wrote in the middle of the night and wee hours of the morning. I typed away while we had breakfast, Sesame Street, and during nap times for the boys. Then I got heavily into reading after I read two famous authors discussing ways to hone your writing skills. They both said to read a lot and write a lot.

I read in bed, on the treadmill, and with toast and Curious George.

As a new writer, I was filled with doubt and insecurity. Writing fiction was a struggle, but I didn't want to write frugal books solely. I wrote four fictional books in those first two years. I felt like a pubescent fool of the writing community—just another silly dreamer. But I kept writing.

How far I have come. I now read books critically, dissecting how the story flows; if I connect to the characters, does the book move me? What is the style that I enjoy or don't enjoy? What makes a book stick with people?

I don't fret over being good enough any longer. I enjoy studying and reading. We need to love our passions and have fun. Who cares if we aren't the next Nicholas Sparks, modern Jane Austen, or Stephen King? We write because it is in our blood.

We just returned from walking to the grocery store. We took Molly with us. Found some deals and got everything on the list for $19.47. A whole chicken, cheese, butter, and even had enough for popcorn. We bought cheap lollipops at the corner market on the way home.

I started a batch of bread in the bread machine but forgot to insert the little paddle-like stirring tool at the bottom of the bread machine pan. We returned to tossed ingredients: wet on the bottom and dry flour on top. I had to start a new batch.

Tonight, Bali will make a huge pot of curry chicken. That will feed us tonight and our guest tomorrow, and maybe the third day will be the left-over sauce and tidbits over spaghetti.

Making double batches of dinner saves me from having to cook the next day, and we can pack a few lunches for Bali during the week. Bulk cooking each time frees up more time, and the bread machine is excellent at taking care of our daily bread.

Homemaking efficiency is what we are working on here. The more we batch cook and streamline the cleaning routines, the more time we have for fun and our creative outlets. Who wants to spend every single day cooking and cleaning laboriously?

Friday

The mornings begin with a hot, bubbly shower, loofah from head to toe, lathering up with lotion, lots of mascara, comfortable stretch capri pants, and a colorful t-shirt. This is my daily uniform, along with my fuzzy slippers. I have another cup of creamy, dreamy, fresh-brewed coffee and spend a little time reading. I finished a book that sucked. I sped-read it. My reading is speeding up considerably with the learned art of skimming. The ending was ridiculous. I'll be giving it two stars on Goodreads.

Cleaning gets old and tiring. However, cleaning has some grand properties. It *is* free therapy; when done often, it helps heal emotions and clear away old thoughts. It is also a way to show gratitude for our homes.

I love our bed because it's big and soft and has many plump pillows, thick comforters, and quilts like a plush nest at night. I enjoy the mornings. I can wake up naturally and linger for a moment to plan the day in my mind. I then get up and wander through the home from stem to stern, pushing buttons, adjusting knobs, and plugging in things. After a few minutes of this work, pushing back curtains and drapes and pouring cream into the frother, I have a sunny, cozy morning home with coffee burbling and music playing in the background.

I made some cookies from my stores of peanut butter and a recipe online. I read the Betty Crocker recipe; it was just too much with its chilling of dough for 2 hours. I live in a house with hungry wolves. No one waits for anything to chill for a couple of hours. Another recipe asked for plain peanut butter *and* chunky. I don't do complicated recipes with too many ingredients or steps.

All my recipes are simple and only require essential ingredients widely used in other everyday dishes in our house. I'm talking about flour, peanut butter, sugar, oil, that sort of thing. And I have a standard way of seasoning. These days everything tastes so much better with just a few flavors. Salt, oil, onions, or garlic, sometimes pepper.

Peanut butter is a big thing in our kitchen. We make no-bake granola bars, thus helping use up my overstocked rolled oats. We make all sorts of peanut butter cookies, sometimes the three-ingredient recipe, and sometimes, like today, I get ambitious and follow a semi-Betty Crocker recipe. I like peanut butter in Steele cut oats. Peanut butter on toast. Peanut butter on a banana or apple. Peanut butter is a miracle pantry food.

Today is Friday, and although I don't do a traditional nine-to-five, and the kids don't finish up a week of public school, I still look forward to Friday night. We do something to make it fun. Movies and popcorn. Maybe a little candy or soda from the corner market.

I didn't want to walk downtown to the grocery store, so I scrounged up the fish sticks and peanut butter cooky ingredients. We still have curry chicken, and I made a fresh batch of steamed rice. We have sour cream, which I love in curry chicken and rice—a buffet of leftovers. There are movies from the thrift store that sells DVDs for a dollar, and we have a big bag of videos and books from the library. That is a good Friday night.

Years ago, I volunteered at a soup kitchen and learned a trick to daily cooking. They served one big meal a day to hundreds of people. It was a big enough meal to sustain a person all day and even that night. They would pass out little bags so diners could save some for dinner. They had a place for the dogs to be cared for and fed separately. It was a fantastic place.

I observed the lunches, which would be something like meat, starch, vegetable, and bread. Then fruit or a dessert. I learned to do this cooking at home. I serve our big meal of the day between 2:30 and 3:30 pm. It has variety, and everyone can eat from this little feast through the day and into the night. Boys love to graze. There is always plenty for that day, the next day, and a packed lunch for Bali, sometimes two lunches. If there are just a few leftovers, I make another dish to go with it. Sometimes I cook daily, and then we have all sorts of leftovers for a couple of days, and we don't mind. I make leftover-friendly meals.

I read three books to Sam this morning while sitting here typing. He made a ceremony out of it. He made a plate of broccoli, bread, cheese, and tortilla chips and sat on my lap despite him being almost too big to sit on my knee. I read him **A Sea Wishing Day**. The wording and poetry of the story are so delightful; it is one of several books I will never give away. **Shrek**, the original story by *William Steig*, and **The Paper Bag Princess** are also fantastic books for children and the writer within. These are such delightful books. The language is inspiring.

Man, oh, man. I should go back to plant-based. I ordered *Sam Turnbull's* **Fuss-Free Vegan** cookbook from the library, hoping to find her gooey cheese and baloney recipe. I still have gluten, tofu, cashews, and tons of nutritional yeast in my pantry.

I can make good baloney with tofu for cheap and a delicious gooey white cheese from cashews. Vegan alternative meats and dairy can be pricy. I will have to make my faux meats, cheeses, and milk from scratch.

I love vegan cooking. I still have many vegan ingredients. The yeast and cashews are the biggest, as are the garlic and onion powder, paprika and gluten wheat, and tapioca powder.

I loved spending a day in the kitchen making milk, cheeses, and meats from plants. It felt good to my conscious. I wasn't harming or eating anything living or using any goods from a living thing. I was eating foods grown in the soil and fed sun and water. That makes for a clear conscience and a clean body. I felt good, had clean breath, never had an underarm odor, and looked younger and fresher.

Since my return to eating meat, my underarms smell foul, and my joints hurt. My finger joints are sore when the kids pull on my fingers. It's the dairy.

Sunday

Bali works locally today; tomorrow is his last day at the old shop. He will take the car in for another minor repair and new front brakes for the truck. The car and truck have been worked on several times this month. He has a good mechanic that does side work at his house. He doesn't charge too much, gets it done in a workday, and is right down the road from the old job. Bali orders parts online for cheap. The one mechanics shop we took the car priced all the jobs at $1200...$1100, and so on. With the home mechanic and ordering the parts online is a few hundred for each big job.

I'm grateful that Bali handles all the vehicle repair and maintenance, tires, and registration. Those are genuinely unpleasant jobs.

Our friends came with their young dog, and we all marched into the woods to play and forest bath. A couple of dogs were off-leash, and I had to block them and then ask the owners to leash them up as it is an equestrian trail and against the rules to let the dog run free. That was not my cup of tea; I had to do it twice. Then on the way home, some dogs escaped their yard and came at us like wild mutts. The owner was running soon behind and caught them both. The one didn't look nice, and the other had no collar for me to grab. I had to block and shoo those dogs off and hold steady until the owner caught them.

The dogs weren't the only issue. The kids were running around like feral dogs themselves, throwing pinecones at each other and disregarding walkers and bikers on the trail. Arjan was yanking poor Molly around on her leash as he skipped about, then let her go when he tried to run from me.

I returned home feeling good from the forest air, sun, and long walk. However, I won't be so quick to walk with two dogs and four misbehaving children. The stress probably circulated my blood more than the walk.

I've spent the rest of the afternoon watering trees because I don't know when winter will return. I made a cup of coffee, wrote out our new budget, and made a big pot of popcorn and the rest of the peanut butter cookies from some dough I saved a few nights ago. We packed so much food for the hike that I don't think we will want a full meal this evening. We had cheese and veggie sandwiches, whole grain fig bars, oranges, apples, carrots, and celery. I have a pot of seasoned pintos on the stove and will make cheese and bean burritos later for the next couple of days.

$300 for the groceries was not easy. I couldn't have done it without the dried pantry staples. But the dog food put us over the mark and close to $400.

Monday

I just made two pans of burritos with leftover rice, beans, and cheese.

In the garden, I found plenty of kale and spinach. We have lovely lettuce, and I'm still harvesting plenty of mustard greens and radishes. We had big smoothies with kale and spinach, frozen bananas, and frozen fruit from WinCo. I found a great way to make oat milk without wasting any pulp. I grind the oats first, add water, blend, and use it all.

I will only buy potatoes, carrots, broccoli, and cauliflower now. When I go for walks, I look at other people's gardens and see that broccoli and cabbage grow well here in the winter, despite the snow.

I'm thanking Spirit for guiding us to some garden success! That and two years of amending the soil with free horse manure, leaves, compost, and grass trimmings.

It has not come to that point where we are almost out of toothpaste, dish soap, or shampoo. I water down everything. I could be more cautious with toothpaste. We brush often, and the boys are far more sparing than I. Although I don't have to be too fanatical, I feel it is one of the most prudent things we can do at home: sparing with everything. It winds up saving us far more money and resources than we know. Because I stretch things out and water things down, I always have plenty. I have time to come across a sale and restock.

I'm on the edge of nerding out on the frugal thing. I won't last, but I work it, and we benefit immensely while it's going strong. This month was tight, and I had my last debt to pay on my side. I was paying off an Amazon credit card I opened before Christmas. I pinched, dragged out, foraged, and scavenged, and we could pay the mortgage early, pay off the debt, and close the card. Paying off the credit card frees up more funds.

I sat on the porch yesterday after our wild walk with all the boys and dogs. Lord, I can't do both dogs *and* boys; one or the other. Ah, but I have no choice sometimes. My little Molly dog is heaven to walk. I don't fear any dog or stress with her. A dog comes around, I pick her up and pat the other dog on the head, and we have peace. She is smart and stays quiet when I deal with drama. She never barks or tries to get involved. She hangs from my arm and observes things from her perch quietly. However, walking a big dog is stressful when another big dog comes untethered. I can't pick up my 40 and 60-lb. dogs to save them.

Another thing I can't deal with is misbehaving boys. Boys act out; this is true. They can be wild and unruly. However, I'm raising my boys to be respectful and well-mannered. Some of their playmates bring out the best, while others bring out the worst. I choose playmates for them that are raised with manners and respect and bring out the best in them.

I'm looking hard at who surrounds us and what experiences we have with them. Who we choose to spend time with is crucial. Is our time with a friend uplifting and positive or unpleasant and toxic?

I brewed a stovetop coffee and watered some trees, sat on the porch, reviewed old recipes I'd copied in a composition book, and found my most recent budget from four months ago. I rewrote a new one with the current bills. This budget saves us $500 to $700.

I'm so relieved that Bali will be working close by. His former boss gave him two free fill-ups on the gas a month, but we paid for the extra fill-ups, and the commute and wear on our old car were too much. If he broke down, it would be expensive to tow the car home. The commuter car has 273,000 miles on it. We need to drive them both less as gas goes up. It's terrific that we can walk everywhere and, most importantly, bike or take the bus. The bus stops across the street all the time. Who knows what will happen with gas prices? We have inflation and now turmoil in Russia.

Hard times come along. Just like good times. We are preparing for the hard times. We live as simply as we can in modern times without going off the grid or becoming big homesteaders. We don't have a goat to milk and hens to throw scratch. We do have gardens and an orchard. That's a start.

The bills are down to the bare bones, and it feels good to have a simple budget. I make dishes from the pantry and make do.

Tuesday

Found two to-go cups discarded at Bali's shop. He said they were left there forever. I need to-go mugs for our coffee. On the way home, I found an old white wicker porch chair with a striped cushion. Very sturdy and cute.

And a wooden deck chair that is perfect for my writing desk.

I was reading a bit in *Dear Kitchen Saints* and came across the part where she shares details about her home. Her husband, Jim, bought the house for $20,000 in 1973, a small run-down house, before he wound up running loose again and in prison. Water bugs infested the house, so she used boric acid to clear them out.

Connie's house was run down, but she said that if a woman *"had a roof over her head and a stove to cook on and running water, and a place to bed down her children and keep them warm and dry...then she can make a home out of anything."*

Amongst other things she said, she also talked about how in the old days, a man looked for suitable land, not a pretty house. The wife got whatever house was on the good land. The land provided food and could earn money. The wife made a home out of what was there. A nice house was not the important thing.

She asks why some people feel they need a fancy home to take care of a family. I agree with her on this one. I think those fancy homes sometimes create debt and hardship for a family.

We bought ugly homes and fixed them up to be sweet cottages. This last home I chose because of the enormous yard, and it was within walking distance to everything; town, trails, library, and stores. We can grow food in this yard, and we can walk everywhere. When hard times come, we don't have to worry about gas and can supplement our groceries from the garden.

We've been tilling, planting, and fixing up the house by hand from day one. Now the house is cute as a button, and things are growing. We still have years of work ahead of us, but what a joy to work on one's property and home.

I'm not too fond of the front yard, and I find that neurotic serpent is rising, wanting to start making big plans requiring money. But there is no money right now for yard scaping. How about we work with what we have? How can we transform the front yard to be fun, productive, enjoyable, and pleasing to the eye without spending money?

We can find free or inexpensive pergolas or shade clothes and set up places to sit and hang out. As the maple tree in front grows large, it will improve the yard. We need to grind down the tree stumps and create sitting spaces and flower beds. Maybe we could use the metal horse troughs people use for garden beds. Or build several beds.

We can use the shade umbrellas we have had for years and the wicker chairs and make beds with scrap wood, compost, and dirt. I want to dig up the side beds along the path leading to the front gate. I'll dig it up after the rains and add compost and fertilizer. Then I'll use it for my herbs, maybe potatoes and such.

The whole idea is to use up every bit of this property. To create a lush oasis for us to lay about reading books lazily in hammocks or cook our summer dinners on the grill and sit outside drinking iced tea and lemonade. So, we set up outdoor kitchens and sitting rooms. We set up places for the boys to play and build.

We have scrap wood and lumber. We are building up the compost. I'm glad the neighbor kept the one big walnut tree because we get piles of leaves and buckets of nuts. We must have collected three buckets of nuts this year and given them all away. They are expensive, and some people love them. Many faux meat dishes call for walnuts. I'm not a walnut person. So, I planted two chestnuts. Now there is a nut! Roast those up with butter and salt, oh boy.

There was a video about the garden foods that truly feed you. These would be beans, squash, potatoes, and corn. These are the foods that do fill you up in such a good way.

We are eating plenty of vegetables these days, and now that the garden is producing so well, I harvest three different greens. We have had big smoothies loaded with kale and spinach every day. With the mustard greens, I gather full pots, let the rows rest, grow for a week, and then harvest the new growth. The best garden year I had was when I bought a $60 greenhouse for the patio at the old house. I planted seeds and watched the homesteading videos on greenhouse gardening. Giving the plants a head start in the greenhouse made all the difference, and we had lots of vegetables through Summer and Fall. I had a tomato patch in the front yard and canned up to 20 quarts of spaghetti sauce I discovered from a video on YouTube. If used properly, YouTube can be a great homeschooling tool for kids and adults.

I've been reminded of the delights of home through movies and books lately. The cousin in the latest **Pride and Prejudice** movie exclaims how wonderful she finds homemaking of one's own home. Connie talks about being poor but proud of having those poor but scrubbed-clean homes. She and her girlfriends, who were also very poor, made do with what they had, acted like they had it all together, and were doing great. They never let the children know they were poor. I know some of her kids went to school; however, later on, she homeschooled all of them. I wonder if it helped her kids not feel so different or out of place from another economic class.

It's too bad people focus on wealth. They are missing out on the true contentment of humble life.

We enjoy the simple things; going out for walks and browsing thrift stores or grocery shopping to refill our pantries. But then I look forward to getting home. I can't sit for very long at another person's house. I long to go home within two hours. I'm eager to get back into my homemaking; that grounds me. I'm anxious to return to my stovetop coffee lattes made just right. I'm like a frequent guest at a plush, cozy Inn. I'm used to things just so and made to suit all my needs. And that is our home, comfortable and tailored toward our needs and wants.

Bali started his new job. No more manager. Not much paperwork, no inventory, and no stocking of coolers and shelves. His new boss doesn't watch over him like a hawk. His former boss was a good guy, but he did weird stuff, like having cameras and speakers in the store. He would watch his employees throughout the day. I say you might as well be present in the store physically if you're going to spend all day at home watching people over the cameras. You could sometimes hear him over the speaker in the store like a mysterious voice from the ceiling. I didn't know it annoyed Bali as much as it did. He never discussed it. But now that he's changed jobs, he seems very happy. He wakes up two hours later, which will make a big difference. It's unnatural to wake up in the middle of the wee morning, such as 3:30 am. Even 5:30 am is a big step toward a better morning. He is close to home, and that makes him feel better. He says the clientele are more pleasant. He has a view of the forest and a lot of light and fresh air in the store, unlike the other store, which was gloomy with fluorescent lights and no air. It's a busy and lively little corner he works. He was pretty pleased with it all when I brought his lunch.

Friday

I started a big project this morning that just kept evolving. I had to call in help. Sam is driven to earn money for the computer and asks for daily chores. You mention tasks and getting paid, and he magically appears.

The kitchen was the big move today. I'm surrounded by misplaced kitchen stuff, and I have a lot of recycling and some garbage to take out.

I was reading more **Dear Kitchen Saints**. I have parts dog-eared and highlighted. I skip her religious and anti-feminist rants and go to the good parts, where you get a glimpse of her frugality and homemaking. I read about her making shelving liners of paper bags. I'm sure she did a lovely job. She said she cut designs in the paper bags. I could barely cut it to fit right. But I like having lined shelves. I clean them with soap and hot water and line the shelves with paper from brown paper bags after they dry. I went through the seasonings and dressings, threw out the expired ones, and organized everything by categories. The central shelf has herbs I use daily or weekly. Then the Indian seasoning shelf. A vegan shelf. Odd seasoning shelf. Vitamin and natural remedy shelf.

I'll clean up now and make dinner. I'll have to finish tomorrow. Our friend is visiting next Wednesday, so we are starting a deep cleaning and purging project now.

A cleaning spree is what I've been doing. I'm almost done with the kitchen. The bathroom had a smell, so I went on to scour that space. A full load of clean and warm laundry awaits me. However, a huge, intense hailstorm complete with lightning and thunder graced us, so we spent some time on the porch enjoying nature being very natury. It's still going.

I may finish tonight. I'm putzing along, and despite feeling I'd gotten in over my head at many points, I managed to get a lot done. I started earlier in my pj's, and the phone wire plugged into my ears to listen to some talks on YouTube. I threw back three cups of coffee. I finally bathed and dressed around lunchtime and made tuna in mac and cheese, a great dish when you're busy with a big project. I did extensive cleaning and moving of furniture earlier while high on the three cups of coffee. I spent the rest of the afternoon labeling pantry items, throwing out old stuff, setting up sections, washing, and organizing. My shelves are lined and tidy, and my kitchen is now set up for scratch cooking.

I enjoy reading about other women homemaking in more ordinary ways. That is why I enjoy Mrs. Sharon White or Connie Hultquist. They live as simple and down-home as you can get. Mrs. Sharon White reminds me to slow down and not try to be the "super moms" out there. Homemaking is enough. Homemaking with scratch cooking is homemaking at its best. Homemaking with scratch cooking and gardening is some gold medal stuff. Making your clothes would be the real Olympic thing. Ain't gonna happen here. I *do* mend things. I repaired some pants of Sammy's and my favorite house sweater. They are not pretty jobs, but things are holding together for now.

I've been getting some great rest of both my mind and body. I needed it. There have been some boring and uncomfortable moments, but I feel more settled with being quieter and more present. The boys are in school twice a week, but I don't enjoy my time without the boys. I feel unmotivated when they aren't around. The house is too quiet and empty of their youthful energy. I think about the future when they leave, and it upsets me. I'll have to do something to stay active and happy when they fly the nest.

I'm thinking about making some vegan butter as we just went through Myoki's $4 butter in a couple of days. I'm also going to find that recipe and make the vegan baloney from Sam Turnbull. Maybe after I write this?

I've got a colorful polka-dotted composition book for recording recipes off the internet when I have some data on my cell phone.

I find that, no matter how much I can adore homemaking, I can also be tired of it quickly. Therefore, I read other people's shares on homemaking, and I stay inspired by memories of Miss B and Miss D, especially now more than ever. I force myself to focus. When I work at home, I am present with the task.

I have no clue how someone working outside the home could keep a clean house or cook from scratch. You can simplify it so it can work, but I'm slow these days. I take my time to get everything done. I don't have that energy from 20 or 30 years ago.

My herbs are doing well as delicate babies on the kitchen table. I feed and water carefully with a jug that I poked holes in the lid. It waters gently.

I have been going through the house and picking out items to donate. I'll put it all out in the front with a free sign as soon as we have several dry days. I have brought home several things these last few months, and now the house is a bit crowded. I'll pass on the extras and clear out some large spaces. I'm getting rid of the faux leather chair and ottoman, a plastic chair, baskets, a stool, a few boxes, some food, and the large chest on the porch.

I look around and make plans for things in my head, and then a couple of days later, if not the next day, I get to work. The front yard is bothering me.

Saturday

Woke up to snow covering the land. Finally, some rain and snow again after two dry months.

My mandarin trees didn't look good, and I think they lacked water because we kept them covered. We uncover them during rain, but I suppose not enough. Now everything will have enough water for a few weeks.

I was reading about the poor but squeaky-clean look of the homes of Connie and her friends when they were struggling young mothers. It inspired me to do some deep cleaning and purging.

My back hurts today—just sore but weak feeling. I will have to exercise today as I skipped yesterday to get into the kitchen project. And that project started in the morning and went past 7:00 pm. The boys broke my beloved new big straw broom last night trying to jump over it. Bali says he'll fix it. It broke in a good place, at least. Some wood glue and gorilla tape, and we have a broom again. I was not happy about this. These boys seem to be destroying my house little by little. The boys will have the amount deducted from their earnings. They now pay for everything they break. They earn money with chores and extra projects. They are saving up for their computer and doing quite well. They are learning how much work it takes or energy expended to earn some money. How long it takes to make enough to buy something of worth, and how quickly and easily that money disappears. This is a lesson for us all. When they destroy something in the house due to being wild and irresponsible, they are held responsible for the item. With money coming out of their accounts for things they break (unless it is a genuine accident), this has helped reduce destruction, and more cautious behavior is employed.

I need to do some grocery shopping. I know what I have and need now that my pantry is getting organized and updated. I keep a tally on the whiteboard for a grocery list. I don't need seasonings, baking soda, or baking powder. I haven't a clue why I have so much baking soda, but I have two containers and a bag. And corn starch! What was I thinking?

I gave us a bigger grocery budget because $300 won't feed a family of four, three dogs, and wild birds. The dog food is $45 for a bag and $34 for a flat of canned dog food, which I use sparingly and stretch by cooking up any bones or carcasses for a broth to put on the food or if I make bacon to flavor food, I save the grease and use that. Then there are toiletries, cleaning ingredients, and laundry soap. I'm stocked up on cleaning supplies, toiletries, and laundry detergent, saving me monthly money. But we need at least $400.

I think I'll make some baloney today. Amish bread and vegan baloney make tasty sandwiches.

I'm cooking up a storm and using up things before they turn. I never have eggs, and many of my **Make A Mix** recipes need eggs. I have a box of powdered vegan eggs I use, and things turn out fine. I often make this sweet Date-Nut bread to use up a large jar of dates that had been with us for a while. I used up the dates, and today, I made it with extra nuts substituting the dates and emptying a couple more jars. I intend to use up everything before we make an extensive stock-up trip again. If we don't, we tend to favor some ingredients over others and waste bulk foods. I've had the oats forever, so I'm going to make plenty of granola and make homemade yogurt from a gallon of milk. A pint of organic yogurt costs a few dollars plus. A gallon of pasture-raised milk will be expensive, but it will make a gallon of healthy yogurt at half the cost.

We can eat healthy food, but we need to shop differently and make it by hand. We should eat within the seasons. There was a book by *Barbara Kingsolver* about that very subject; **Animal, Vegetable, Miracle; A Year Of Food Life**. Her family ate with the seasons, and I believe locally. I don't find it hard to eat within the seasons as produce only tastes good in its season. To go all organic is expensive; thus, we grow food.

I think we will keep the garden small this year. I grew confident with the other house and that yard. We dug that yard up by hand with a shovel. After a load of horse manure, it produced well. This garden has been a bevy of mistakes for a few seasons. However, we are eating from it now, and it's winter! We eat mixed lettuce for salads, plenty of kale and spinach for smoothies, and sauteed mustard greens.

In April, I start the melons.

I'm saving every can. I poke holes in the bottoms and fill them with a bag of potting soil I have in the laundry room. I grow the seeds into tiny plants and then put them in the greenhouse.

I've switched us to mostly brown rice. I put wheat bran and wheat germ in everything; bread, pizza dough, and tortillas. I'm on a health kick.

I've noticed our taste buds changing. We like cleaner yet hardier foods. Heavy wheat bread or roasted vegetables and baked chicken. Brown rice and a roast or homemade vegetable pizza on rich whole grain crust and homemade sauce.

We make steamed rice, sauté vegetables, peppers, and onions from our deep freezer, and the boys had the veggies piled on the rice. They had a filling meal with a little teriyaki sauce or soy sauce to season, which I bought in bulk. Then I sauteed a small packet of grass-fed beef with the leftover veggies and peppers. I added cans of tomato sauce, canned diced tomatoes, and plenty of seasonings. I used some of it to mix up with elbow macaroni; the remaining sauce can be used for regular spaghetti tomorrow.

Then we made a Date-Nut bread without dates. A vegan baloney roll is steaming on the stove. Tomorrow I will make a couple of loaves of Amish bread, and while I wait for it to rise a couple of times, I'll haul everything to the street with free signs. Spring cleanup is early this year.

I've been exercising every other day for half-hour faithfully for some time. How much time, I have no idea. I want to say a couple of months. I don't mind it since it's so quick and easy of a routine. I'm getting a combination of stronger but still often sore. I keep at it.

The next move is self-homeschooling. I will need to spend a few hours working on my writing craft. I have books to read, notes to take, writing to begin, and more novels to read. I'm always looking forward to something throughout the day with all my books, drawing projects, studies, movies, and documentaries.

We watched the **Babushkas Of Chernobyl**. The documentary is about elders that snuck back to their homes in Chornobyl after the Nuclear Plant accident in the 80s. Some of them outlived their neighbors that were evacuated and never returned.

Here they eat fish from nuclear-contaminated waters and breathe the air, growing their food in the contaminated soil and eating foraged mushrooms that are notorious for cleaning up toxins, and yet, they were healthy and outlived their neighbors who did not return to the contaminated lands. They felt many of their neighbors passed on early from being homesick and heartbroken, having been removed from their lands.

Is it home that can keep us so well? I think so. When we love where we are, we are so much happier.

This house is bizarre and requires a lot of cleaning work because it has many layers. It's hard to explain, but I need buckets with hot bubbly cleaning solution and rags, toothbrushes, brooms, and vacuums. I try to streamline the process, but I have two and three-layered baseboards in some rooms and layers in windowsills, crevices, and cracks everywhere. My tub always looks dirty, no matter how scrubbed clean it is.

I like the old look, the poor but scrubbed and clean look. I don't know why I find it fun to be on a budget or why it turns into this challenge. Most people hate not having money. They feel sad or deprived. No one enjoys being poor all the time, but if you are working towards a goal, such as school or writing, building a business, or saving for a home, being broke for a while is not so bad. You make a game of it and find ways to thrive with very little cash at hand.

If I were single and had no kids, I would want the internet, money, and all sorts of things to keep me happy. I would be working and need comfort. But having a full house makes for a full life. Yes, I get frustrated with being a parent 24/7, and housework gets old. But then I recall how I used to get up early with an alarm clock and work all the time for other people. I worked with the public all the time, and I worked hard. I have worked since my first job as a nurse's assistant at a convalescent hospital at the tender age of sixteen. The next job was busing at a steak house, and after that, I worked two jobs and went to school on the side for decades, spinning my wheels.

All I ever wanted was my own home and stability. I have my own home and peace today, and I can stay home. I don't have to work outside the home. It helps that I have passive income from my years of self-publishing, and I'm grateful that I was so productive during that period.

I have the luxury of taking some time off. Perhaps a sabbatical, as I do get some monthly royalties. I can be in my warm home with my little boys and feel safe.

We don't suffer or feel sorry for ourselves when tight on money. We have a home with everything we could enjoy; art supplies, books, movies, and toys. We eat well. It's simple cooking these days, but the food is quality, has tasty flavors, and is nutritious. We have treats with my daily baking.

It's surprising how little you need and how simple your pantry can be. As we use up everything, I have an idea for simplifying my pantry. I only use a handful of ingredients these days. I need lots of wheat flour for bread and very little white all-purpose for cakes or cookies, waffles, and biscuits. Maybe some blackstrap molasses for the best ginger snap cookies. Then some brown rice, very little white rice. Pintos are the best and cheapest. Wheat and brown rice are also the most affordable. With seasonings and bullion, you can make all kinds of delicious comfort foods.

There is a channel on YouTube, *Il Rifugio Perfetto (The Perfect Home).* She cooks the most budget-friendly dishes. Her main ingredients are very cheap items such as flour, cabbage, carrots, a little cheese, very little meat, eggs, oil, some salt, and yeast. Very cheap, basic ingredients, but she makes tasty, simple dishes.

Sunday

Bali has his days off again. He worked every day for a couple of weeks as he transitioned to the other station and is there now full-time, and he likes it. I was surprised he wanted to take this job. I thought it would bore him. There are no employees, and it's just a tiny station competing with a couple of big stations with stores. This place used to have a tire and oil change shop attached, but it's empty now. It can get a bit slow over there.

He says the clients and atmosphere are very different and upbeat. He enjoys talking to the people he meets—a lot of interesting foreigners. The locals are friendly. He doesn't manage the gas station or deal with other employees. He runs the station alone, and it's quiet and slow, so he can read or listen to his radio. But of course, he cleans and organizes because he's like his wife, and we can't sit still. He cleaned up the whole shop and put it right.

He gave me grocery money last night. It's the 6th of the month, so I'll try to drag it out, use up everything, and then make a trip to Grocery Outlet and WinCo. We will take a trip down to the valley and pick up library books. I have a lot of level 1 books coming for Sammy. We need to start ordering books and movies from the local library here in our town. We have continued with the library from our old town because Bali still worked in that town, and we never switched over during the quarantine.

I'm planting some watermelon seeds today and maybe some loofah. Maybe some gourds. We had two days of rain, hail, and snow. Not a lot, but thankful for what we got.

I need a lemon tree for my porch. We will plant kiwi soon as well.

Later that night...

I have been looking around the house and yards, eyeing it all with a critical eye. I have tried to motivate each day and didn't get far. The last few days have been this excellent, slow, steady work from morning to night. Before returning to work, I often rest with a book, meal, or coffee. I have put many hours and days into setting up my kitchen, and now it is suitable for all the baking and cooking I do daily.

Today, with help from Sammy, I dragged so much stuff to the street. The house was getting crowded. Tomorrow I'll do a deep clean and last purge, and the next day I'll do a big grocery shop. M will be here in two days, and Sammy's birthday is in three days. In preparation for the day, I have decorations from Dollar Tree that I bought for $5 and used for all the birthdays last year, including M's. I will make everything from scratch. Sam wants a strawberry layered cake and broccoli beef. It turns out these two dishes are super easy. When we were at the library today, I found two excellent recipes on YouTube, watched the videos once through, and wrote them down in a new recipe book I started. I won't need to buy that many ingredients, either.

I have all this bulk food. Some of it has lasted me so long. The oats and the kidney beans have lasted years, so this budget is doing a great job of using up stuff before it turns.

I'm getting better each day at immersing myself in housework and getting the home in good shape. Some moments are so enjoyable. When it's warm outside, I'm harvesting greens in the sunny garden or in the kitchen, making a meal from pantry ingredients.

Monday

I did something this morning that I haven't done in ages. I brewed some coffee, took a hot, bubbly shower, packed a to-go mug of coffee, made a grocery list, and packed up my bags to go into the village and shop all by myself.

It was early, and that was the best time. The stores are clean and restocked, and quiet. I had no children. Which means I can think clearly. It means I can finish a sentence. Or not start one at all. I can chat up the checker and stay within budget because I'm not distracted by children and their antics.

Tuesday

I'm up this morning with Bali. We are having coffee and giving the dogs bread treats as they sit here staring expectingly, but it's too early for their breakfast. It's 6:00 am. I've been awake for a long time.

Bali is so much happier at this job. I'm pleased for him— no need for anyone to have a stressful job if they can get by on a small income.

Yesterday was busy. I had my morning shopping trip to the grocery store, where I kept under $200 and stocked up on pantry items and the main groceries. Then over to the health food store to get a 25lb of organic all-purpose flour. I don't use so much white anymore but for cookies, cakes, and tortillas. Wheat is healthier and much cheaper. I also bought organic popcorn in bulk. Then after the boys had some homeschooling and music lessons, we drove down to the valley. I dropped off and picked up books and movies from the library, went to a hole-in-the-wall thrift store with dollar DVDs, and found ten winners. Then to WinCo, where I carefully shopped and added things in my head so as not to go over. I only do the cash now, so I have to be careful. I spent another $77.

Then, because the fun didn't stop there, we went to the old gas station and picked up four wine barrels filled with giant pink geraniums, a small fig tree, and a grapevine. The former boss said no one watered them, and Bali could take them. Bali planted all those flowers when he opened the shop six years ago. A homeless lady helped herself to most of the plants, so he trimmed branches off geraniums from a neighbor's plants, with permission, and propagated those. Today they are lush and large. I was thrilled to bring them home. I'm trying to fix up our front yard without spending any money.

Not spending money is becoming our thing. Bali seems to be going in another direction. He wanted to spend all this money on a small battery-operated jeep for Sam to drive around our property. First off, it was hundreds of dollars, and that irked me as the boys are getting too big for that sort of thing, and it is a jeep for a large property, not our little quarter acre that is quickly filling with trees and plants. He wanted to buy something else, and I felt like that person stamping big red DENIED on everything at the desk. We don't have funds for frivolous things, so I have to be the bad guy.

I love having money envelopes. I feel like I have boundaries and freedom at the same time.

I feel good about how we are living right now. I never buy gas anymore, so I'm clueless, but I sure saw the prices yesterday at $5.49 just for regular. I never remember gas being so high. Bali said it's been at $5 during 2007 or 2008.

Is this the beginning of a hard-core recession? Inflation, the war in Russia or Ukraine, and high gas prices at the tail end of a pandemic?

I learned a lot from the quarantine. I know we all did. Much of it was valuable and good. It depends on how you look at it. I learned to stock the pantries with what was available at the stores. We bought bidets for both toilets. I learned to substitute and use different ingredients when other ingredients were out of stock.

And cooking, so much cooking and baking. I prepared Amish bread yesterday and had it doing its last rise when we were gone to town. I threw the three loaves in the oven when we got home. I use the bread maker almost daily, but I'll need to go back to hand-making the bread as I can make up to five or six loaves at once, which will cover the week. We eat sandwiches and toast all the time.

I am sitting in bed with coffee, typing this, and talking with Sam. It's a school day, and Sam wants to stay home this week. I need to clean like a whirling dervish today. I'll sweep, vacuum, wash all the floors, take apart the bidet and scrub the bathroom.

I also will make brown rice and some Indian kidney bean soup with ground beef. There are so many mustard greens in the garden. I gave a bag to the music teacher. I'm not sure he knew what to do with them, but he politely took the bag.

We now eat as much as possible from the garden, and I refrain from buying vegetables. I only buy big bags of organic carrots and onions. I only buy apples, mandarins, and bananas for fruit as they are in season now and cheap.

I look forward to the days when our trees produce lots of fruit and nuts, and the garden feeds us three seasons out of the year, to have such organic, fresh food packed with vitamins and the money saved.

Much later in the evening...

I replanted my tomatoes. I took my seedlings to the greenhouse, and the tomatoes didn't make it. The cucumbers are hardy little things; they made it. So, starting in the greenhouse from day one would be best. And my mandarins look bad. Upon some research, it seemed they were too dry. We keep them covered in the winter but pull the plastic back when it rains. We may not have removed it enough, and they didn't get all the rain. We covered them last year, and they were fine. We even had snow last year, but not like this year. Hey, I have a master gardener next door, so I'll ask him.

It's stressful when plants, especially trees, don't do well. It takes so long to get them up and running and producing. One gets attached to the trees.

I'm done with chores for the day. I swept, vacuumed, mopped every room in the house, and washed the throw rugs. I scoured the bathroom with half a container of Comet and took the bidet apart to get it clean. I have been deep cleaning for months, so a good clean is quick since the place is in good shape. I even washed walls, doors, cabinets, and baseboards, but only wiping quickly since I had done all this wall and baseboard cleaning a while back and had to use a toothbrush and hot soapy water to get into all the old cracks of this charming old house.

I made a quick dinner with hamburger in mac and cheese and sautéed vegetables. I meant to make Punjabi kidney beans but got caught up in the cleaning and had no time. If I want to tackle big cooking on the same day as house cleaning, it needs to be set up in the morning and have it simmering most of the day. It should be either a crock pot dinner or a casserole.

Well, I'm off to copy some recipes from cookbooks I ordered from the library.

Saturday

We are sitting in the truck in the library parking lot. The library is closed, but WIFI is available. The sound of explosions and cars racing is going on in the back seat, where the boys are playing video games with joy and glee.

I just downloaded a video on my channel. I wanted to show some fun things we are doing and how I'm stretching a smaller income.

As we spent a couple of hours in the library parking lot, I observed a woman who lives in her van. Maybe she doesn't live there, but she's there whenever we are here. She parks off to the side in a white van. She is a plump blond in her 40's. A few people are living in their cars or vans. They keep to themselves and stay under the radar. I don't know why I picked up on them today.

I wonder how they pass their days. Do they read all day or watch things on a cell phone? To be older and living in a van alone must be hard. I know the van life channels are popular on YouTube, and parts of life look carefree, like a dash of lounging in new and exciting places. It could be an adventure if you have some funding and traveling, especially if you have a companion. What about people having no choice but to live in a car or van and not wanting to do this? What about working and trying to live normally out of a van or spending weekends in a van? You'd have to be an avid reader to pass the time.

The rents and housing costs are out of control, and a plug should have been put in the whole thing long ago. The average income won't afford a person housing and a comfortable life.

Housing is considered an investment, and it shouldn't be. It is for homes and should be made available to all. A solid and permanent home gives people confidence and makes families feel safe. It's a shameful scam what is happening.

Families need a home they can afford, not a home with a separate bedroom for every person. It doesn't hurt children to share rooms. Living in a small house doesn't harm a family's sanity and contentment. Even an old house that is a bit funky. What hurts a family is being kicked out of their home and living on the streets.

We have old vehicles and an old, old house. The house has panel wood in the living room and slanting floors. But the cars get us everywhere without breaking down, and the house is solid, warm, and dry.

Because I'm not online or on social media, I don't struggle with comparisons and jealousy. I don't see other houses and want different things. I focus on what I have, and if it doesn't suit me, I find ways to improve or change it with what is already available, or we can find free or cheap. Such as using old paint found in the shed to brighten up the rooms or finding free furniture on Craigslist. It doesn't take much to make a cute home. It does require we not be too prideful or try to be like everyone else. My home is no Home and Gardens layout, that is for sure. I could never hold a candle to these new suburban homes. But I have a solid home. I love it best in the morning when it's warm and smells of freshly brewed coffee.

Nothing matches inside our home except the kitchen, which sports a lot of red because I ordered too much chalk paint by accident and then painted everything in the kitchen with the barn red. The home is comfortable and offers all the basic creature comforts. We eat wholesome meals, drink creamy lattes, have board games, and have a small library filled with books and DVD movies. We have soft beds and ample pillows. We have a TV for movies. What more is needed?

Sunday

The neighbor wanted to get rid of his wild roses. We dug up several, and Bali planted them everywhere. These are probably naturally propagated from roses over a hundred years old. An excellent gift today that only costs some digging and replanting.

The small news clip I found on YouTube of **America's Most Frugal Moms** inspired me in a few ways. The single mother paid off her house in five years, and she didn't make any home improvements until the house was paid off and officially hers. That's smart. I haven't been so willing to pay for work since. I don't even want to do the floors unless we have money saved for that specific job. We have only planned to buy kiwi trees, and I need a few packets of vegetable seeds.

Aunt M will return tomorrow and spend a couple more days with us; what a blessing to have family and friends visiting again, although she was one of our rare friends that *did* visit during the quarantine. It just feels almost normal again. Normal, but we have all been changed in some way. I sure learned how to be just fine at home with my family and not need to run about and socialize all the time. I have learned to be content with a quieter lifestyle. I enjoy the company of my family more than ever. The boys are fun and playful. They don't talk about weird stuff like these adults are prone to do. They teach me to be in the moment and keep it light.

On to another topic, segueing as Dawn would say, I was thinking of the Appalachian mother who had raised 13 children. Most of her kids stayed close to home. They were all good, salt of the Earth folks, and poor as ever. They were in the Appalachian mountains with no work available, so they were all on government assistance. One mother used an old ringer washer and used collected rainwater. They would collect moss, mushrooms, and ginseng from the forest for extra cash.

It seemed inferred that the mother had raised the children alone as the father was an alcoholic. She grew enormous gardens and was able to kill a chicken with just a swing of it in her hand. She kept the roof over their heads, kept all the children alive, and they all loved her deeply. What a strong mother. They were all poor but devoted to their families and always had food on the table. And that is the biggest thing after shelter. You can handle life if you have good food nourishing your body, shelter, and nurturing relationships.

I think hard times are coming, and they will be necessary to bring things into balance. Housing costs too much, which in turn, makes everything else a struggle. We have to stop chasing money and 'things.' Once we humble ourselves and our lives, we will find all the hidden jewels and gems.

We had a roasted chicken with only carrots as I had no potatoes, but we love roasted carrots with some olive oil and salt and roasted in the chicken juices. We ate a pan of sauteed mustard greens and fresh steamed brown rice. It was such a lovely meal, and I joked that it was a perfect dish for a fancy organic restaurant, and we would call it the Peasant Dish. It looked like gourmet health food, but it was a very cheap meal. The chicken was pricy because it has no hormones and is organic. Brown rice is as cheap as you can go, carrots are affordable, even organic for a huge bag, and the greens are from our garden. People pay big money to have organic, fresh garden food cooked for them.

We have been having smoothies every other day with kale and spinach. We will have a salad from the garden with the leftover rice and chicken tomorrow night.

I'm doing great with the grocery money, even with Sam's birthday dinner, and I stocked up on 25 lbs. of organic white baking flour and a big bag of bulk organic popcorn. Two big containers of coconut oil and other oils as well. If I'm careful and only shop twice a month, I can feed us well, dogs included, and continue to stock up. I watched some woman who talked about continuing to stock up all the time. I can't remember who it was I watched, but it wasn't in a prepping prepper way, just a way of staying up on your pantry. You want to keep things stocked throughout the house, and when you need to cut spending or save up, you can go a few months without buying food, toiletries, or cleaning solutions. Create a little store in your pantries.

I've yet to master the three months. I can stock up for a couple of months at most.

Monday

M returned from her trip today. She'll be here for a couple of days. I ran the vacuum through the whole house and the one big area rug in the little living room yesterday. Today we washed linens, cooked up a pot of pintos, and made two loaves of Amish bread and one loaf of organic honey wheat in the bread maker. I made a big batch of cheese and bean enchiladas for our supper and gave the kitchen a good sweep.

Today I sent a form for our former house insurance to be canceled, and the money is coming back. We just filed our taxes, and not only do we not pay for capital gains, but we have $9000 coming back. Yahoo!

I was somewhat concerned about having less money to live on. Bali brought home so little. Trying to live under that without my side work would take some navigating. But the minute I decided to follow through and do family and home, I received a check in the mail from the bank. Something about overcharging customers: this bank is always in trouble. Then our tax lady told us how much was coming back, and we owed nothing. Now this house insurance money. It affirms that I can take some time off and focus on the home without money worries.

My new tomato starts are coming up fast. I planted a couple of loofahs and still waiting on more cucumbers.

I had so much coffee stocked up, but we are now down to a big bucket of Maxwell House. I will never complain. Coffee is grand no matter what brand. Yes, I have had lousy coffee, but not often. You can't go wrong with Maxwell House or Folgers on a small budget. I learned that from Miss B. She used to buy Medium roast Maxwell House, and I found it pretty good. It had a warm, deep-brewed flavor for a cheap coffee.

Now that the budget is simple and small, and I have one checking account to monitor and a grocery envelope, I have no worries. Now that I have no goals or deadlines (self-imposed), I feel no pressure. I don't worry about money. And money shows up. I try not to think about it at all. I get a bill, and I pay it. In the middle of the month, I pay the mortgage. The rest of the accounts are auto-pay, so I don't have to think about them. Soon we will pay ourselves, and I've got all kinds of envelopes for everything: vet, car repair, home décor, grocery, dental, garden, and entertainment. We will put half in savings and half divided up amongst the envelopes.

In the meantime, shopping at Grocery Outlet and WinCo is saving me a lot. Finding the hospice thrift down the road was a blessing.

We are getting an above-the-ground pool for the summer. The boys had fun with the small inflatable. It was a good 10 feet around but didn't quite cut it. This pool will be significant and sturdy, and they can swim and play. It will bring them so much fun and exercise this summer. I need a simple pergola, and I can hang out with the boys while they swim and read my novels.

We need to do the fence and the bathroom, and then we can relax and focus on growing things and making the yard an oasis. I see a lot of propagating in the future. It's free, and if you've seen Ron Finley's Master Class or clips on him, you will know that he grew a garden of Eden in this backyard in an empty pool. He said it was mainly propagating trees and plants. And that is what you do when you have no money. You play and figure things out.

Lucky for me, Bali loves to propagate and keeps things simple. I get too intense, and things die. He sticks stuff in the ground, and they grow. He has such a green thumb but became a little too confident when he tried to plant the Christmas tree one year. He was sure he could bring it back.

Tuesday

Kids went to school, and M and I had time to talk without being interrupted for a few hours.

We had burritos with the batch of pintos from the enchiladas. I made tortillas and picked salad out of the garden. It is the best lettuce I have ever grown. I also made a vegan chocolate cake, and the frosting was fantastic. I had to redeem myself with another cake after the strawberry sand cake. I still need to make a batch of confectioners' sugar to know it works. I used store-bought powdered, but it would save a bit to make my own.

A dishwasher. That is what I would install in my kitchen. I would love a dishwasher. I wash dishes so many times a day. With a dishwasher, you keep loading it, hidden away and not in the sink. Once full, you run it, and it does all your work. I have been washing my dishes for over five years, a beautiful meditation act. And I'm done with it. Alas, I will be washing all the dishes for a long time.

I can't wait to have the house paid off and no mortgage. It will free up so much money each month. Then we don't have to rustle up the mortgage every month.

Wednesday

Where I live matters, where I raise the boy's matters, and where Bali works matters, the only requirement is that we are happy and content with our surroundings. I don't care what Bali does if he doesn't mind his work. I don't care if my kids make their living collecting acorns in the future if they are happy and fulfilled.

When we lived in the first home we bought, I loved the house after we cleaned it, painted the rooms, and pulled up the stained rugs to expose old wood floors. We dug up the little yards front and back with a shovel and planted vegetable gardens and fruit trees. It was an adorable house. But I wasn't crazy about the location, and we had rough apartments across from us. During the house inspection, I knew these units were a big problem, and I had massive anxiety before moving in. I kept wanting to cancel during the inspection. We bought the house anyway. I gained some 30 lbs. during the move and right after. I felt exhausted during this move, barely able to finish our last day of cleaning and moving the previous items. I remember feeling like I was dragging an anchor, and I bought a bunch of soda and junk food at FoodMaxx to keep me going. Like a drug addict, it's all that kept me going—good ol' sugar and salt.

After we moved in, I suffered odd maladies and more weight gain. I didn't feel that thrill of owning our first house, that sweet contentment as I nested, and we started gardens and brought in chickens. The units across the street were not dangerous, but they were filled with wounded souls, and the police graced the apartments weekly, and every other week we would have a night visit by a team of cops, sometimes a swat team or close to it. The back street was glum as well, and there were times I would be out in the garden and have to call the police for whatever was happening in the back street. Fortunately, we had a good neighbor behind us, so that cushioned the drama.

I suffered some anxiety, but I knew how to numb myself. I just became desensitized. But I had weird esophageal spasms that made me feel like I was having strokes. I was not, and a glass of water would soothe the issue. I grew to over 200 lbs. when I'm usually 170 lbs. and have been for decades. I had a few illnesses and went through some stress and depression. Most of it was mild and came and went. Overall, I found ways to be happy and loved the house. I also got busy growing a channel on YouTube and writing books. The town and people grew on me, and the town was in a state of significant improvement and clean-up as the city people started moving in. I am not a valley or flat lander. I love forests and mountains or the seaside. I can even live in a less desirable town if it has some old charm and I'm looking at the ocean or sitting in a thick forest.

I discovered this town (where we live now) during a trip with the boys. I was taking the boys hiking and headed up to the mountains. I stumbled upon an outdoor school for kids. I was in love at first encounter and knew immediately that this was where I had to bring my ducklings and raise them amongst the trees and like-minded people. I joined the health food store coop and enrolled my kids in a homeschool charter and the outdoor forest school. We came up here once a week, and it was a beautiful escape to a dream town.

For two years, I dreamt of moving up here. I made dream boards and wish boxes and worked on manifesting. I listened to Abraham Hicks and set my intentions. But nothing happened. Faith without works is dead. That is the truth. I woke up one morning in the third year with this sudden urging to make it happen. I had a small window to make it happen; it was about a year, and it might close forever.

Bali wasn't so on board. He had a job down the street and a small mortgage. He had his eggplant and peppers growing well in the valley heat. He was content. Then he wound up with a part-time job up here in the mountains. Bali had a new boss, and the hours had been severely cut. A friend of his guided him to a part-time job. He was charmed when he began working in a little store in a wooded neighborhood. He was captivated by the area's beauty, and the people influenced him. He said it was another culture up here with friendly and well-mannered people. Then he was on board. It's delightful how the Universe works.

We both began working like crazy, working as much as possible, saving every penny, and looking at fixer-uppers in that town. I sold lots of books and grew the channel, and Bali started working double shifts when the other two employees went to India for months. Our garden produced into the Fall, and we ate whatever it gave us. People blessed us with grocery cards and money gifts. The Universe conspired to aid us through extra work and people's generous help. It wasn't easy, and we went through many homes before finding this house. We almost ran out of time and options, but at the last minute, this house happened. It took a whole year of long hours of work and many disappointments, deals falling through, weird situations, and letdowns.

When we moved up here, I had tons of energy. I was thrilled and packed with glee daily. I am pretty sure I got Covid during the time we were packing. It was a significant bronchial illness, but I was so happy and didn't listen to the news, so I knew nothing about Covid. I packed and cleaned daily with some rest during that time.

When we follow our dreams and the right paths for us, live in places we love because they suit us, and do what we enjoy, we feel good and energetic. When we go in the wrong direction, we feel it in the form of sadness, exhaustion, and overeating. I got fat, sick, and tired moving to the first house because I knew it wasn't the forever home. I knew the neighbors would be a big problem. I didn't love the town. I was drawn to the town because it was smaller and quieter than the city, and I loved that. I grew to adore many things in that town because I chose to find contentment there. However, it was never the perfect match for our family.

But moving here was joyful. Bali and I worked diligently on our home and land all through the quarantine. It may not be our forever home, but we love the town and being surrounded by forests. Our neighborhood is peaceful, and the walkability of everything is a gift. We spent the first year painting rooms, planting fruit trees, and working in the yard. We worked hard, and I was healthy through it all. My health has improved. I have lost very little weight, but I'm more fit than I have been in a long time. I look happier and calmer than ever.

The most important thing is to find a place to live that you love. That is crucial to our overall happiness. Next, we need a solid shelter and some land. This can be an ugly fixer-upper with a small back and front yard. Who cares? If the neighborhood is decent and you love the location, that is all that matters. If you have even a tiny yard, you can create. You can plant and build, add outdoor chairs, shade trees, dwarf fruit trees, and a small kitchen garden. This will provide you with free organic food and some free therapy, as gardening is so good for the soul. The house is easy. It can be as simple as scrubbing and painting, adding a window, or redoing floors. But if your home has "good bones," you can learn to do the rest or hire a handyman to help.

We watch YouTube videos to learn how to do house renovations, and Bali does a lot of DIY on plumbing, cars, house repairs, and improvements.

Thursday

Yesterday I filled up on some uplifting videos. I watched **The Secret**, then **How To Cook Your Life**, and wrapped it up with **Rocky 2**. The Rocky movies are inspiring. I enjoyed the second one.

I was sluggish today. I hung on the phone and walked Molly in the mini forest. It felt more like I dragged Molly most of the time. She was a bit of a Mule since she has a particular path she likes to take, and when I go the opposite way, she tries to dig in her little paws and stiffen her two-inch legs. After picking up the boys from classes, I set about doing light cleaning and cooking. I added Jennie O's Italian sausage turkey to the grass-fed ground beef. After sauteing it and adding some Italian seasoning, salt, and the .88-cent cans of basic Spaghetti sauce, I let it simmer while boiling pasta. I purchased a pasta maker and can't wait to try it out soon.

I've been focusing on clearing the house a little more. I ponder this and that, but I can't seem to motivate or get it done. I have a vision in my mind. No, I have an idea or feeling of what I need with my home. I observe the minimalist that aren't so extreme. They have cute little apartments with charm, and it's just an effortless charm. My aunt was so good at this. Her homes were simple but sweet, with little areas set up with small decor. She kept the house very clean and tidy. I need this home to be easy to clean and tidy. I love a clean home and don't mind life messes such as artwork or books strewn about, but It feels like there are still too many layers and stuff.

I want us to get out and about more. As the weather gets warm and sunny, we must go for walks and be away from the house. I want more time to read and sit outside in the hammock. I want more time to sit and just have a coffee and think. I get tired of daily mass cleaning, cooking, and baking. It was fun for a while but needs streamlining and a schedule. If I were running an Inn with a café, I would have days I did inventory, days or times I baked, and times or days for certain cleaning or laundry. I would have schedules and firmly set routines to run things smoothly.

A simplified house and schedule would make these dreams come true. Then I could focus on boys, outdoors, getting out and about, exploring, or just going into town for ice cream or something at the store. I will have more time for reading to Sam, homeschooling, studying, writing, and reading.

Yesterday was the beginning of the month for our new Mint Mobil plans. I was allotted 4 GB, which translates to either 8 hours of video or 48 hours of articles and blogs. I enjoyed a documentary on people who had chosen to retire early and live in their vans and small RVs. Part of me would love that experience, but I know it would get old after a year. Or maybe not? I think about the days when the old dogs pass and the boys move out. Will I suffer from loneliness and boredom, and would traveling in a small RV be a solution? I could travel, write, drink coffee in different states, and meet new people. I'll put that on the back burner for thought in 10 or 15 years.

Saturday

I was hungry all day yesterday but found nothing appetizing, and nothing filled me. I made pasta with the best sauce yet. However, I felt hungry after eating. I craved fast food. I saw the neighbor carrying a bag of greasy fast food, which made me dream of sloppy burgers and greasy fries.

Today I made three cookie sheets loaded with empanadas. I didn't have eggs for the proper dough, so I made pizza dough and didn't give it time to rise. If it sits and rises, it makes a fluffy dough, which isn't great for empanadas. I used a small package of ground beef, five cans of vegetables to bulk it up, and Cream of Mushroom for the gravy. It could have used some sage and salt. I seasoned it with pepper and called it a day, not knowing it wouldn't be all that much flavor. Even so, the boys and I enjoyed many of these empanadas.

I made some bread that didn't rise too well. I made bread with all wheat and a cup of wheat germ and bran. I used to use primarily all-purpose white flour but have been switching to all whole wheat and adding wheat germ and bran to everything. It makes a dense bread, but it's so healthy. When I use the bread maker, it turns out a little less like a brick.

I woke up renewed today. I've been a bit lazy. I didn't exercise for five days, and I felt it. By the fifth day, I felt funky. I've been hungry but not motivated to eat much, perhaps bored with what is available in the pantry. Then there is the purging. I'm unsure of what I'm doing, but I need less clutter. I was enjoying my friend's visit and being slow and present.

Today I had my coffee with a side of ambition. I did my workout, finished **Empty Planet**, and washed linens and clothes. I did some purging, put all the comforters and blankets on a shelf in my closet, made the empanadas and bread, filmed a video, put all the laundry away, and cleaned and tidied. I meant to harvest greens today, but it drizzled all day, and I didn't make it out to the garden. Tomorrow I will gather plenty, and we'll have brown rice and greens for dinner.

And salad. The salad is so beautiful. I have no idea what I planted, but it's colorful and crisp, the best I have ever grown, and the first time I've had success with lettuce or any greens.

I still have grocery money, and the month is closing.

We are watching **Cinderella Man**. It's hard to watch the beginning with all the suffering of the Depression Era. After reading all the books about this historical period, I don't have much of a stomach for it. I am sure another recession is coming but let's hope it never gets like that, although some "experts" in the financial field have claimed we will have a crash far worse than the Depression Era.

And so, I start my money envelopes, work the pantry to its full potential, and find ways to save a coin daily. I have a change jar made from a pickle jar and our budget written out. Bali brought home his first paycheck from the new job, and he is earning more. He drives a few minutes instead of two hours a day in commute.

With gas starting at $5.50 and up, it is a blessing we don't need to drive anywhere now. Bali could bike to work and even has a bike. We can walk to three big grocery stores, the library, the downtown, and even the medical and dental clinic if necessary. I have a canvas wagon to drag to the store to put our groceries. We have a bus that stops across the street.

Life feels full and abundant, but there *is* this feeling we might be preparing for hard times. I don't think we would suffer much because we have no debt or credit cards, no car payments, and a small mortgage, but it is a time to prepare for changing times.

I don't know anything about the stock market, and, like a suspicious old lady, I don't trust it. I could learn, but I have no interest. I plant fruit and nut trees. I stock up on seeds, quilts, cloth napkins, and anything sustainable and reusable. We squirrel money away when we can. That is what I know. I'm taking all the advice; pay yourself first, have money envelopes for everything, save, and scrimp. I think of Miss B often, how she lived, and what she used to do to get by or make her home comfortable on her small allotment. I think of her when I go to my favorite hospice thrift, use the lotions I've stocked up over time, or drink Maxwell House in the big, blue can. She used to drink that all the time because it was the cheapest. She would get the medium roast, and I always liked it.

We buy quality meats and as much organic as possible, but I use the clean 15 lists for that, and I buy cheap coffee. I'm only shopping at Grocery Outlet and WinCo now. I ordered nothing online and was hitting the thrift stores now and then, but I don't even do that right now. I'll wait for 50% off sales beginning of the month.

This budget and cooking from scratch are using up all the ingredients I've been stocking up. It's terrific now because nothing goes to waste. And after two days of working on organizing my kitchen, cleaning out the old stuff, and doing a thorough inventory, I know exactly what I have, and I have a lot of herbs and seasoning. I have a lot more baking powder than I'll ever use, so I'll add that to a free box. And corn starch, I kept buying it, not knowing I had stocked up already. Baking soda is OK to have plenty. You can use it for a list of cleaning, not just cooking.

Friday

I sat on the bench with **Nicholas Sparks'** latest book, **The Wish**, which Dawn has sworn to be a good book, and being that she has led me to some good books, two out of three times thus far, I'm giving it a whirl despite not being a big Nicholas fan. I had my second cup of homemade latte to perk me up this afternoon. I have laundry to fold and the house to sweep. I swept the kitchen this morning and had to double sweep it with all the nutritional yeast and salt that seemed to be in layers on the floor after being spilled during my organizing. I swept barefoot and could feel every granule.

I watched a big FedEx truck pass by and realized I hadn't had a delivery except for Sammy's laser tag set in over a month. I would naturally perk up upon seeing a FedEx truck or big, brown UPS truck in the neighborhood. I still sit up a bit when one passes but quickly realize it won't be stopping at our gate.

The weight has been lifted with a basic budget for shelter and utilities and no ordering things online. Our monthly budget is straightforward. It frees my mind of that hamster wheel where we go over the bills, what is coming up, what needs paying, when the paydays are, and if they will be on time. The dread of looking at the accounts is gone, and I don't fuss over bills. I know there is always enough to cover everything. I don't need to check any longer.

Life feels rich. I picked up movies and books at our library here. We often go to the library in the town a few miles up the road because it's enormous and we can tuck away in the large computer room. They have a vast selection of excellent movies. I discovered this the other day, and the librarians taught me how to order on Link plus, which enables us to order anything and everything in the state.

A whole new world has opened its doors. Bali used to pick up books from our old library in the valley when he still commuted there. Now things are open, and we are familiarizing ourselves with the local libraries. They are fantastic!

I'm playing laser tag with Sam. It's easy since Sam keeps hiding in the bedroom and getting himself cornered.

I've used up all my data. Yes, I itch to watch a few videos, but I don't mind waiting until the library or next month fills up my data. I get messages from Mint Mobil titled, "Oops, looks like this isn't the right plan for you!" Bali says I need to change it. But that is how we think, right? We need more and right away. Absolute long-term satisfaction is in waiting and looking forward to something. If I have all the data I want and watch videos anytime, I begin to watch videos I don't even care about because I'm now in the habit. If I can only watch videos now and then, I choose wisely and watch quality over quantity. I don't waste time on junk.

We watch the best movies and read such good books. There are no commercials, none of the outside world pollution and influence. I even accidentally found a fantastic new radio station playing this new hit music. It is very dance, hip, new age stuff. It's fun and upbeat. I was growing tired of the 80s and 90s music day in and out. This station plays minimal commercials and very little news!

I feel like there are days I wonder how long we will go without the internet. Will we tire of this before a year? I know this is a new age, and computers are a massive part of it. Kids love playing games, watching YouTube videos, and coding. I know, eventually, that I'll have to bring the internet back, and the boys will need individual computers for school and life.

But then I see the kids spending whole days outside and Arjan reading all day or both talking busily with imaginations in full gear, and I know this is healthy. I am learning the art of hanging out on the porch with my iced water or coffee, just as the old timers did decades before TV. This house has been around long before TV and movies. So, I sit and watch the trees waive in the breeze, the clouds pass over head, the walkers stride down the street, the squirrels busy playing and burying walnuts, and the black cat claiming at least three houses as his territory on this street. I watch the Camelias, ever so slowly, open their hot pink blossoms. I watch Molly being so darn cute it should be illegal. Her legs are so short. Some neighbors commented, "she has no legs!" And she hardly does. She has maybe two inches from the main sausage body to her paws. She's like a caterpillar.

I've been saving boxes and filling them up with household things. I have put so much stuff out on the street lately. The house feels open and airy, and I can quickly run a broom through the whole place and have clean floors within minutes. Clean floors are delightful, especially with us barefoot in the house. I don't mind a busy home with books here and there and a productive kitchen table. But I love clean floors, made beds and washed dishes, wiped counters, and clean bathrooms. Now I have it so I can wipe, sweep, and tidy up quickly.

I also have a stocked pantry, and I buy minimal groceries. With the storage of beans, rice, and flour and the garden producing so many greens, I only need some onions, carrots, potatoes, creamer, butter, and eggs. We eat very little meat, and I have a storage of canned tuna and some canned chicken I make for sandwiches or throw into mac and cheese. I'm getting better with the grocery money each month. This month was the second one, with me working from an actual cash envelope, and it was more straightforward.

I see a lot of videos on YouTube and books about living on very little. Frugal this and frugal that and how to live on $1,000 a month or how "I live on less than a thousand a month." People want that magic formula; heck, I want the magic formula. I want all the tricks. But once you know the tricks, finding anything new to impress is rare.

Each grocery trip, I buy a couple of whole chickens, a few packets of grass-fed beef, and then stock up on, say, 25 lbs. of flour or two big jars of coconut oil and a few tubes of toothpaste at .99 cents a box. I continue to stock up a little bit each shopping trip.

Someone suggested the **Meanqueen-Superscrimper** channel. She talks about how she isn't so concerned with rising prices because she's been living within her means for so long.

I try to get the bills down more each month, but we can only go so low until this mortgage is paid off. We need to thrive. You can only be extremely frugal for so long, which then turns into feelings of deprivation.

I think people want to work less, and it is understandable. People have been working themselves into the ground for decades; now, everyone works. There is no balance. If we had one person at home and one working four days a week? This would make for a very content and calm home. Everyone would have time to enjoy life and relax. No after-school programs for already tired and maxed out children, no daycares separating mothers and babies, no stressed parents working and rushing around all week only to run around all weekend. And for what? Prepare for another fast-paced week of commuting, working, grabbing to-go dinners, and picking up kids—a bummer life. But excel for what and whom? Themselves and their dreams? Mostly to excel and get those corporate jobs that pay well and have great packages but will use you up and spit you out so fast you won't know where all that life went.

People are now asking these questions and the next question is how can we cut down on work and slowdown in life?

For each person and family, it will look different. Some people need to cut out the extra stuff slowly, one by one, and adjust so they don't go into shock. Some families or individuals get rid of the old life overnight and start fresh. We need to see significant changes fast, or we won't continue on the path. However, we must slow down after the initial changes and feel each decision.

If one of you would like to stay home, you may need to move to a cheaper house, get rid of leased cars, switch to bikes and buses, or downsize to one car. Or maybe cutting coupons, shutting off the cable, and growing a fruit and vegetable garden will do it. Some families will have to do it all; cheaper home, garden, coupons, thrifting for household items, and school clothes.

Friday

Today's theme was hormones and eating. I'm burnt out on all this scratch cooking. I feel accomplished cooking all these dishes, but I need a break. I did some grocery shopping, staying within the allotment for the week, but I switched it up a bit with some new items and easy dishes. I made sure I had my Chinese vegetable pot stickers and found a big bag of plant-based chicken patties for cheap and some boxes of mac and cheese since that is always an excellent quick meal with some salad and vegetables sauteed with onions. I bought crackers and small round cheeses. I have a cracker mix, but I have no ambition to roll out crackers.

I enjoy making things in my kitchen, but I can spend hours making a dish, and then the family devours it in minutes. I feel a little hostile watching food shoved down quickly and recalling the laboring hours in the kitchen, making it from start to finish. They see a plate of goodness. I see a dish that took three hours to bring to fruition.

For years, I have been thinking, drinking, eating, talking, writing, filming, blogging, and reading about homemaking, frugality, thrift, and sustainability. From the day I became a housewife, I was into it. From the frugal journey when we moved to the fruit farm and lived on Bali's small paychecks to when I started writing, blogging, and building the channel, it has been none stop with homesteading and homemaking. I can't seem to think outside this homemaking box. It's a problem for my fictional writing because I start with a good plot, and then the characters wind up on budgets and gardening. I can't think past stocking a pantry or living on a small budget.

And it's getting old. It's what I do; it's my life. However, lately, when I sit down to make a video on frugality or homemaking, I can feel the energy drain from my body. I can feel my mind turn away as if to say, "I can't. I can't do this topic any longer!!" And it leaves me to sit there mumbling and fumbling until I turn off the camera and delete the boring speech.

So, it's time to change. It's time to change it all. I need new material for the channel or to do it a whole new way, or it dies. It's time to work on the fiction wholeheartedly and let the homemaking rest. Maybe down the road, or perhaps I journal for a year and publish those writings, but I want to be entirely fictional.

To become a fictional writer, I'll need to immerse myself in a new world of imagination and observation of the human spirit and stories. I have to look at the world differently. Move on from the daily grind and enter the realm of fantasy and other worlds.

Sunday

I woke up early with Bali yesterday and started his coffee and eggs. I began my NaNoWriMo April camp project. I've started reading **How To Write A Damn Good Novel**. I'm still not there, but there is a spark.

Yesterday was houseplant care day. I washed, soaked, trimmed, and fed all the houseplants. I created a space in front of the living room window to move several plants stuck in the house's dark and lonely areas. It feels good to be so nurturing to the plants.

Inspiration came over me to rearrange the living room. The piano was in a dark and stuck corner, and I felt the need to feng shui the whole house. Most rooms are in good order, but the living room needed work. The neighbor gave me a leather recliner that was so comfortable and clean. I had just given away the faux leather chair with an ottoman. I was wondering if I had made a mistake and if it was the loveseat that needed to go. When I brought home the recliner, Arjan and I dragged the loveseat out onto the street. It took a couple of days for someone to pick it up. I was relieved when it disappeared. I had removed some big pieces, and now the living room looked uncomfortable. I redid the whole room and washed and cleaned every inch of it and all the furniture. We even washed the big window and Windexed the TV with its many little paw prints.

When I finished, the room looked amazing. Open yet cozy, lush, and green with all the plants lined up in the big window. The piano is by the sunny window, and everything looks right now. That is feng shui to me. Not what the books will say to do. It is when you look around and feel good. The room feels good. There's a flow.

Today I have a pile of laundry waiting for me. I'll need to bring it in and watch a movie to get me through the pile. The living room is so warm with this heater. I am trying not to run the whole house heat because gas is getting pricy.

Bali is outside with the neighbor working on the fence. He and the neighbor are doing it together and saving $2,000. It's slow work because he can only do it on the weekends, and he's been called into work or had appointments one of the days each week. Today they are putting in the frame and then the boards. Bali wants to do all the work on this property and house himself. It will save us thousands of dollars. Handymen are great, and I loved when the carpenter would come, and the house echoed with the sounds of hammers and saws. Unfortunately, they are vague about when they can show up; sometimes, the carpenter and his help don't even show up. They often mess up, or Bali must come behind them and fix things. There is some work and big jobs we need help with, but now we are down to easy-to-learn projects like switching out a sink or building a fence.

I opened to verse 56 in the Tao Te Ching. It's long, but the gist is to find wisdom in silence and not be swayed by outside desires, profits, or losses. I had someone text me yesterday. Some families won't see us because they are afraid of covid, but I can no longer get involved with someone else's dramas and struggles. It is not my business. There is a saying in Buddhism; Let go or be dragged.

So, I read this verse and fold over the pages so I can ponder this over and over. I could use the reminder to keep my mouth shut. Sometimes I want to be honest, but it wouldn't be a good idea in many cases.

I'm content these days, and I know it is due to being home, minding my business, and limiting contact with others. I have people wanting to get to know me and hang out. I keep it light. I have no energy to start new relationships. I used to want a huge family and many friends, but I have learned over the years that more family and friends mean more energy expended, and not always in a good way. Relationships take work and time to nurture. It is the time taken from my creativity and family. I have just enough energy for my little family and my housework, then a little left over for creativity.

I'm breaking everything down into moments these days. When I homeschool, I focus on that one page or math problem and don't rush or overwhelm us with several subjects or tasks. Instead, I focus on figuring out one problem, or word, at a time.

Even the garden has taken on a new plan. I started a few seedlings, and as they did well, I gained the courage to plant more. This winter crop has produced so much it has built up my faith. Focus on the trees and garden we have and focus on what we have now and not expand until we are in a strong place with knowing how to keep our plants and trees alive.

Focus on what matters. Focus on what we love. Family, garden, home. Do hobbies daily, like reading, art, writing, and learning. Play music and make coffee often throughout the day. Eat food that is alive and fresh, and organic. Exercise daily.

I have an excellent little 30-minute workout I do every other day. Sometimes I miss a few days, but I take walks and clean the house on those days. I keep it short and straightforward, but there is cardio, my 5 lb. weights, and squats. I've been doing this workout for months.

Monday

What a weekend. We built a fence from Saturday afternoon to Sunday night.

We drove to the valley to pick up an above-ground pool at Habitat For Humanity. Bali knows the family that runs it, and we get great deals, sometimes free things on the way to the dump, such as sinks and priced-down windows. This pool is 22 feet long and 4 feet deep. It is a sturdy above-ground pool to set up permanently. It was priced online for over $1600, but we got it for $350 at the store. Since we were in the valley and gas is almost $6 a gallon, we did several errands. We stopped by the Punjabi grocery store and stocked up on Moong beans, Chana Kala, and some Masalas for making bean dishes. I then talked Bali into a quick trip to WinCo. I love that place; we don't have one in our town. I stocked up on cream of mushroom, cans of Hunt's spaghetti sauce for .92 cents (can't beat that), and pasta. I bought us some small cheeses to eat on the way back home. We packed fruit, bars, and water, so we didn't eat out.

The pool is exciting, but we need to finish the fence, and then there will be a lot of cleaning up, and we need to lay a good foundation for the pool. Bali will build a frame and layer with tarps and sand to set up the pool. Public pools are fun, and the kids can play with other kids, but they are not so cheap anymore. Who knows if they are open this summer, they have been closed for two years. With the quarantine, we learned to set up everything we wanted or needed at home. Does the public pool close? Build your pool and fun backyard. Social distancing? Need a passport proving you've been inoculated? Build a sanctuary at home. Learn to make life enjoyable at home. Set up barbeques, pools, and stock up on movies and library books. Who needs to go out? Well, we do need to go out, but you get what I mean.

The other thing about gym pools and public pools is that they are cesspools of filth, urine, fecal matter, and bacteria. The one summer we all swam at the outdoor gym pool every afternoon, my kids were chronically sick to the point of me taking them to urgent care to see what the heck was happening. We were healthy all winter when it's flu and cold season but sick all summer? The doctor said it was the public pool and all the germs it breeds. It never had the same appeal.

Long ago, I watched a news clip about a frugal mother that found an above-ground pool on craigslist for cheap, and they filmed the kids swimming in it during a hot spell in the summer when the air conditioning had broken down and they didn't have money to fix it. But they had that great pool and a big fan in the kitchen as the mom busily worked on the budget at the table. Things like that inspire me and stick. I was determined to get this pool one day for a deal. We had a free pool we found on craigslist last summer, but it was a small 10-foot kid pool that was more for sitting in cold water and not so much for having fun. Finding this big above-ground pool has taken us a couple of years.

We got back, and Bali started on the fence with the neighbor, but he had been up since dawn and pooped out in the afternoon. I went out and helped Bali finish the neighbor's side that evening. I kept spacing out, and Bali said I wouldn't be hired back if it were a real job. I finally got the rhythm down, and we got it done. Bali and I got out there and built our side the following day after some strong coffee and fried eggs. We finished the fence around 6 pm. Bali stayed out there and cleaned up junk, wire, and old wood, loading it in the truck to dump at work. We can use the bin anytime, and it helps because we have a lot of scrap wood and such to clean up. I took a scalding hot shower and was never so happy to nestle into my recliner. I had been cooking and building a fence all day.

The days have been in the 80s, but we have had wind for two days, and the wind was icy last night. Today we woke to plenty of rain and fog. I was thrilled as I planted a big garden patch with my summer stuff the other day. We are to have more rain in a couple of days. Us Californians are very greedy about rain.

Today I worked in my kitchen all day. I took Molly to the chiropractor for her doggie adjustment. She was in pain, and I took her in a couple of times, and she's right as rain now. After her appointment, I committed to working in my lovely kitchen. The counters were crowded with cans and bags since I had never unpacked from our valley trip to WinCo.

I put my pantry items away, cleaned, washed dishes, filled the bread machine and set it to work, made a huge batch of pasta and spaghetti sauce, peeled ripe bananas and froze them for our smoothies, and had the boys take out my garbage and recycling, took out the compost, and swept the floors. I also washed all the bedding and clothes.

Babu had his dental surgery at last. It took eight months to finally get the old boy in, but now he's done. Deep cleaning, and they pulled two teeth. I dread taking pets to the vet. They're so excited about the car ride then they are delivered to what they probably register as hell. You can't explain it to them; they are high as a kite and miserable when you pick them up. They look at you accusingly, then spend the rest of the day whining and acting strange. Then you have days of antibiotics and softening foods. I've got two elders now and a young girl, and they all seem to need dental or chiropractic work, special food or pee pads, or just to be let out five times in the middle of the night. Bless their dog souls. I'm running a senior dog center at this point.

Let's talk about the *'Gansta Gardener,'* Ron Finley.

Ron Finley was a fashion designer selling his clothing line to upper-crust stores such as Nordstroms. He did well in his career and put his three kids through private schools. Then the recession of 2008 hit and his work dried up. He took a gardening class and became hooked. If you look at his backyard today, it's a garden paradise, but when you get an aerial view, you realize that he has no land. He has a cement patio surrounding an empty cement pool, and this pool and cement patio are thick with pots, containers, and garden beds filled with fruit trees, banana trees, and vegetables. He planted food in the grass strips along the sidewalk so his neighbors could pick and eat good produce because he lives in a part of LA that is plagued with cigarette and liquor stores but no actual grocery stores with real food. Thus, a movement began.

Ron Finley got in trouble for planting food in the empty lots and strips along the sidewalk. Before, there was garbage, and he cleaned it up and gardened. The city fined him and demanded he remove his gardens. The first time he complied, but then he did it again, and the second time he was fined and told to get rid of it, he started a petition and started some significant change. Because of him, the laws have been changed, and we, in California at least, can now garden in our front yards and the strips along sidewalks and empty lots.

This movement started decades ago in New York with an older woman named Hattie Carthan, who began planting trees in red-lined neighborhoods that had been badly neglected. She led groups to plant trees in all the neighborhoods. She became known as "the tree lady of Brooklyn." Her story is impressive. She started a significant movement, saved historical sites, and planted over 1500 trees with the help of the local kids. She turned the Brownstones into the Magnolia Earth Tree Center, a place for children to come and get an environmental education.

The following New York City woman to start such a movement was *Liz Christy* in 1973. The city was suffering the deterioration of abandonment, and Liz and her friends started a group called the Green Guerillas. They would plant in empty lots, clean them up, fence them off, and fill them with gardens. The city tried to stop it, but Liz called in the press to bring attention to the movement, and the city backed off. The city began selling off lots for a dollar, and community gardening exploded. Over the years, gardeners had to fight for their spaces from being sold off and bulldozed to build houses, but they have won many battles.

Talk about a silver lining. Ron Finely lost the one prestigious job that made him good money, tried something new, and found his passion. His passion turned into something big. He's been on countless news channels, has a Master Class on Masterclass.com, and projects all over the place. He is helping people grow food for themselves in food deserts and low-income neighborhoods, even if they don't have land or yards.

During the quarantine, Ron was busy gardening and happy despite what was happening. He was able to feed himself well from his garden and rarely left the house except to buy fish.

Watching all the interviews inspired me. I searched for clips and articles about the yard because I was impressed that he grows so much in a cement yard. I came home and planted corn, summer squash, and carrots. I started melons in the greenhouse Bali made me, and I am babying my tomatoes, cucumbers, and herbs in the kitchen. I move them from window to window and a little bit outside.

I put used coffee grounds in my houseplants and make banana peel juice to feed them. Some ladies told me about this excellent plant food you can make by soaking banana peels in a big container of water for a few days, then soaking your houseplants and feeding them some banana juice. I soak the peels for days to make them strong and then water the plants well and feed them, maybe every six months. I add eggshells and coffee grounds, wash the leaves and add more soil if needed. The plants are lush and deep green.

We had a little money blessing with Babu's dental surgery. The vet's office called the night before and said it would be a few hundred more than what they had initially estimated due to the cost of everything going up. I stressed at first and almost canceled, but then I looked at Babu and his sweet face and thought about how important he was, and I wouldn't want him to get infected teeth and suffer in any way. Why was I acting poor? Why did I make money more important than our fur child? I decided to have faith and let it go, and that night I thought, "what if the tax return money shows up in the bank tomorrow?" And the following day, before taking Babu to the vet for his surgery, I checked our accounts, and sure enough, there was the IRS tax return money.

It wasn't the estimated $9,000. It was $5,000. But we didn't have to pay capital gains on the property we sold last year, and getting money back was a tremendous gift. I had told Bali the night before that he should not count on the total amount. We are blessed to get what we did.

Originally, Bali had wanted to put it all in savings, and I had agreed, but when it was almost half as much, I asked that we use it in other ways. We have been so hardcore frugal for months, but with the new job and budget, we can afford to relax just a wee bit. With this tax return, we paid off some small remaining debt, took care of Babu, stocked up the pantry a bit, and I intend to do more stocking up this week. I stocked up on eyeglasses and lip balm at Dollar Tree, sunscreen, a straw hat for me, and summer sandals for the boys. I bought garden seeds and pee pads for Clyde. Tomorrow I'll go into Grocery Outlet and stock up on frozen meats, vegetables, and fruit for the chest freezer and toiletries. I paid the mortgage early and put an extra $100 plus on all the utilities.

So, a recession is looming. That is what the "experts" claim. I'm not a bright cookie with adding numbers or financial economies. However, it doesn't take a brilliant soul with a math mind or understanding of the simple workings of the economy to see the interest rates going up, gas prices going up, and the housing market out of control. It is like a slow-motion domino lineup. Who knows what will happen? Experts are as accurate as weathermen. The government is as honest as it serves them. They say rain, and we get an 80-degree sunny day. But something is going to happen. Something has been building for a long time. When it gets some air to it, it may be intense. Who knows.

But, like the quarantine, there is always a silver lining. There is always an upside, lessons to be learned, and experiences to be had, and we are often made to repeat what we didn't learn the first time. We can find new lives in a dilapidated situation. We are reintroduced to ourselves or our families in challenging times. We see many hidden gifts in a new roughly-hewn chapter of life. Sometimes being broke is the best thing to happen to a person or family. Believe it or not. You won't know until it happens.

Tuesday

Today was library day, much to the boy's delight. They played games, and I downloaded a video and watched some videos. I browsed through the DVDs, choosing a pile to keep us busy for the week, and moseyed into the children's section, which was so very charming, and found beginner readers for Sam and a few big dragon Novels for Arjan. We then headed to Grocery Outlet, where I spent $313 to restock my chest freezer. I bought frozen fruit, berries, vegetables of all sorts, fish, and some vegan alternative meats. There were whole organic chickens, grass-fed beef, some oat milk, zero sugar caramel macchiato creamer I had to try, and lots of fresh fruits, vegetables, and bags of salad mixes.

Thursday

I just made a video. Far too long, as usual, and I didn't relay the message the way I wanted to have it inspire others. I don't know how to package or serve this way of life to show others how good life is on this side of the fence.

We are already in an economic free fall. How far it will go and how challenging it will be, we don't know. Who will it hit the hardest? The poor or the investors? The ones living in cheap shacks or big mansions? The banks? The small businesses? The housing market. Gas is so high that everything goes up because we rely on gas to deliver and do everything. If it costs more, food costs more, deliveries cost more, and getting to work costs more. Then people start cutting back, and shops and companies start cutting back on employees. Then a two-income family paying an outrageous mortgage will no longer be able to make the payments they were barely making in the first place. Renters will be moving. Houses will become empty as foreclosures fill the lands once more.

People are looking for the magic formula to survive with little money, and there is no magic formula. It's a step-by-step plan to make life easy and sustainable through economic challenges. You buy a house, not rent, so you never have to deal with rent increases or must move because the landlord is selling. You buy a cheap house, be it a trailer or fixer-upper. You fix the house up yourself. You grow food.

We save hundreds on organic produce. I figure the amount of kale, lettuce, and mustard greens I harvest almost daily could run as high as $20 a day. That's $560 a month. How much will we save with all the fruit and garden vegetables come summer? We will easily consume $600 plus each month because we will eat what we grow and not buy any produce at the store. Nuts are coming too, and that will be hundreds of dollars. At the health food store, nectarines were $4 a lb. Each nectarine was about a lb. If we have a nectarine tree that produces well, we will eat at least 4 to 8 nectarines daily for our family of four. That is $16 to $32 a day. Organic food is expensive and so good for you. You are eating food rich in vitamins and minerals and void of chemicals and pesticides.

We have many reusables (another huge money saver); feminine cloth pads, cloth napkins and towels, cloth mops, and rags for cleaning made of old clothing unsuited for the thrift store. I bought reusable straws and a straw cleaner brush. I bought everything to make the best coffees; the stove top percolator, Italian stovetop espresso maker, and handheld milk frother. I keep stocked up in flavored creamers and plant milk, coffee and cocoas, honey, monk fruit sugar, and all sorts of things to create a café in my kitchen. I can make any fancy coffee drink the coffee heart might desire: lattes, mochas, seasonal drinks like the pumpkin latte or peppermint mocha, cappuccinos, and good old-fashioned coffee.

The pantry is stocked with 25 lb. and 50 lb. bags of flour and beans, rice, sugar, and polenta. It's also stocked with canned goods and pasta. I have more seasoning than you can shake a stick at. I've learned how to make almost anything out of scratch. Because I loved my vegan days and learned to veganized things, I also learned how to make plant-based milk, butter, cheese, cheese sauce, baloney, and gluten steaks right in my kitchen without milking or butchering anything, and it's so cheap to make your oat milk or vegan butter. You can also make these things and avoid a trip to the store in a pinch. Learning to cook vegan is a big money saver. You don't have to be vegan to enjoy vegan substitutes.

Turn your pantry into a small grocery store for convenience and money-saving. Grow your produce aisle.

Learn to make everything. I've never made soap, but I have made tons of laundry soap, which ultimately doesn't work for me. But I've also learned to make house cleaners, which work great. The more I cook from scratch, the more money is saved on groceries. I've learned how to make replicas of the packaged stuff we love, like perogies and pizzas, Chinese food, Indian food, and layered cakes.

Saturday

Easter is tomorrow. I've already baked the ham. We eat all weekend if I bake a big ol' ham on Friday. I baked potatoes as well and made *Plantiful Kiki's* vegan cheese sauce. I don't have to cook all weekend and not even on Easter. Brilliant.

I had a very dark day yesterday. I felt downright depressed and burnt out on all thing's homemaking and child-rearing. I'm burnt out on cooking from scratch and cleaning. God, so sick of cleaning!

Arjan is incredible when I need to have some quiet and downtime. He reads and does his thing, but Sam is still that little boy, the baby that wants momma all the time and can't stand not having that connection all the time. He wails if I wish to take some space, taking it personally. I need to set some small, clear boundaries with everyone in this house. I haven't had a break in 10 years. I have no grandparents, sisters, or in-laws to help or support me. I have needed a break for years and can't get one. Bali works outside and gardens when home, or he's on his phone reading Punjabi news. It's time he stops the work and takes the kids out for bonding—father and sons before it's too late. The boys are stuck to me like barnacles, but they aren't interested in dad. We need to work on that. As the family's matriarch, I must take serious charge here. Dad needs to take the boys and give me peace and time to refuel.

Days and days later....

I've over-garlicked and salted the greens for dinner tonight. There are six rows of mustard greens, according to my garden map. I have been out there weeding after each bout of rain, and I love being there so much. It's healing. I think of what a friend said about getting your hands in the dirt for healing. Also, the documentary *Grounded* taught me so much about having bare feet to connect to the earth and heal. I worked barefoot in the dark, damp earth and weeded until my hips were sore from crouching on that footstool.

Molly is by me in her kitchen bed, asleep after our long walk. I was going to take her to the woods for a minute, but Arjan wanted to go downtown, which sounded fun. I slathered on the sunscreen, donned my new straw hat, and donned the bag I wear across my body. I love this bag. Small, black knit, the strap goes across my body, so I don't have to hold it. It's like the days of the fanny pack but without the embarrassment. Although, I don't think I would be embarrassed. Anything that creates a way for me to carry less is up my alley. I had Molly and my to-go tumbler filled with ice water. My fabulous small bag held my cell, lip gloss, hand lotion, and billfold. Finally, at age 51, I'm organized somewhat.

The downsizing of the house is helping tremendously. The house is getting easier to clean and tidy up. It would take me over two or three hours to clean, and now it's half the time. I feel more motivated with the freed-up space and time, and I'm doing the extras now, such as scrubbing out dog dishes and dismantling the bidet to clean thoroughly.

Today was one of those excellent days. The boys, Molly, and I walked to town and around the backway. The walk was enjoyable, and Molly needed that long stretch to work those little legs. I put a chicken in the oven to bake since Bali was home to watch it, but we made it back in an hour and fifteen minutes, even with the long stop at the corner market.

I spend the rest of the day doing more cleaning projects. In the morning, I did the most dreaded chores, taking apart the bidet for a deep clean. Once that was done, I felt energized with the obstacle job out of the way. I've been doing the small chores the last couple of days, such as washing the vacuum filters and boiling toothbrushes with bleach and Dawn. I need to take our old pillows to the laundry mat and wash them. They have large front loaders that wash big pillows perfectly.

Speaking of laundry. I hung the first load outside today. I will be honest, the dryer spoiled me, and I was so tempted to throw the laundry in it and be done, but I made myself do the green thing. I had forgotten what an enjoyable task it is to hang laundry outside.

After lunch, I pulled my espresso machine from atop the fridge and made a fancy, creamy little drink to take with me out to the garden. I spent the rest of my day weeding.

Sunday

The garden is now weeded. It looked like a wild jungle. It was the most daunting thing the first time I saw it a few days ago. I needed a trowel, which took forever to get through a few rows. After three days of heavy rain that soaked the ground deep down, even the most mammoth weeds came out easily by hand. I took my straw hat and espresso out there and watched all the bees humming around the mustard greens that had bolted and blossomed. I didn't touch those leaving them for the bees. I have left a few rows of weeds for the ladybugs and didn't weed the outer edges of the garden, leaving that wild for the good bugs. And the worms! This garden is alive.

When we moved here two years ago, the backyard was gravel and clay with some wild dandelion and chamomile straggling here and there. Now it's this rich, brown soil, and there are ladybugs, bees of all varieties, worms, caterpillars, and other unknown bugs teaming in this lush, wild garden. And it is finally producing. We have eaten pounds of greens for weeks now. The soil is alive, and our garden is successful. Organic farmers say it takes three years to get the soil ready to produce well. We have been amending the soil for two years with compost and three truckloads of horse manure and straw, and I did that rye cover crop one winter, and it's still growing. Now things that didn't grow last year are coming up this year.

We have had an absolute junk food weekend. I feel like celebrating for a few reasons. First, we will be done entirely paying off our debts by the end of this month and will still have money in the bank. Thanks to a better-paying job for Bali and our tax returns, our new budget cuts, and being super frugal the last few months, we have been able to pay off a debt that I thought would take at least five months—thrilled about that.

I'm a rewards kind of gal. I find that we are all so much more productive if there are rewards of some sort. Rewards are not expensive. It could be hours at the library or feeling good once a task is completed. I'm thinking of the bathroom cupboard as I type. I need to do that today, and the boy's room needs a helping hand.

So, rewards can be the joy of being done with the work, picking up books and movies from the library, or finding goodies during the 50% off sale at the Hospice Thrift. That is where I do most shopping sprees.

I have a play and shopping date with a friend that lives here. We wait for the first week of the month when some thrift stores have a 50% off everything. I don't need much these days, but I love to browse. I might find better stirring spoons or a few good DVDs.

We are in heaven with the movies. I have this sweet pink bee bag I take to the library weekly and fill with movies and books for us all. I found a five-book series for Arjan that he loves, *Aru Shah Adventures*, and I get beginner reader books for Sam and mystery novels for me. Then I choose some emotional movies for me, Rocky movies for Bali, and adventure movies for the boys.

Bali is not the best movie companion for me. It's like watching movies with the Amish. He thinks everything is either weird or inappropriate. He only likes old movies, such as westerns, Little House On The Prairie, Some Madea movies (he loves Madea movies), and old Elvis movies. I cringe, trying to watch what I like and having him sit there frowning and the inevitable moment when he comments on its morals. Not that I watch weird stuff, and I don't watch grown-up movies with the boys around, but Bali didn't get *The Big Chill*, he can't stand *Melissa McCarthy* (whom I enjoy very much), and anything American and mature.

He loves Rocky movies, Rambo movies, and any kid movie by DreamWorks, Disney, and Pixar.

I watch my movies when no one is around so I don't get reprimanded. I just finished the book *Girl On The Train* and was eager to watch the movie. However, the movie was dark, confusing, and far too much "naked embracing" for my comfort. They could always "hint" at it like they used to do in the old days. I didn't enjoy it and left it unfinished.

I do prefer old movies and musicals. You don't have to cringe at the rapid-fire cussing or have the remote ready to fast-forward any inappropriate scene.

We have a fantastic movie library right here at home, and it's about to get even more fantastic because I earned a $22 gift card from being an Amazon Affiliate and ordered *Hello, Dolly!* And some reusable casserole pans.

Tuesday

I was thinking about all I have learned as far as cleaning goes. Cleaning used to be the regular schedule of washing dishes and sweeping. But to have a spotless home, I now pull-out furniture and appliances to clean the floors, walls, and sides of things. Wash pillows at the laundromat with bleach and detergent. Boil toothbrushes with bleach and Dawn. Use bleach spray and a cloth to clean all doorknobs, light switches, computers, laptops, and cell phones. Scrub dog bowls often. Take apart the bidet and clean the toilet inside and out and around the floor—Wash shower curtains. Wash walls and baseboards, and windowsills. Wash throw rugs. Even take apart and wash vacuum filters.

I probably need a schedule—something like the old song about baking on Tuesday, Ironing on Wednesday, etc.

The bulk cooking is one I'm excited to do, but I need a minute to figure out what we need. I will need some casseroles, lasagna, and enchiladas to freeze. We could make cracker mix, waffle mix, and bread machine mix. I could return to making big bowls of potato and macaroni. I can bake ahead and freeze the Amish bread and the wheat bread.

Saturday

All the little efforts are adding up to wonderful results. The short workout routine I do every other day (more like every few days) is starting to work its magic. I believe I have been doing this half-hour routine for a few months now, and although I'm not as regular as I'd like, I'm feeling so much stronger, and it was so evident the other day. House cleaning gets easier; things feel lighter when I lift and push, and I feel a bounce in my step instead of being heavy and weighted down. I'm feeling lighter and stronger. I feel more energetic daily. I also did not become winded up the stairs on the way home from downtown. I usually poop out on that climb, but I didn't even notice until I was at the top of the stairs.

Wednesday

Homesteading off-grid is a young person's game. I thought about living off the grid and how often most people start enthusiastic enough and eventually throw in the towel. It's isolating and hard labor all the time. Got to build a house, then a garden, then the deer and bear eat the garden, then build a shed, then chop enough wood for winter, canning for the winter, hunting, fishing. It sounds like a dream to a mountain man or woman at heart, but it sounds like too much work and not enough reading time.

We only have a quarter acre, and we are farming less than half of that, and it's been nonstop work for days. We need to do the most challenging work now, so when we are old, we just maintain the garden and prune the orchard.

I passed an old Victorian that is on the road near downtown. It's run down with paint peeling, but the woman has big plastic tubs set about her porch and yard. She grows tomatoes and flowers in them. Our place would quickly get run down if I didn't have Bali to do all the hard stuff. The house would be clean and tidy inside and out but would start to look worn. I think about homemakers that became single in their older age and must live on so little and keep up a house on their own.

It is why so many are borderline obsessed about how to live on less and less. But there is more behind this quest to live on so little these days. It is a desire to have some freedom. These days, the big talk is about the "big resignation" or "quiet quitting." More people are buying tiny homes or starting lives in vans and RVs. Since the quarantine, we all learned how dispensable and disposable we truly are in jobs and with friends and family.

Thursday

Sam is with me today, sick and hacking. We dropped Arjan off and went to the outside produce cart a block from dad's work. I bought two big bags of oranges and some other produce.

And, of course, I bought some starts; melon, summer squash, and corn. I planted those and some melon seeds.

Friday

It's been a slow-moving day. Washed the dog's pans and hung out a load of laundry. Funny, I don't feel valid in saying I did laundry unless I hang it on the line. Who washes the laundry? The washer. But I hung it all up. Thus, I did half the work.

I felt very homey this week. I took each day slowly. Start brewing coffee and opening curtains to fill the little house with morning light. Sip coffee and don't plan things. Don't plan the day. Just have the coffee and see what the day brings. We have Spring weather now, and sometimes I want to take a long walk into town. Maybe we need more movies to make it through the weekend. Maybe I want hot dog buns. So, I walk to the library or the market downtown. Some days I want to sit on my small stool in the garden and weed for hours. The big rains have passed, so the last of the easy weeding is over. I leave some weeds for the bugs anyway. My garden doesn't need to look like a spread for Home And Gardens. I need to be able to find vegetables, that's all.

I think of *Ron Finley* when I get frustrated with the quality of our soil and the parts of the yard we can't dig up. He planted a fruit and vegetable farm complete with trees in a cement backyard with an empty inground pool; everything is in containers. I think of that mother in Nova Scotia that feeds her family of five seven months out of the year in her tiny yard with her terrible soil and short, foggy summers. You can find her video on YouTube, **My Urban Garden**. I think of the Darvea's family **Urban Homestead**. They only had a 4000-square foot backyard, and yet it was filled with goats, ducks, and hens, and they grew enough organic food to sell to fancy restaurants and feed themselves. You don't need nearly as much land as you think, and the land can be turned from awful to fruitful with some work and layering amendments.

And you can also stock a pantry well *without* a garden or home canning. ***A Year With Out The Grocery Store*** by *Karen Morris* is a quick motivational read. The woman had no garden and didn't can or preserve food when she began stocking the pantry for up to a year. Not everyone wants to farm or preserve their food. I find it habit-forming once I get into it myself. However, canning is daunting, and gardening can be disheartening. But you are hooked once you can your first few batches of sauce, and the first season you have a successful garden.

What ***Vivi Did Next*** is a great channel to explore. Vivi is a retired nurse and had to live off her plots in the UK. She had to retire early due to health issues and had to live on very little. So, she rented a big plot in a community garden and started growing and freezing enough food to feed herself all year. Her videos are inspiring.

I have a big yard to do all kinds of creative things. I can grow things and build until it is all filled up and jungly. Sam started planning out the back fence area with the pool. He said he wanted a sanctuary in the back. Part of the yard is a driveway with cement and dirt, so we would have to plant in containers like Ron Finely's backyard.

The sky's the limit when you have a decent backyard.

Today was very cozy in my kitchen. I made a delicious tuna casserole. I didn't add salt because I've been oversalting everything. Bali asked what was going on with me and the salt last night when he tried the fish. But I had luck with the tuna dish and baked some date/nut muffins. My reusable aluminum casserole pans arrived. I will do bulk cooking with the reusable pans, the chest freezer, and my Make A Mix books.

When I feel burnt out on cooking and baking, I can shop from my chest freezer and shelves instead of going to a store and buying packaged and premade foods loaded with chemicals. I'll have containers filled with homemade Bisquick mixes and cereals. I can make granola bars and breakfast cakes in bulk.

I love writing in my kitchen. I'm putting the desk back in the boy's room as I don't use it at all, and they claim to have a great need for a desk (and they haven't used it since). I prefer to sit in the kitchen and type while preparing supper. I love to brew a small pot of coffee and write in my kitchen.

It's fun browsing through my cookbooks. I have the **Make Your Own Groceries** and **More Make Your Own Groceries**. I have the **Cheap And Good** scratch cooking book created for food stamp budgets. **Better Than Store Bought** and **Make Your Own Convenience Foods**. I do have a few dump dinners and desert books as well. These are all scratch cookbooks. I can learn to make Ranch dressing, candy, cheese sauces, boxed mixes, bread, and the list goes on.

Thursday

Ah, coffee and morning sun. Some writing. The boys snuck off with my cell. I want to read some homemaking blogs. *Life With Dee* is a good one. *Legacy Of Home with Mrs. Sharon White* is calming. I enjoy going on *Rhonda's blog, If You Do Stuff, Stuff Gets Done*, because she always has a long list of good blogs in her library that I love to check out. *gDonna.com* is another enjoyable homemaking blog.

The boys are watching the movie, **The Secret Life Of Walter Mitty**. It's such a good movie. It is about a man who finally climbs out of his small world. He has a wonderful imagination, but he lives a plain life. Due to a missing photo needed for a magazine spread, he is forced to step into a real adventure. As the movie continues, you learn that he used to be an adventurous kid, but when his father died, he stepped into the role of being responsible for his mother and sister and lost that adventurous part of himself. But the Universe will call you back onto the path when the time is right.

Sometimes we need to jump right in when life calls. Leap into the unknown to have the most profound experiences.

Tomorrow is library day. I run around in the morning getting chores done, my dogs are exercised and walked, and I work out. Then I shower, brew coffee, pack up the laptop, snacks, and to-go coffee mug, and we head to the library for four hours of internet bliss and a building filled with free books and movies. This library is vast and spacious, with big windows looking out to the forest.

I feel immensely grateful for the library. It is pretty dreamy to bring home a bag loaded with good movies and hit novels and not have to pay for it. You can be flat-out broke and have these books and movies. How can one feel poor when watching such good films and having popcorn? Or having a coffee and reading a good thriller?

I feel grateful for YouTube and KDP Amazon. I can be at home and make a living. I can write about things I adore. I can film at my kitchen table and make money doing it. I don't have to go out and work. I don't have to leave my house. I can make money in my home, work for myself, doing what I love to do. That is a tremendous gift.

So, we can experience some broke times, but we can still have so much and find creative ways to make money. That is the joy of this day and age of the internet.

I still don't want to bring it back into the house. I only miss my Pandora with my musicals and opera. But that is a small price to pay.

I have my **Hello, Dolly!** That is a wonderful addition to our library. **South Pacific** is the next one I'll order.

I have a lot of purging and cleaning in the laundry room and boys' room today. I also did a little studying on thready vegetable starts. My tomatoes are so thin and thready. I saw a technique to save them. I have learned that I can't start seedlings in this house. None of the windows have full sun all day.

I'm trying a few melon starts in the greenhouse Bali made.

Later that day...

I created a super flu-buster drink. Arjan liked it very much. I found it bitter and weird, and Sam refused to drink it. I put Vitamin C packets in large jars with ice, freshly squeezed lemon juice, water, a tsp powdered high potency vitamin C, Himalayan salt, and some sugar. It is a big electrolyte drink loaded with vitamin C and other vitamins. I feel pretty good after drinking it.

I repotted all the cucumbers and tomatoes. Fed some watered-down fish emulsion and put them in the greenhouse. The melons I planted in the greenhouse are doing great, so I guess Bali's plastic-covered frame is fine.

I'm enjoying a couple of carrot dogs on sprouted wheat buns. I still eat some meat and dairy, but less each day. My skin always looks much more moist and supple, my eyes are clear and white, and I feel much better when I eat more vegetables and less dead stuff.

I was thinking about my childhood when most of my friends were poor as we were. We had the same furniture for years. I don't recall my mother ever replacing a coach or buying a new piece of furniture. My friend's homes were simply furnished with school photos framed on the wall. No one was doing big decorating jobs. They just kept the house clean and took care of everything they had. People didn't order as they do now. We had to fill out a form, enclose a check, and then wait six to eight weeks for the package to arrive. You had to save up for everything. So, we ordered only the things we needed or were very special.

When I was a child, I had a wooden doll house, and sometimes little stores would sell small pieces of Victorian doll house furniture and kitchen items such as tea sets. I would get a piece when we went to these stores, and slowly I decorated my doll house. I also had a teenager that would watch me now and then, and she was very good at crafting. She taught me how to build a doll house out of cardboard boxes and to make furniture out of small strawberry baskets or egg crates. I tried it recently with Sam, and it was a mess of stuff and glue, but he had fun doing it. I forgot about the matchboxes—big ones for beds with a drawer or small ones for making side tables with drawers.

Now we have the Amazon effect. The Dollar Tree effect. We get things so cheap that we can decorate and trash and repeat. It's unsustainable. I feel like people are slowing down, and Minimalism and simple living are all the rage now. However, we still have the lovers of Dollar Tree and Walmart "hauls."

I have gotten out of the habit of shopping online. I can't even do it on my phone as something happened with my password, so I can't order. I just do a looky Lou and save wishful items in my cart for when I come to my senses and remove things from the cart. I was offered free things a few doors down when a shop had a weekend garage sale and wanted to eliminate all that was left over. She offered me anything for free, but I only left with the Mix It And Forget It cookbooks and a couple of big, lime green mixing bowls for all my mixes.

Reduce your needs, and you reduce your spending, thus making life easier.

I was thinking back to when we sold our rental property and made a tidy profit. Bali and I sat about dreaming big. We even talked about putting in an inground pool. That was a five-minute dream as it cost around $60,000. We dreamed of getting an RV or a new car. But when the check was in hand, we put it toward our mortgage, thus paying half of it off.

I read a book that keeps me on track with making smart choices regarding money; *Evicted: Poverty And Profit in America* by *Matthew Desmond*. I read about people's hardships with renting and losing home after home. With rents going up so astronomically, people will always be in this state of hardship. I bought a house so my family would never experience sudden homelessness. I looked past the ugly and dirty parts and dead backyards, the bug infestations, and old parts because I saw a house that could be turned into a haven with some scrubbing and paint. I saw a yard that was a blank canvas, and I saw organic gardens and fruit orchards replace weedy lawns and dirt driveways.

A house is not a profit or money gamble. It is security and safety. It is a property that, if worked well and properly, can feed you and provide you and your loved ones with a sanctuary.

Sunday

It's Mother's Day today. Bali bought me a kiwi tree. The nursery only had one left. You need a male and female to pollinate and produce fruit, but this is a unique kiwi that is male and female in one. Good thing, too, as it grows up to 25 feet tall and long. I think one kiwi on the front fence with a built arbor or lattice will do well.

I have refused to work at all today.

Wednesday

It was a day to leave the house. We love being home; then there are days we need to burst into the world, roam, and be a part of our community. We started the morning with some basic studies, and I watered my starts in the greenhouse. I'll be planting the big plants from the nursery this week. We had some rain, hail, and snow the other day, and here it's May. However, I believe that we will be heading quickly into the hot summer months—

time to be grateful for each day without a wildfire close by and clear skies.

Arjan's birthday is tomorrow, and he has chosen shrimp Chow Mein and orange cake with orange cream cheese frosting for his birthday feast. I have found the best channel, **Seonkyoung Longest,** for making Chinese food. The recipes are easy and quick and taste just like a good restaurant. The orange cake was from allrecipes.com online.

We spent a few hours in the library, and I didn't feel like being home when we returned, so I donned my straw hat and leashed up Molly, and all of us walked to town. I wanted a book called *Gaining Ground* by *Forrest Pritchard*. I've been reading a lot of murder mysteries and need to change the material to something more positive, perhaps some farming talk.

We tried a café on Main street. It had Israeli and Arabic foods, all organic. We sat on the street and enjoyed the food. It tasted alive and fresh, so I didn't mind the price. Most food at restaurants tastes dead and reheated. That is the only time I'm hostile about forking out money when it's on poor-quality foods.

We took our time going home. It was the first time I didn't care to be home in a long time. Home means chores and work. I'm working on changing that daily. Every day I purge and organize, trying to find that sweet spot.

Friday

We had our glorious four hours at the library today. The library is open on Saturdays now! The night before, Sam will ask if the next day is "library day" to ensure we are on schedule. We pack water, bars, my laptop, and a mug filled with hot, creamy coffee. We get there at 10 AM, pressing our eager faces to the glass doors and waiting for the librarian to let us enter the kingdom.

I brought home a bag full of movies for the week and spent the rest of the afternoon planting the healthy starts I purchased at one of our local nurseries. Bali planted a male/female combo kiwi tree and two more blueberries on Arjan's birthday. We have the Spring fever for sure.

I watched a movie and ate leftover cake from Arjan's day, and then right before Bali returned home, I made pizza dough and used a can of tomato sauce and Basil I grew last year and shredded Pizza mix cheese, and voila! Quick pizzas.

I have a wonderfully clean kitchen, coffee pot, and espresso maker filled and ready for the morning. I love when the evening closes like that.

Saturday

I was awakened by my bladder and then kept awake by an ambitious bird at 4 am. I'm up now, and the sun is glorious and lighting my kitchen. I've made some Bread

Maker Mix from the most recent Make A Mix book and tried it out in the bread maker. It cuts down on the many ingredients I usually add to the bread maker.

I will put on a better brazier and head out to water the front and side yard. I have a cotton sports bra I wear to bed. It is so comfortable. This is not a sports bra to do any activity besides laying down or having morning coffee as it is soft cotton and has no real support. It's just nice for sleeping and holding it all together. But for outdoor or any daily activity, we get on the super bras that hold everything up and together. I have had to let go of a couple of worn-out bras. All it takes is a photo or reflection in a window to help me see when certain clothing items are not improving things.

I have lots of watering today, and it's one of my favorite things. I have learned that despite my data being used up, I can still download videos and articles. I'm really into listening to shows while working. **Timothy Ward** is great to listen to; he is fun and talks a lot. He thinks like I do but in man form. Timothy is about finding your bliss and keeping life simple. Of course, he has no children or dogs, so it is easier to be free and wild. This morning I fell down the hole of RV living and all those videos. I love watching videos about RV or van living. It's a fantasy, but I would always have to have a home base.

Some of the videos were news clips of Silicon Valley people living in vans and RVs because rents are through the roof. The average house rent is over $4,000 a month.

It's insane everywhere. What are people to do but get very creative? It makes me wonder how helpful all this frugal living is if a person can't afford basic shelter. Your housing cost will make or break you. Car payments and gas will add to the challenge. The only way to make it through tough financial times and rising prices is to buy a cheap house. A decent neighborhood is crucial as you can fix the house but not the whole neighborhood. You may be a good influence, but some things don't change fast enough, like bad neighbors.

Having paid for cars and a cheap mortgage is the only way to go. No debt, no credit cards. Then learning to garden is the next step, along with learning to cook from scratch. Then you can live an easy life no matter what recession may come. Sadly, so many people don't know how to live under their means or budget in the most basic ways.

Later ...

Sam and I are having homemade sandwiches; mine is veggie with Violife vegan cream cheese (I won't repurchase it, as it is too sweet), and Sam is a ham and veggie.

I spent the morning having coffee with the family and then cooked a tofu scramble for Arjan and me and fried eggs for Sam. I went out and watered the front and side yards and what I missed last night. The boys and I walked to town with Molly, carrying a backpack and ice water.

We picked up two novels at the library for me, and I deposited a check at our bank right across the street. We bought some groceries at the store around the corner. It isn't the best store, but I was surprised by all the organics. The produce department was half organics, at least. I remember when the organics section in a market made up a tiny section in the corner swarming with fruit flies. The organic sections have grown to almost half the produce section in most big stores.

We had our tasty sandwiches and watched movies between small chores, and the boys stole my phone again. I don't know how they watch things. I have no data.

I'll cook chicken in a pan and heat the leftover rice for dinner. I'm in my pj's and washed my face. I suds up a bar of Ivory soap and sprinkle a little cornmeal on a washcloth to exfoliate. I don't use the cornmeal nightly, maybe weekly. I lather my face in coconut butter I purchase at Grocery Outlet in big containers for little cost.

It is that sweet time of the evening when the busy day has ended, and it's time to relax, cook a little, watch movies or read if the kids choose a movie we've watched five times already

I think I'll use the toaster oven. Today was very warm; summer has begun. I'll pull out the crock pot and use the toaster oven to keep the kitchen cool and reduce gas usage. Our bill was $84 last month. I know those Presto heaters are helping so much. I turn on the heat in the morning to take the chill out of the air. The vents and doors are closed to the rooms not in use, and I use the Presto heaters in the rooms we hang out in; the kitchen or living room. Using the bread maker instead of the oven to save gas, using natural light from the windows during the day, and having energy-efficient appliances have kept our bills small. I would only turn on the whole house heat a few times a day when necessary, but I mostly close off rooms and run the Presto heaters. We were always warm with an oversized area rug, curtains to hold in the heat at night, extra blankets, and comforters on the beds. Rolling up towels and pushing them against the front and back doors also helped.

Sunday

We will be preparing an area for the above-ground pool today. I'm not looking forward to more labor, but I will consider it an exercise to feel a little sunnier about it all. We have so much to do, and Bali is big on us doing it all on our own to save money and because we can't count on anyone. I miss Dave, the carpenter; I love the sound of saws and hammers when we have workers here. Productivity, I love that sound. But he is not reliable and doesn't show up sometimes. We saved so much doing our fence, and now Bali thinks he can do it all, and he can, with my help, do most of it, but I think we need help with some things.

Another crucial thing is preparing for unseen issues. We were all surprised when the quarantine happened and even more surprised when it went on for a year and a half (longer for some countries) instead of the predicted few weeks. We all learned a lesson about preparedness. It is wise to have backup plans and emergency plans. We don't have to go crazy, bonkers. Just be prepared. For example, having a well-stocked pantry has been great for our budget, and it's wise to have a few months of groceries for winter storms, unforeseen job loss, or illness. It is keeping your car gas tank full. Have clean water set aside. Have exit plans for the summer fire season or flood season. Have a first aid kit in the house and car—that sort of thing.

But if we are talking about getting by on a small paycheck, we have other ways to save ourselves from challenges. For example, we live in town, so we can walk, bike, or take the bus anywhere if we want or if we can't afford gas or the cars break down. I have a full pantry. If we can't afford groceries for a few months or get out to buy groceries for any reason, we are fine for a long while. We bought a house with a quarter acre. We may not have needed even that much, but we got lucky. We can garden like mad and grow our own free, organic food. By learning to garden, you save a ton of money on organics, feed your family clean food, and practice self-reliance.

We have solar, and I find it expensive because we rent the solar and are also connected to PG&E. However, electricity keeps rising, and I hear people paying huge sums. So, I guess it does help. Solar covers us most of the time. Gas is going up, so learning to use more electricity than gas is essential. We hang clothes out and use toaster ovens and crock pots.

We have learned to improvise on everything. We couldn't afford a lovely new house, so we bought old fixers and learned to do the work by hand with YouTube. Certain foods are getting pricy, so we buy other things. Meat is expensive now, so we cook more beans and tofu. Sometimes the solutions to challenges will bring you to a better place in life, health, and even levels of joy.

Later in the early evening….

Well, it turned into some Spring cleaning. I went for it and swept, vacuumed, and washed all the floors. I shampooed the area rug. I made the cleaning solution with homemade lemon vinegar, a squirt of Dawn dish soap, and hot water. To make lemon vinegar cleaner, you soak lemon slices or rinds from lemons in white vinegar for a few weeks. Making the solution will save you at least $9 to $15 for bottled, toxic stuff. I don't have babies crawling and playing on the floor anymore, but my little Molly dog is so low to the ground with her two-inch legs. I feel good not using the chemicals, but I love that super clean chemical scent. Boy, oh boy, I do.

I have a small Hoover carpet cleaner, and I love that thing. We had two throw-ups and a spilled coffee in the last couple of weeks, so cleaning the rug was necessary. Buying this carpet cleaner was smart. It only costs $99, and it's so light and small I can store it in the corner of a closet. It's easy to maneuver. With dogs and kids, I use it every other month. If you rent a shampooer at Walmart, it can cost $29.99 plus tax. Maybe there's a deposit? And the thing looks cumbersome. You have to load it in the car, unload it, and load it again. And you must clean it well—what a pain. With my Hoover, it paid for itself two years ago, and I go into the guest room, pull it out of the closet, use my homemade cleaner and get to work.

I cooked a simple meal of stovetop drumsticks, leftover rice, garden salad, and homemade ranch or bottled blue cheese. I was inspired to make the last batch of chocolate chip cookies and do some writing. It's too late for a small coffee drink. Drats.

Bali is still outside working. We started the foundation for the above-ground pool. He felt it necessary to remove a few tree stumps, so that took up the day. Arjan helped him with sawing on the stumps. I started cleaning and decorating our front porch. It is now porch weather, and ours was looking ratty. I rearranged porch furniture and plants, swept, and hosed it down. The goal is always to work with what we already have. We have quite a lot of little things here and there.

When the pool is set up and the red brick patio built, I will set up a pergola and get out the long plastic table, add the barbecue and chairs, and we will have a summer retreat! I have planned a simple, almost free summer vacation. We will swim, barbecue, garden, and go to the library. The boys have some friends that might spend some time with us this summer. Then all the reading and being lazy. What a dreamy life. It's the same at a resort. You splash about, drink organic smoothies, and read your NY Times Bestsellers. Same here at Resort De Singh's. And it's free—organic vegetables from the garden and lots of sunscreen.

It's not complicated to have a good life. People equate being poor or broke with being in a bad state. It can most certainly mean that; however, if you want a good life and search out how to do this, you will find books, YouTube channels, and blogs for free on how to live on a budget.

The basics that make for a good life are simply a home you love being in, healthy and delicious foods, lots of rest and good nights of sleep, a safe and nurturing family or friend network, and being able to pay the bills effortlessly. All this is attainable whether we live in a tent, trailer, bus, or stick house. We have to learn how to do it in each environment. YouTube is great for that. You can learn anything you want to transform your life on there and with books from the library or blogs by others on similar journeys.

But searching for a simple life can quickly become an obsession or nervous habit. Frugal living should be natural, but some people become too intense. A well-stocked pantry was a way of life for our grandmothers or great-grandmothers because stores weren't readily available until the 1900s, and only a few sprouted up in the early years. Recessions have come and gone, and inflation has been worse, but now we have social media and YouTube, which can be as much a curse as a blessing. Nervous people make channels about obsessively prepping. Fear mongering pays well, and the news channels know it. But not everyone is trying to make a buck by scaring the pants off people. Some people are nervous and scared and share this stress with others. A friend told me about a psychologist that analyzes psychotic types and specific personalities. He did a video on Preppers and talked about how most of them are the nervous or anxious types, and prepping feeds into their nervousness and feels normal to them. They have a constant sense of foreboding.

Prepping and preparedness are very important, but it's not healthy if it becomes fear-related, constant, or obsessive.

People are obsessed with this inflation, but it's been worse in past decades. I think it's 7%, but in 1981, it was 14.5%, so we have had worse inflation, gas shortages, and recessions. But we now have social media to scare us all into a dither.

I'll tell you what I'm obsessed with: bulk cooking for the freezer. I found **TheSimplifiedSaver** on YouTube, and I love all these easy crock pot meals, freezer grab and dump crockpot meals, and other freezer meal ideas.

Monday

Piano and school lessons today. I woke up, filled the percolator and Italian espresso maker, and set them on the stove to perk. I reached for my cell phone to listen to a show while I washed up some pots from last night. Despite a pan or pot, the kitchen has been clean and tidy each morning. Nothing starts the day better than a clean kitchen.

The cell phone is dead. I don't know if it's the boys; it seems they have the opposite of the Midas touch, and every electronic device they play with soon dies. I will need a new phone, and they are now forbidden to touch it. These cell phones are old anyway. I need a phone with excellent color and a mic for filming.

This morning I had my coffee and did a home pedicure. My feet were in despair with all the bare footedness. I watered my baby seeds and plants in the garden and gave the bathroom a deep scrub. Finally organized and cleaned the cabinet in the bathroom, and now there's room for all the towels. I was surprised to find four deodorants and a lot of conditioners.

Buying the pedicure set and foot tub that heats and massages was a good idea. I can do full pedicures anytime and save myself $30. I have built a homemade spa with the pedicure tub and set, the hair-cutting kit, my laser wand, and the glycolic peels. It costs $25 plus for a Pedi and hundreds for laser or glycolic treatments. I do it all at home. I also have hand gloves for exfoliating in the shower and an exfoliating pad for the face. And let us not forget a lot of sunscreens.

The boys have friends over now, and Bali is still working on preparing the foundation for the pool.

Lunch was leftover black beans with sauteed Jennie O turkey sausage. I chopped the remaining tomatoes and garden lettuce and made flour tortillas. It was a nice lunch. I hid the surviving cookies from last night and will dole them out soon. Made a little espresso for my afternoon chores.

Wednesday

The boys unstacked all the lumber so I could retrieve my garden bed planks. I have enough boards and fitted corner bricks to make two beds in the front yard. I'm pleased about this. I have a lot of melons in the greenhouse and would like a melon bed and another wildflower bed. The front yard is too bear.

So, today we have material for two beds and the ingredients to fill them all for free! The lumber and bricks were from the first house when we used raised beds for our garden.

I watched a little YouTube and found this delightful video on **Rob Greenfields'** channel. It was about a man who used his stimulus checks to build a garden for his family and neighborhood. Just a short clip, and I know so many people did this with their stimulus checks, and I love seeing it. It's what we did with our stimulus checks and advanced child tax credits. We squirreled some into savings, and the rest bought trees and seeds. The minute the government shut things down, we raced off to a big garden nursery and Grocery Outlet, stocked up the pantry, and got busy planting fruit trees, nuts trees, and berry bushes and amending our clay garden soil.

You couldn't find a bread maker or yeast to save yourself at that time. People got smart and began baking their bread and planting kitchen gardens.

Speaking of bread makers, mine is working hard on the counter. I made a big batch of the Bread Machine Mix in the recent **Make A Mix** book. It's fantastic. It turns out perfect in the machine and tastes so good. It's soft enough for sandwiches, which is necessary. We love sandwiches of all kinds, especially veggie ones or our basic PB & J.

Sam and I ventured about town yesterday and dropped into a deli. The potato salad was $11.99 a lb. I can make the best organic, vegan potato salad for ¼ of that cost. We enjoy going out to eat now and then, and I like to look over the prices and think about how cheap it is to make at home and how much we save with home cooking. We still need to eat out sometimes.

Getting movies from the library and making popcorn in a pot on the stove cost a few dollars. Going to the theater and buying sodas and popcorn for four people runs about $70 in our town. When we look at things like that, it makes sense to stay home for the most part.

Thoughts for the day...

I had my coffee chat with Dawn, and we explored incomes and households over the decades. We were talking about timelines, and it seems that around the 80s, homemakers started entering the work force. This changed a lot of things. More malls and fast food because a family had more disposable income with two incomes. People started buying bigger houses and extra cars. This changed the housing market and traffic. It changed a lot of things, and not all for the best.

I don't care who stays home, but I see these kids around me now; some of them are getting into trouble and gangs or selling drugs and acting foul at very young ages, and I believe, without a doubt, that it's because no one is home. These kids need at least one parent, preferably two, to be with them, take a deep interest in their lives, be aware of the friends the kids are hanging out with, and be present in all things. If people are going to have a family, someone needs to be home.

However, with rents and mortgages so high now, how can a family survive on one income when society is now geared toward double-income earners?

We started as a two-income household; however, a month before I had Arjan, I came home, and we had to tailor our life to one income for years. We are a family of four living on an average of $33K to $35K. With my book and YouTube royalties, each month is different. Some months the money flows in, and other months it's lean. We save whenever possible, and we allow some extravagances.

The only way someone can stay home is to find a cheap house. I say buy the cheapest home you can. Have NO debt and have paid off vehicles.

We had to work hard, think far, far, far ahead, make wise choices in everything, save like crazy, live well below our means all the time, and learn to garden, be frugal, repurpose, and find cheaper alternatives to everything from beauty to car repair.

We bought a HUD house for $130K in a small town and fixed it up by hand. It was an old house that squatters had taken over. It was filthy, and the yard was infested with bugs, not the friendly kind. Years later, we bought another old house that needed work. It had a plain, neglected yard with two giant dead trees in the front and was infested with wood bugs. We bought this house for $250K. We bought this house right before the quarantine. Today we would not be able to afford a house in this area or any areas nearby, or even in our old town. We would struggle with rent. The average rent for a three-bedroom and a yard is $2300 to $2800. Our mortgage is $1300. I would never suggest that renting is more frugal than owning your own property. I would suggest buying a house with a mortgage that can be paid on one income.

We have lived in questionable neighborhoods. We drive ugly cars. We buy funky old houses. We live like our grandparents. Amy Dacyczyn of the frugal world has educated me. I have tried many things to save and pinch the dollars. I have been highly motivated by the desire to stay home. I have spent most of my life in the workforce and doing commutes, working two or three jobs a week. This life at home is heaven.

Chapter 3

Summer Begins

Wednesday

Well, well, well, it has been a busy week. My allergies started mildly, and then the big winds from the North came and blew the pollen right up into my very marrow, and I felt like I celebrated two months of allergies condensed into two days. I'm happy to get it over quickly. That's efficiency for you. And I had a few days to loll about in bed and watch **Rob Greenfield** videos and this Japanese documentary about *Granny Mochi*, a 95-year-old woman famous for her mochi. I filled up on positive people and drifted off in the sunbeam across my bed. Arjan stayed by my side, brought me snacks, water, and wads of tissue, and kept me company all day. Bali had to deal with his chores, the house, the cooking, and Sam.

That whole day off must have reset and recharged everything because the next day, I had the most fun fictional idea inspired by Molly. She follows me about as if being even a few feet apart would be dreadful. I wondered what she would be like as a human companion, which led to this idea. I spent all day typing up the beginnings of a story. I've been inspired to write fiction for the first time in years. I stayed in bed one more day and the boys put away all that laundry I kept shifting from bed to floor. They folded and hung-up clothes only as an eight and 10-year-old do, but I was thrilled to have them put away instead of winding up on my floors.

By the third day, I thought I would go mad if I didn't clean. What the heck is with the house falling apart in just a few days? Why can't it look nice and keep itself together for a week or so? Bali kept up on the dishes, but the house was awful grubby and sticky everywhere.

I finally drank a whole cup of coffee. That is the worst about being sick, the inability to down a coffee. Then I got to work. I washed all the bedding and did all the laundry. I hung it all out as I now have no excuse to use the dryer with the warm weather and high gas cost. I hung out four loads. Washed the dogs out by the pear tree. I took apart the bidet and scrubbed with heavy cleaners. I swept and vacuumed, and washed down counters and fronts of counters, all doors, fridge, walls, baseboards, and shelving. I was busy all day.

The next day I was inspired to work on the front yard, which had bothered me for two years. Bali built me two beds filled with dirt from the pool area he's leveling. I took a wheelbarrow, shovel, and pitchfork and filled up the beds with composted leaves and hay from Babu's second house under the stairs. It's summer; he doesn't need the hay anymore. I filled up buckets, a big broken basket, and pots I found lying here and there, layering dirt, straw, and mulch, then planted wildflower seeds. Sam and I carried the little wooden table and faux wicker chairs and set up a place to sit in this new garden. I found an old Lock Smith sign from the woods ages ago, and Bali hung it on the trees behind the sitting area. The front yard looks charming in that shabby chic way with the beds and sitting areas and then clustering all the pots and baskets. And I used everything we already had in the yard or house.

Ah, but I wasn't done there. The rest of the afternoon, I weeded in the garden. Some mustard greens have lost their blossoms and have become like trees. I pulled up rows of this forest and then planted the melon starts in the ground.

Today was the fourth day of working madness. It was also a very painful healing day. I watched **The Book Of Henry** last night, and although it was a good movie, it touched on the death of a beloved child and other heavy topics of child abuse that was ignored because the abuser was an influential figure in the community. It was an intense movie with a good ending, except for the eldest son's passing, which sent me over the edge. I was so disturbed because the boy was so much like Arjan. The scene of him dying in the hospital killed me. So, then I watched a movie on two married couples, **Dinner With Friends**, which touched on infidelity and aging couples, questioning lifelong friends that suddenly become other people, and so on. The two movies combined touched so many buttons of my own childhood, being abused and no one stepping in, and then my fears of losing my children, aging, marriage, and not always being content, friendships that I thought would last forever and are gone since the quarantine.

I stayed up until 3 in the morning writing out all my feelings since I can't seem to get a damn therapist in this town. I've tried three times, but I don't have the fears and problems most people have right now, and the counselors may be overwhelmed with patients. So, I'll do my own therapy. I wrote for hours and cried. I feel abandoned by many, deceived, and forgotten over the years. I have hurts and pains that are just surfacing now. I know it's a clean sweep of the old as I change, but sometimes I can't do the spiritual. Sometimes I feel hurt and abandoned, whether or not it's a cosmically good thing. I need to sit in the pain for now.

I woke with a heavy heart and such sadness. I brewed coffee and called my natural healer friend who gets this stuff. I cried and talked for an hour and a half. In the end, I felt drained. I spent the rest of the morning watering and weeding while listening to *Kyle Cease* on YouTube. By the afternoon, I felt healed. Sam cleaned the fridge, organized the red kitchen shelves, and made me a tomato and cheese sandwich. The boys helped me with another purge that included nerf guns, toys, and a rug. The boys are earning a playdate and library day. They are finishing up their school days with some studies and piano. I swept the whole house after rolling up the big carpet in the living room and storing it for summer. I got rid of the kid's rug. It was cream-colored with flowers and showed all the dirt. I think it's best to have no carpets with the boys, dogs, and a pool soon. I have a little braided rug in front of the couch.

I dusted, took out the garbage and recycling, and made a huge pasta pot with a creamy, meaty vegetable sauce. Then I went out to the garden and harvested a huge amount of salad. I've never had such success with lettuce; now, we eat it daily. Dinner was delicious, and there was plenty for two days.

I've had days of this incredible energy, no back pain, and inspired work. I am amazed at all I've done this week. It is not always like this at all. I don't know if it was the day lounging with my cold or what.

And the healing. I genuinely feel it's all this time offline. I have time to go within deeply and start working on the old stuff I didn't make time to heal before. I'm not keeping my mind busy with blogs and videos. I spend days outside, in the garden, and without distractions. It creates space for old pangs to appear.

Gas prices are going up and up. It was bound to happen, and now we can see just how the oil and car companies have created such a dependence on cars. We must find other ways. People used to build small, walkable towns, and people walked everywhere. There is a silver lining, but I don't dare share that right now, as people may come after me with torches and pitchforks. All I will say is that we need to start living differently.

I will pull out the crock pot and already have the bread maker on the counter. I use the toaster oven and limit the use of the gas oven. But who wants hot food in the summer, anyhow? We love vegetable sandwiches and salads now. And watermelons and fruits! Smoothies!

The truck has been parked for days. We walk to the stores and local library to pick up books. We only drive to Grocery Outlet or the big library in the next town three miles away to hang out and use the computers.

Days are getting warmer, so I open all the windows at night to fill the house with cool air. It stays nice and cool during the day if I close the house up by noon.

Wednesday

I haven't written in a long time. I was beginning the painstaking task of editing. However, I've had so many moments and thoughts lately, and I want to record them before I forget.

I've been listening to *Kyle Cease* and working in the garden. The combination has been a very effective therapy tool. I felt like my old self by the next day after I had a crying bender over coffee the other day. I've felt the release of yet another layer of old pains, hurts, and perceived abandonments. I feel lighter inside and burrow deeper into being present. Each day since and in each moment, just as the old anxiety begins to poke at me, reminding me that I have lists and agendas to get to, another voice is now present that tells the nervous, busy person to relax, be present at this moment, there is nothing else to "get to, rush toward, return to doing and getting done." The difference today is that I *feel* this in my soul. I *listen because I feel it's the truth and will save my life*.

My family and I took a trip to the valley to return the PO Box keys. I am discontinuing it. I don't want or need anything, although I have loved all the cards, letters and gifts. I'd rather people enjoy being with me while I ponder life and drink coffee. I don't want the obligation of performing, and I don't want anyone to feel the need to send me gifts. I've been on a purging kick for years now and don't want to bring anything else.

Bali agreed to a side trip to WinCo, and when we arrived, I said to the family, "Please do not rush me. Do not be in a hurry. We have nowhere to be and nothing to do at home. Let's be in this moment and enjoy the time here." I meant it. I'm inevitably pressured to move along by one member or another each time we shop. Sometimes, I put pressure on myself as if I have a job to get back to before I am caught and fired for not finishing a task. It is an inner slave driver, really. But it is often manifest in Bali's words to tell me to hurry or that Sam is ready to go.

As for me, I see how I've been driving myself. I'm sure it comes from childhood issues. But I'm exhausted emotionally from exploring the past or being driven by forgotten demons. So, I am in a state of sweet surrender. The much-earned vacation of letting go. Whenever I think I need to rush or get back to something, I say, "just be in this moment and nothing else."

I have felt spent the last couple of days. It's a good spent, but it is the uncoiling of decades of inner stress. Worrying, fear of life and the world on the deepest levels, and feelings that I'm running out of time, I've fallen behind somehow.

I have days full of energy and enthusiasm and get so much done in the house and garden. Then I want to rest on the couch and have one movie after the next take me away from reality.

I've been scrolling on the phone, despite being out of data. I looked up news articles for the first time in a year. I did this for an hour or so one night and stopped myself. But it was too late, and I suffered mild anxiety the next day. I detest feeling so off, not having that contentment in the morning, only fear of the unknown. The news and information out there are toxic, and it only takes a small amount of time to be infected, but it takes a day or two of inner work to get right again.

How fragile we all are with our inner worlds. A book, a movie, or news clips and our deepest fears are unpacked. While it's good to embrace the old pains and give them your attention so you may benefit from healing, subjecting oneself to social media and news is never good unless you are called to do something about the situation. Most often, we can't do anything, and most often, a lot of the drama on the news or social media is drama mixed with other people's opinions.

I'm reading **The Invisible Life Of Addie La Rue,** by V.E. *Schwab.* In the story, an elder named Estele loved living alone in the forest. She loved her nature and preferred to keep to herself. She is a role model for me right now. Society says we should be out and about being social and getting our kids into all sorts of activities. We should be striving and climbing and going, going, going. We should set goals and reach new heights, being challenged to be worth our salt. But many people are burnt out and miserable, constantly pounding themselves into the ground. People are allowing themselves to be driven by unseen forces and bombarded with online life filled with other people's opinions and arguments, false or overblown reports, and fearmongering in all forms. Then they go to a therapist, happily taking their money and dragging therapy out for decades without life-changing results. The therapy is coupled with a pill or drink, or drug of choice.

In our society, mental illness, homelessness, depression, and stress are so common that all of it is now normal. It isn't normal to be wholesome or happy. Contentment is fleeting with most. The diet industries and liquor stores are thriving. There is a "wellness" guru on every corner of the internet.

The Internet offers wonderful things and learning but must be handled with wisdom and care. Most people do the internet as a child would handle a bag of candy handed to them. They gorge on it all, and even when it's making them sick mentally and emotionally and disconnecting them spiritually, they continue to gorge.

Unplug and then only use the internet for things such as a cooking lesson, gardening advice, or positive subjects that lift you up emotionally. Walk outside as much as possible and get into nature as much as possible. Be sober. That one is hard for most but being clear of mind is imperative. Surround yourself with good people; if you aren't sure what that looks like, then be alone for some time. Let yourself cry and heal. Clear out anything toxic; people, work, maybe a bad neighborhood. Work toward a healthier life. Eat real food. Learn to cook and bake. Cut way back on work hours, so you have more life. Live humbly.

Sunday

It's June 5th, and raining steadily. I rushed from my morning chores to have my coffee on the porch and watch this miracle in Northern California and what will be the last time we enjoy the cool weather and smell of rain this summer. It is a light but steady rain that started last night. I can't believe it! We had rain start in September and now ends in June. Very unusual for our area. I had to chase some very large ants from my wicker porch chair to sit and watch MotherNatures' gift. I decided to add more coffee to the cup and do some writing out here.

I am grateful to live in a forest town. I'm grateful I don't look out on buildings or ugly suburban homes with yards filled with junk. My neighbor's yard has redwoods, and the apartments across the street have giant trees blocking most of them.

I almost forced myself to finish the dishes and make the bed before coming out here, but then I thought, "this is the last rain for months; dishes will always be here reproducing," Then, as I sat out here enjoying the sounds of rain and the smells of wet earth, I wanted to get the cell phone and do some recording, but I stopped myself. I have this inner drive that isn't always so positive. I have a list of "to-dos" instead of just walking into the moment and sitting with it. To-dos can wait. They are always there. Beds are messy each morning, dirty dishes multiply, and they sit and wait patiently, all night if they must. But nature has its own agenda and doesn't wait for us.

I started thinking of the negatives in the world. How it's so crowded, and they keep expanding roads and tearing down rainforests so we can drive more and glut ourselves more on crap foods. It's making a handful of smart business people rich, but we are the fools. We get fatter and dumber as we scroll through our phones while waiting for our double whopper with plastic cheese. We pave over green lands and build ugly suburbs where lovely forests and fields once lived for centuries. It hasn't taken man very long to destroy all that is natural and good. But it's only a handful of mafias that are doing all this, but they have lured us with their flute music and shiny baubles. Oil companies, car companies, big Pharma, and the fast-food industry. They get more affluent and prosperous, and the planet and the ignorant get poorer, sicker, fatter, and more depressed.

But people are waking up, and grassroots groups are sprouting up everywhere. People are reclaiming city streets for their children, for themselves to walk, bike, and play. After the quarantine, some city streets never opened back up to cars because the people woke up and said, "Hell no! Our children want to run around, and we want to stroll and sip espressos without being run over by cars!"

All over Europe, massive rewilding projects are in full motion. Forests and jungles are being replanted. People are starting to bike and walk more, and sales on Ebikes are spiking. Trains are coming back, and cities are being beautified and greened up. Instead of expanding roads to allow more cars, which is never a solution, road diets are happening to reduce cars, pollution, and dangers to those who bike. We must wake up fast, take back our lives and cities, and do what is good and right for nature.

But we don't see all the good happening, do we? No, because all mainstream news and media are filled with violence, nonsense, and drama. There is no news about all the great things happening, the love being shared, or the community's people are developing. I saw a headline for Australian News about how New York City shows signs of social decay. What a laugh. There has been social decay since man began. It was a ploy to get one to click on the video and take the poison. But the news wants you to click on their shows and articles so they get the ratings and money. They don't care that they ruin your day or fill you with fear that keeps you up all night. They want money, and it's like that with most of these media sites and companies. They only want your money. And if you get sick? Great! That means more money for Pharma and all the pills they seem to invent weekly with all the fantastic side effects. It used to be just dry mouth and loose stools, but now they give you suicidal thoughts and actions. The pills for social anxiety gave you a dry mouth and maybe made you poop yourself, which I think doesn't help out in public if you can't talk now because your tongue is stuck to the roof of your mouth and you have a fear of spattering your pants. But now, the pills for depression make you want to kill yourself and sometimes give you just the push to do it.

You can question things and don't need to go too deep to see that things aren't right.

But here is nature. Gorgeous, free, and offers clean food, medicine, and therapy, but we allow developers to pave over it with thick cement and burn Her down.

Times are changing. I hate the internet the longer I'm off it. It's been six months now, and with its spell broken, I can not only see but feel how toxic it is. I've had to delete channels and constantly hit "do not show again" or "don't suggest channel." I need to focus on where I need to go and what I need to learn before I get on there so I don't get lost down some rough alley and poisoned to emotional and mental death.

I had five boys at one time several times last week. I asked them how much they felt social media was causing all this mental health deterioration. They said social media was to blame for at least 65%. That was the first answer, but when I asked if that was all, they said, "we're being generous. The truth is that all the media out there is causing 95% of mental illness and short attention spans."

These are ten and 12-year-olds that already get it.

The longer I'm offline, the more I see how it affects me deeply, even after taking in one short article or news clip. I truly, in the deepest part of my soul, believe that one solution to mental health and well-being is to limit the internet. Go back to having a cell phone that can only call or text and make short visits online when you want to look something up or learn something new. The internet has a good side and a dark side, but we live there and take it all in. Too much information and stimulation makes one feel crazy and overwhelmed by the world. I wonder how many suicides during the quarantine were from being isolated and how many were due to being on the internet, taking in all the toxic drama and fearmongering.

Anyone who takes away your hope and instills fear is not a friend. The news is not your friend. The news channel's motto is "keeping you informed and sharing both sides of current events." This statement could not be farthest from the truth. The news channel will give you the information the sponsors have paid them to give. And They don't care about keeping you informed. Don't be fooled. They are there to make money and be top-ranking. They don't share both sides. They share one side and keep the other side quiet. They are paid puppets.

I only read **Positive. news** or **Livekindly.com**. I stopped with Future Crunch because it felt like they started having an agenda. I don't want information from groups that subtly push a political party's agenda or hail the Pharma companies.

Believe it or not, some of the more popular YouTube creators are doing good work. **Mr. Beast** and **Mark Rober** have been on colossal tree planting missions, ocean clean-ups, beach clean-ups, helping the less fortunate, setting up food pantries during the quarantine, and more. There are many good people and great things going on out there. But you have to search it out. Once you do, more will flow to your suggested feeds.

Another thing I'm losing my taste for is shopping. I have only shopped online once in a month or more. I needed natural pesticides and copper spray for my fruit and nut trees.

Mostly we shop right here in town. I only order online if I can't get something here. I love this town, so I am putting my money into it now. But I used to shop for everything online. I'll pay extra to stay local.

There was a good video by **Kyle Cease** about this very subject. He discussed how most of us could go at least a year without buying a thing and be just fine. We all have so much. We could find fortunes of stuff in our closets, attics, garages, and storage units. We have surpluses of things. And so many people live with just the bare essentials and get by just fine. We only "think" we need stuff, but if we take the time to think it through, we often have it or don't really need it.

It is what I've struggled with for years. It is another spell that needs time to fade. So, I don't shop. We have moments, make memories, and create experiences, but we don't shop. We don't purchase things and stuff.

Thursday

What a busy time it's been. I haven't written in some days. The weather is heating up, but rain is reportedly happening on Sunday, which is wild for NorCal! Mid-June and rain again. Wow, thanks, Mother Nature! I would love to live where it rains in the summer so I can always smell that earthy smell, have my coffee out on the porch, and watch the world having a cleansing shower.

The pool is still not set up. We have only weekends to work on digging up a flat foundation on our backyard slope, and it's taking some time. We have more dirt than we know what to do with. Time for building more beds is what I say! I spent days weeding the garden after two days of rain. Weeds came up so easily. I listened to **Kyle Cease** with earphones and weeded all day until the garden looked tidy. Later I dug up rows, hoed, and planted watermelon, cantaloupe, pumpkin, corn, butternut squash, and beans. The garden is thriving. It gives a real sense of faith in all things when a garden grows lush and produces well after two years of struggling. I think my cherry tree is recovering. I have one dead apple, a mandarin that didn't make winter, two pluot plums that aren't leafing out, and that cherry that was on its way out. I used some natural pesticides and some not-as-natural stuff for the boring peach pest I suspect attacking the cherry. We have lost a lot of trees over the two years. I've had no such luck with pluot trees. Lost three now, and all the gardeners say they grow great here. I'm not even wild about pluot, I didn't even have one until I was in my late 40s, but now I *must* have this pluot. It's a real tragedy when an established tree gives you a great harvest, and it dies. The bugs are thick here, and the lessons are continuous.

On the bright side, many trees are doing great. The nut trees are flourishing, the nectarine seems happy, the pear we brought from the other house is lush, and two apples and two cherries are healthy. The pomegranates are well. The biggest suffered the frost but is leafing out. The maple is growing strong. The wildflowers reseeded themselves in the front bed. Some things are strong and came back when I thought they wouldn't. The crepe myrtle was one. I thought all the trees had died, but they are thick with leaves, even the one Bali planted in a stump. He stuck the remains of a myrtle in a hollowed-out part of a dead stump, which is healthy. Funny how you can stick a part of a tree clumsily in the ground, and it grows strong, but the trees I've worried and fussed over have kicked the bucket.

We've been having a lot of Arjan and Sam's friends over. Arjan's good friend stayed with us for a couple of days and a night. He is charming and a delight, with a great sense of humor, but he has no life skills. He is brilliant, but the simple act of making a sandwich confounds him, and he says spaghetti is too much work with all the twirling of noodles. I've seen his eyes glaze over with the job of putting leftovers in a container. This makes my work a bit harder as extra boys now need care and feeding. But all the boys are well-mannered and show gratitude. I let them walk to town when it's a pack of them. Arjan and one of the older boys are wise about crossing streets and avoiding weird situations.

Many parents are into this free-range style of homeschooling, and I can't say it works for me. I'm around kids who still can't read or write but are intelligent. I'm pretty lax with the schoolwork, but we do reading, writing, and math daily, along with the piano. I raised the boys with the classics, read the Bible, Greek mythology, Homer's tales of the Odyssey and Iliad, and fairy tales, and we watched musicals and listened to classical music, old rock and roll, opera, and everything outside that and in between. They know how to do quite a lot of cooking and meal prep, some cleaning and tidying, and basic gardening.

As far as homeschooling goes, there must be some daily routine, and the basics of writing, reading, and math should be practiced. Then I let the boys choose whatever interests them in history, science, and social studies. Whatever they are passionate about, I support it by supplying tools, documentaries, toys, books, and art supplies. I encourage art and music. I encourage good movies and books. We don't study long, and we don't make it complicated. It has taken me years to relax, be patient, and enjoy the process. Take it slow, make it all safe, and encourage the boys to dive in and not fear mistakes. Mistakes are vital as you learn so many things from mistakes. Making mistakes is like planting a tree that branches out in many directions. Every branch is an experience and learning opportunity. I also don't push a lesson. If Arjan says he can't do the math that day, we don't do it. Stress and pushing through creates blocks and slows the brain flow.

Chapter 4

Deep Summer

I have rested from my writing for weeks, maybe over a month. Tomorrow will be July, and the weather has been interesting. Fires have already begun, and the library has a table spread with pamphlets and magnets to put on the fridge with your zone, so when you get an alert, you don't run about like a chicken with its head missing. Precisely what we did last year when we received our first evacuation notice. We had no idea what zone we were in and became nervous idiots packing clothes and dog food. Bali started packing the pantry food as if we were going underground for the next three months. Lots of weird behavior was displayed, and it turned out the fire was in a whole other county, and people were being evacuated to our town.

Lesson learned. Today I have us linked and registered with reverse 911 and RedAlerts for fire updates. Our zone is written clearly on a fridge magnet from the library, and I know exactly what to pack and can do it in a hot second. Important documents are in a safety deposit box at the bank. I download all the other stuff onto a USB port and keep it close to throw in my purse. But if all goes, all goes, and we are free to cry about it and start a new life. To create something fun and interesting.

I would be very sad to lose this town—this house. We talk about moving sometimes. Maybe a new country far away, but I have memories here now which are hard to separate from when they are warm and sweet memories. The kind that overwhelms you with feel-good nostalgia. I was cooking pork chops from the food bank boxes (I'll get into that more in a bit), and it is the second time I've made them with cream of mushroom. I felt this warm nostalgia come over me and had a memory I savored. Funny thing: the memory was only made a few weeks ago, but it felt like an old memory. It was of me cooking up the pork chops for dinner, the boys watching a movie, the summer's evening light just so in the kitchen, and the flavors of the meal being so comforting.

We have memories now. Good, happy memories. They whisper to me when I water the garden, cook a meal, sit on the porch with my hot coffee, or swing in the hammock with a mystery novel I can't put down. I remember times when I was reading a great thriller and half listening to the chimes on the porch or making caramel corn for an excellent movie we had waited months to get from the library.

All the memories are of being at home doing life. None of the memories are of going on trips or spending significant amounts of money to do a thing. They are free life stuff.

The allotted budget is now down to $2,500 a month. This is relatively new, and we have been overdrawn at the bank because I went to the store twice for ingredients. I didn't have to buy those ingredients; if I hadn't, we would have been fine, and the car insurance payment wouldn't have put us over. But I give myself grace as the family accountant since I'm working with a true-blue shoestring budget.

We want for nothing, and it seems we have been cured of the consumerism bug. I no longer order things except some natural bug stuff for my trees since I couldn't get them in town, and I order books from Thrift Books. You can't wrong a person for books. The new rule is that we can buy books and art supplies, clay, writing supplies, and garden stuff, but that is it. We don't need a thing.

It's freeing to want little. You know, to find great comfort and little joys in the simplest things, such as a well-made homemade latte in the morning, when you get it just right with the creamer and honey. The anticipation and excitement of waking up to library day. Finding a book you enjoy so much you rush through making dinner to get back to it, thinking about the last chapter the whole time you wash the dishes, pondering the next chapter.

Arjan and Sam don't ask for things anymore. They don't even wander much when we go to the Dollar Store. I don't order things online, and I've skipped the last few 50% off weeks at the Hospice Thrift down the road. We sometimes watch movies for breakfast and make caramel popcorn from what we have in the pantry. Arjan and I have books in hand, even when dad thinks we shouldn't read at the table. We live a very different life right now, and if anything, I want to record it so that when the day comes that we turn the internet back on, we remember this and maybe are inspired to turn it back off again.

The library is our hang-out. They serve brown bag lunches to the kids during the summer. The bags are loaded with great snacks. This is a thrill for the boys, especially Sam, because it's foods we don't eat. It's enough to cover breakfast, lunch, and a snack. I love it because I get a break from making meals until supper time on those days. The library is also working on setting up a gaming room. They had rehabilitated animals the other day, and Sam could touch an alligator. The amount of free wonderment and community information is vast. I adore the library ladies and have received excellent advice during small chats. They suggest good books for Arjan and TV series for me.

The boys made a new friend who knows all the jewels the library has to offer and introduced them to the lunches, the animals, and the promise of the gaming room. He teaches Sam new games, and they all play their video games together. Since all this bounty, Sam, who had trouble adjusting and often hollered and begged to have the internet reconnected, has fallen in love with the library. We only have five months left, but he has decided a year is prudent. I'm relieved as Arjan and I aren't in a hurry to get internet back in our house.

There are days I feel like I'm done and want to turn it back on. If we have another lockdown drama or the covid scare arises again, and they shut down the library, we may. The only thing I still miss is Pandora. You have to pay for it on the phone, and I won't do it. I miss operas and musicals. I miss good music. The radio sucks after a while. I love the Dahlila show at night, but the reception is crappy, and the one local station that comes in plays this bubble gum pop most of the time. I'm not sure what crowd they are catering to, but it doesn't seem like it fits with this town. It's more geared toward suburban teeny boppers, less mountain folk, and this village's artsy, hippy, radical thinkers. We have the "other" local station with the blues hour and plays Hawaiian music on Sundays along with some old gospel and NPR. That is more like it for here. I usually shut it down when they play NPR. I wouldn't say I like the depressing and all-is-going-to-hell opinions of the speakers.

Last year when it felt like all of California was on fire, one of the speakers said it was like an apocalypse and would only worsen each year. I remember working in the kitchen, looking out the window at the smoke-filled skies, and feeling hopeless. I was in the middle of filling a bucket with black beans, and I thought, with utter despair, "What is the damn use!" That's what that sort of BS talk does. It robs everyone of hope and creates depression. Well, this year, they were interviewing someone, I started listening halfway through, but he was a forest expert or something rather. He said that much of California is actually dependent on fires for healthy growth. Some animals and trees need fire to propagate and thrive. Some seeds don't sprout without the heat from a fire. He said there used to be many fires from Native Americans and natural or controlled burns. At least 4 million acres would burn yearly, keeping the forest healthy and thriving. What a new and refreshing perspective on all this. I was getting so tired of hearing about the tinder box we live in and how California is "on fire!". People run to fear and then date it and reproduce many fearful children, figuratively.

When I hear of a fire, I think, "Well, that area will regrow healthy and strong next year." Isn't that a happier way to think? And probably more correct.

The garden is doing well, but my plants aren't as big or lush as other gardens I see around here. My plants are a bit stunted and slow to grow. It's much better this year; winter greens were incredible, but we still need to add all sorts of amendments and cover crops. I have three bags of chicken manure pellets and have been throwing them in the garden. I feed the fruit and nut trees to make them strong, but there won't be fruit this year. My pluot trees are dead, and the apple tree in the back is dead. One cherry tree is trying to move toward the eternal light, but I think I saved it. Now, the berries are thriving! They were just one long and sad vine each year, but all three vines bushed out this year and are producing. Some trees are doing great despite the late frost. I'll replant a few trees this Fall.

Unsuccessful gardening and dead fruit trees are very disheartening. But each year, there are minor improvements.

I just came in from watering the back orchard, and I'm pleased that some trees look strong and healthy. A good pruning this winter, and I hope they continue to grow. And the birds! My garden is full of birds. I moved the bird bath under the old pear tree and hung another bird feeder. Bali hung two bird feeders in the garden. With the earwig population explosion, I need these birds to feast and clear them out, or I'll have to borrow the neighbor's hens.

I left my laundry out for days, and the laundry basket was on the ground for days. When I did collect the laundry and bring it in yesterday, I playfully poured it out on Arjan, and he pushed it onto the floor. Much to my horror, a herd of earwigs began scuttling from the pile. I ran for my slipper and commanded the boys to start whacking at them before they could spread through the house and set up communities. I tried to be a brave mother but caved after a minute of smacking bugs and seeing them pour out of my sunbaked clothes lying on the carpet. I did what all girls do when encountering the grotesque. I cried out, "Ahhh, I'm freaking out! I'm freaking out!" My brave sons did battle by my side until every bug was terminated.

We won this battle, but it unnerved me to the core. My yard is alive. Maybe there's more life than my constitution can handle. It sent me on a cleaning frenzy that lasted all day into the late evening. I cleaned and scrubbed things I had neglected or had never cleaned before. Molly's little staircase to get up to the bed was a cheap plastic thing that once had felt cloth on the steps. They became unglued, and the goop left behind became black with dirt. I kept eyeing it as I passed the ugly thing daily but thought, "for another day, for another day." I've thought that about a lot of things over the years. I've had projects in mind but just put them off for that special time when all the planets align.

In the last few days, the planets have aligned. I put the stairs in the shower, and with a liberal amount of Ajax and scrubber, the stairs are sparkling and clean. I did the same with the garbage can under the sink. It was white, showing all the filth inside, and dribbled brown stuff down all four sides. It is scrubbed, left in the sun all day, and is pure white again. Then I pulled out the stove, and I'm always amazed at the accumulated grunge that collects within a season. The next thing that happened was something I'd dreamed of for a long time.

The dryer stopped working, much to my liking. I dragged it outside, pulled out the washer, and gave the whole pantry/laundry room floor a good sweep and scrub. I moved the big wooden clothes rack into the room and set it up by the washer. I love this for many reasons. I was reading a women's account of their high electric bill, and once she stopped using the dryer completely, her monthly bill went from hundreds to $50. Something like that. It was impressive enough for me. I'm always tempted to use any excuse to use the dryer. Hanging laundry is not a remarkable feat, but I get lazy in small areas. Without the dryer, the pantry will stay cooler, we will save a lot of money on the electric bill, and there will be more room in the pantry.

I have several buckets I used for my bulk dried foods, but as we cook everything from scratch and use up the mass amounts of dried goods in the pantry, the buckets have emptied. This is great as some of the oats and grains began to turn. We have wasted nothing. I don't plan on ever stocking up like that again. It's taken two years to get through the oats, and still working on the last 10 lbs. We have kidney beans that have lasted years.

I have a neighbor that helps run a dog and cat food pantry. People donate food that is sometimes new; sometimes, they donate because their pets were allergic or didn't like the kibble. She asked me if I needed dog food as they had a surplus about to expire, and they were throwing it out. I was thrilled and went the next day to pick up a few bags. Well, they had tons. It filled the back of our truck. I kept half and gave half to some friends who live on wild land and have rescued some five dogs plus their own, and I know they struggle financially. It was enough to feed all their dogs for months.

I had all the dog bags, tapped up and some with holes, stacked carelessly on the floor, but when I went on the big cleaning frenzy, I poured them all into sealed buckets so we don't attract mice and bugs. We even had canned food, treats, pig ears, and toys for Molly. I would say we have enough dog food for 8 to 10 months. That saves us $180 a month.

Friday

There is nothing like washing your face at night. I use a lot of sunscreen during the day, so I lather a washcloth liberally with Ivory soap. The bars are cheap and gentle for the face. After rinsing well, I rub coconut and shea butter all over my face and neck, which is refreshing: that and getting my pajamas on and a soft cotton sports bra. I'm in heaven.

We had a long library day, and the kids had free lunches. Their friend said they could eat in the library, and I was quite surprised, but I made them eat outside. I don't want them getting into the habit of eating in front of the TV or laptop. It turns out you CAN'T eat in the library, much to my relief. The sounds of crinkling bags make me crazy, and all the food is everywhere.

I'm less interested in YouTube; I find it hard to find something I can sink my teeth into. I can't stomach another frugal or thrifty video, but I love easy meal ideas. I did find a good video on Freegan living. A man in

Singapore said he works and has a home but is always worried about money. He started dumpster diving and finding free vegetables after Farmer Markets when they throw away the excess. He found great stuff, and his wife gave him a room to keep it. He said at first, his family was embarrassed, but as he found expensive purses for his wife and coins and jewelry for his father, now they love when he goes out scavenging. He also works with a food bank that rescues expired foods and has a community of freegans that share. He has a room filled with good stuff to share, like shoes, purses, bags, a telescope, etc. There is a food stand called Junk Food, and they make meals from leftover stuff in the dumpsters or from the vegetables markets are throwing out.

I'm a little bit Freegan. I have found so many great things on the street, and the food bank keeps putting food across the street on certain days. It sits there for days before the management throws it out and cleans up. Sam and I have gone over when it's dropped off and collected what looks safe and promising. We have filled our chest freezer with chicken, pork chops, corn tortillas, and cheese shreds. I have filled pantry shelves with peanut butter, jelly, canned tomato sauce, tuna, and chicken. Once again, I'm thrilled with the free bounty, which helps save on groceries.

Sam and I have filled up backpacks with good, canned food on other streets where we find boxes left out. We are not taking from others. The boxes are there for days sometimes. We take what we need. *We* also always put things on the street: food, clothing, books, furniture, DVDs, and lovely knick-knacks. It is the cycle of giving and receiving; lately, the abundance is ample.

Saturday

Speaking of abundance, yesterday was overflowing. Arjan had his best friend over for the day, and this boy will only eat my smoothies and PB & J sandwiches. I had slacked on my bread-making duties, so we walked to Safeway to find a cheap loaf of bread. On the way, we passed two garage sales and some free items. I found a faux fur pillow and faux fur blanket, which washed up beautifully and are now on the couch, giving it a more bohemian look along with the Indian spreads. I found an upholstered chair I adored, but they wanted $20, so I waited for the evening when all the garage sale items that didn't sell wound up on the curb. I did have some cash and bought a bin full of hot wheels cars and tracks (looked almost new) for Sam, along with a big stack of Pete The Cat reader books. That only cost $7 for all that.

And then I made the mistake of paying $20 for a push mower, thinking we would be so green and not need gas for the mower anymore. I had visions of mowing the back forty with my iced tea and keeping it all neat and tidy. When I tried mowing around the fruit trees, it was hell. I tried all levels on the mower and went over and over spots, but it only managed to beat down hearty weeds but cut nothing. Sweaty and frustrated, I dragged it down the street back to the seller. She is a lovely neighbor, so I didn't have the heart to ask for my money back. America's cheapest family, we are NOT. I asked to exchange it for a glossy, maple wood (probably not, but it looks like it) swivel desk chair. We pushed it home. I'm sure the neighbors are sitting on their porches with their lemonades to watch the show of Kate dragging things back and forth during garage sale weekends.

Later, after I fed dad, Sam and I took the car and prowled the neighborhood for all the things we thought would be on the street for free after a full day of garage sales. I found my upholstered chair (that I wanted earlier, but they wanted $20) for free on the street! I don't know how I got it in the back seat, but I wasn't leaving without that treasure. Then we drove about town and the next town. We came home with fuzzy rainbow arm or leg sleeves that look like they should be in some night club get-up, a stuffed raccoon, a sun dress for me, a Stephen King book for me and a Tolkien novel for Arjan, some canned mixed veggies, sugar-free cookies, and a small bag of lollipops. We went out hunting and dragged home some great stuff.

Our home is absolutely perfect now. It took two years of purging and collecting, but it is so adorable and bohemian without being too busy. It's colorful and easy to clean and maintain.

I feel good about decorating for free and finding all these great finds. I feel good not spending money. Lately, when I do spend money, it is always disappointing in one way or another. The last time we had fast food, it was so gross and made us feel ill from its greasiness. The place was Burger King, who was King of sad and gross. The place was dirty and dark from all the advertisements covering the windows, miserable employees, and an empty dining area (which should have been our first red flag). We watched them microwave our onion rings. I mulled over the loss of money and digestive enzymes to the foul food for two days, but in the end, it put a full stop to our desire to have fast food. We haven't purchased to go anything since. Most restaurant food has been a grave mistake of oil slicks and nausea. The food always tastes reheated and dead as dead can be.

The last time I ordered books online, it was also a bummer. You think about all the manpower, trains, trucks, and postal workers it takes to get a small package to you, and then it sucks. This has to stop. Amazon is not benefiting the environment or people's wallets. I ordered **America's Cheapest Family** and skimmed it, bored from the first page. It was nothing like my beloved **Complete Tightwad Gazette** that is lovingly dog-eared and highlighted, worn from many evenings perusing to keep my frugal spirits up.

I read Connie Hultquist's book about the poor but "scrubbed clean" house. It has inspired me to scrub this house from every nook and cranny. To take such pride in what we have and not buy anything more. And I will stick to the freegan lifestyle somewhat because I'm not happy with the things I buy, and it feels harder to part with that hard-earned cash.

The goal is to pay off the house in four or five years. Bali says two years. However, unless we win the lottery or one of my books makes it big, that's crazy talk.

Monday

The pool is up and full! It took almost two months to get that slope leveled and the foundation of sand and tarps, then setting up the pool and filter system. We were so fortunate that all the pieces were present. So many people have complained of missing a crucial piece, but we were short one filter pipe we found at the pool store. This pool is over $1600 online, and we got it for $350 at Habitat For Humanity. We searched for over a year. The kids are in there now, having a great time. It's the 4th of July and in the 70s this week. Bizarre weather for a California summer. Arjan and Sam have been playing since this morning with only one break so we could shop for fresh produce at Grocery Outlet.

I'm reading **A Happy Pocket Full Of Money**. It is about metaphysics and quantum physics, creating prosperity and abundance in your life by understanding the Laws of the Universe. The book had so many rave reviews. I've read many of these books and enjoyed listening to Abraham Hicks for years. Even those most well-versed on this topic say this book was fantastic and life-changing. I got this book idea from **Timothy Ward** on YouTube. I love his channel and often listen to his streams of thought when outside gardening. He has been through living the "American Dream" and depression, the work treadmill, then let it all go and started traveling and working at large parks and Country Inns. He talks about getting off the news and getting out of the working mill, letting go of the stuff and ideas of how we "should be living," and to go forth finding our dreams, following our happiness.

He made a video called "Turn off the news and read these books!" (he's changed the title since to "11 books that changed my life") and listed all the books he felt changed his life. I ordered half of them, and this *Pocket Full Of Money* was one of them. He almost didn't read it because he doesn't care much about money, but he was so glad he did and feels it has changed his life and prosperity in grand ways.

I'm pretty content with our financial life, but I love learning metaphysics.

Wednesday

We will be going to the library every day this week. I can't remember why I agreed to this, but it is happening. I'm already over it, and at the same time, I woke up this morning feeling like I was ready for this home unplugging to be terminated.

The pool is complete, and the boys swim for hours every day. We go to the library for a few hours, then they come home and eat the free lunch from the library, then off to the pool for hours of play and swimming about like little fish. They sleep so well at night, Arjan snores now, and he never snores, but they are wiped out from all the exercise.

I'm baking some chicken legs we got free from the box, brown rice, and frozen vegetables. Last night I plucked a large zucchini, a small yellow zucchini, and a large onion from our scant vegetable garden. The onion and zucchini filled the large pan. Everything was sauteed with oil, salt, and pepper and spooned over fresh steamed brown rice. It was so simple, probably cost a dollar for the whole dinner, and so delicious.

In the Fall, we will add some sand, more horse manure, all the compost from the two piles, and more leaves from the colossal Walnut tree, and then we will have a fantastic garden. Each year the harvest will become more abundant.

And I saved seeds already! I saved one giant mustard green bush and dried it. It saved the equivalent of three or four packets of store-bought seeds. Thrilled. I hadn't planned on doing that. Baby steps.

Ah, sometimes we must stop and go over everything we have accomplished.

Monday

I woke up in the seventh month of not having internet in the house and felt done. We had been going to the library daily, thinking it would be fun, but it wasn't. Arjan and I felt a little bored and depressed by the third day. Arjan said the one day a week was something to look forward to, but daily was overkill. I didn't enjoy having a schedule, getting up each day, and getting things done to leave the house by late morning. I didn't enjoy being absent from the house and my daily chores. The floor was collecting dog hair in the corners. The laundry was piling up. I missed sitting in my comfortable pj's, sipping homemade lattes, and doing my writing. I missed tidying and sweeping the house and leisurely planning the day's main meal.

Going out also requires driving in traffic that suddenly seemed thick in this little town and dealing with people. Even if we don't talk to each person, we take in their energy, and in today's soup of chaotic energy, it is unsettling at times. We examine the population's fears, worries, hopelessness, and anger. Yes, there are so many times I enjoy interactions with others, but I then need alone time on my porch reading fiction and detaching.

So, for a few mornings, I felt like I was done with this time of not having internet. I investigated Xfinity, but what a price tag! And you had to commit for two years!

The solution was found at the librarian's front desk. I'd seen signs for Hot Spots and a stack of small boxes. You check one out like a book, take it home, turn it on, and have wireless internet! We can keep it for two weeks and renew it if no one is in line for it. When we return it, we get right back on the waiting list. What a thrill!

I have my Pandora back! Which is indeed what I missed overall. I can do my screen recordings, a trick I learned, and watch my favorite authortube.

Yes, we had drama the first day. We had to make some hard, clear rules and there is still work to do, but I have to say the thrill of having Pandora on again and watching channels on YouTube in the evening while I write and bake cookies is so dreamy.

Speaking of, there is a charming and fun little channel called **Your Daily Orange Juice**. I love this channel! She has been watching me for years and is a part of the community of *Coffee With Kate*, but I had no idea she had a tiny channel. She is a homemaker, and they don't make much money. They frequent the food bank and food pantry (not sure what the difference is), and they make do big time. They have no washer or dryer. They line-dry the clothes after washing them in a big tub in the yard. There is a greenhouse and some garden beds made of halved barrels. I love seeing how other people make things work. The mother shows what recipes she makes from the food pantry items. I think this is very useful for many people right now.

Thursday

I had a bit of a scare the other day. I have lost a couple of nights of sleep over it. Our mortgage went from $1330 to $1548 overnight. Upon inquiry, it is our taxes that went up. I spent all day on the phone calling Assessors, mortgage company agents, and friends for comfort. No one gave me a clear answer. The assessor...I still have no clue what she was talking about, but she went on about percentages and property values and said my taxes would probably go up $3000 a year faithfully. I was peeing myself and packing our bags to find a FREE cave in Utah at that point. Then every agent I spoke to with my mortgage company kept trying to sell me something. I hung up on one girl because she kept sniffling on the phone and "upselling" me on taking equity out of my house even after I told her I was trying to pay my mortgage *off*, not get into more debt. She didn't know what she was talking about, so I cut that relationship loose.

Finally, I called the Treasure Tax Collector and got a woman on the phone who was present in this Universe and clear and concise about the subject. The only reason my taxes went up is that we are now paying our adjusted house value. So, last year we were still paying what the previous owner paid for a house valued at $142K. This year our proper taxes for our house value of $257K kicked in. We pay $2700 a year in taxes. That is all. I have no idea what that assessor was talking about. I asked a simple question, "why did our taxes go up so much now?" She did a complicated calculus equation while standing on her head and exploring physics simultaneously. She lost me a night of sleep, and I started thinking I'd have to find this Daniel Suelo and learn how to live for free.

I devoured the book, **The Man Who Quit Money,** about Daniel Suelo. It was far more profound than I thought it would be. I love how his friend (who wrote this book about him) explored Daniel's life ruled by religion and money from childhood. This led to a life of exploring the depths of his own spiritual beliefs, his sexuality (he is gay and raised in a hard-core religious family), and all his years of service in social work seeing the truth of money and humanity. For him, money caused stress and fear. In letting it go, he found a sense of peace and freedom and lived well for decades. But it was a journey to get to that place of absolute faith that he would be ok without it. One day, after testing the Universe for years, he left the last of his money in a phone booth and never used it again. He did volunteer work on farms, in a battered woman's shelter, and a free meal program. He exchanged work for a meal or produce, dumpster dived, foraged, ate roadkill, and family and friends fed him now and then. He also fed them from his finds. He lived in small caves in the Utah desert and was part of a large community. He was not isolated and poor at all. He had many friends, the farms, and projects, then he started a blog and frequented the library to post his writings to a large following. I believe he now lives with his mother to take care of her in her last years. He has a YouTube channel. There was a video of the "chariot" he built onto his bike to ride his mother around.

Sunday

So much has changed in my inner world in the past so many days. I don't know where to begin.

First, we brought home a Hot Spot from the library. It's a small disk that you turn on, and voila! You have wireless internet. It is not the strongest, as we learned over some days. We can play simple games on the computer, and the Chromebook does excellent with it. We can watch YouTube and do simple things but streaming free movies is out. (Later we would find that some Hot Spots are stronger, and we can stream movies and be on several computers fine, this was an old Hot Spot).

We were thrilled at first. I blared my Pandora, so jolly to be reunited with my musicals again. They boys jumped on the chrome book. I even ordered another computer as the boys had worked all year and saved their birthday to earn $500 for a new one.

Then the drama and fight began. The new computer sucked (refurbished), and we had to return it. I quickly became bored with YouTube. By day seven, Arjan looked blue, and when I asked what was bothering him, he said,

"I don't like having the internet here. You brought it back too soon. I liked when we went to the library once a week. We had something to look forward to." Sam agreed. I agreed. I was surprised and ever so pleased that they felt this way. We took it back that day and spent hours in the library working and playing. It's our social center, after all.

I did recheck the Hot Spot out this weekend to do some screen recording and work. We will return it tonight.

But then other things started happening. Marcy was talking about her guides and reminded me we must invite them to join us and help us. They are on standby until we invite them in. I remember this from years ago but forgot until she mentioned this.

While washing the morning dishes, I talked to my guides. I said, "All the guides around me that mean well and have my best interest in mind, please join me, guide me and work with me."

The next thing you know, I started having these thoughts, and I kept flashing on the tall stack of books I had yet to read and the inner work I kept putting off. I had the overwhelming hunch to get on my channel and delete all the future videos I had posted for the next five weeks. It was hard to do since it had been hours of filming. I had something like ten long videos up. But I did it without much drama. I know from years of work that a hunch is all you need to stay on the path. Those hunches are crucial.

I have no regrets. I have one video to put up, and that's it. I tried to make a screen recording of how to publish on KDP Amazon, but I messed up part of it and can't go back. I was recording myself publishing the cookbook that I published this morning—just another sign.

Then I watch this movie with Molly Shannon, **Year Of The Dog**. It was a good movie but a little hard to watch because the main character loses her mind a bit before she genuinely finds her most authentic self and calling. I may watch it again now that I know things turn out well. But that is self-discovery. It can be painful, confusing, and embarrassing. We lose people and things during the process. Then when we finally surrender to our destiny, it all flows, and we find ourselves surrounded by the right people and situations. Life is whole and prosperous when we find the right place for ourselves in this world.

Another sign.

A fellow YouTube creator from the UK, a friend of mine, emailed and she talked about her electricity not working in their house. An old Indian man came out to try and fix it. She said he exuded such inner peace and kindness it was moving. When she mentioned him at the rental office and how kind he was, they said they felt like the Dahli Lama had visited them when he came to the office. It made me think about what his life and his inner world must be like. He is probably present in every moment; whether he has tea or works on someone's electrical issue, he is present. I doubt he would work on two

YouTube channels and load his plate daily with chores, goals, and child-rearing. He focuses on one thing at a time, and being an electrician is probably all he puts his energy into. He may lead a calm and serene life. He probably chews his food and tastes it.

When you genuinely chew your food and taste it, you discover many foods you aren't that into—just one insight.

Another sign.

Then I return to my book, **Bird by Bird by Anne Lamott**. I begin the chapter on Perfectionism. She talks about the killer of freedom, imagination, and creativity. I can't wait to get back to it.

Another sign.

I keep "preparing" for some time to go off into the wilderness, but then I forget that I'm on a soul quest and get busy. Or something happens to make me nervous about our finances, so I get busy. I distract myself from the inner work I need to do. Well, no more! That is the message. No more. I deleted the videos scheduled for next month, scraped today's work for the other channel, and I'm done. I need to focus right now, this minute.

Monday

It's time. I need to move even deeper into the forest. I asked for guidance. *Florence Scovel Shinn* always said, "Never ignore a hunch."

I watched two movies yesterday that resonated with me for different reasons. **Year Of The Dog** with Molly Shannon and **Land** with Robyn Write. **Year Of The Dog** is about a woman living a neat and tidy life with her sweet dog Pencil. She is a good friend and supportive secretary, loves Pencil, lives in a suburbia setting, and works in a newer corporate office. She is kind and never disagrees with anyone. She goes along with everyone's stuff without expressing an opinion. Then Pencil gets poisoned and dyes. She mourns the loss but soon adopts another dog with the encouragement of a dog rescuer who saw her at the hospital the day Pencil passed.

The dog is difficult, but the dog rescuer works with him, and a romance between the woman and the dog fanatic seems to blossom. He's vegan, and this inspires her to explore it. She begins learning about factory farming and all the cruelty around animal testing and so on. It is her journey toward becoming a vegan and animal rights activist. It's hard to watch most of this movie because, as we know, change can be messy and painful. We embarrass ourselves when we find a new passion and want our family and friends to jump on board. They humor us and hope we get over this new fad and return to the person they know and love. Eventually, she loses her mind a bit from this profound inner change and becomes so different from the people surrounding her. Her passions for animal activism consume her. Her romance doesn't happen because the dog man is celibate. When we travel the road to transformation, things go wrong as they do, and she winds up having a breakdown. Eventually, she finds balance and tries to resume her life. The problem is that she has changed too much. She is someone else, and her life no longer fits her. The end of this movie is worth all the cringy parts. She writes a mass email explaining that she just isn't that person anymore and must move on and walks off the job and leaves her home. The next scene is her on a bus with all the Peta activists. She has found her people and her place in her new life.

I think of all the times I've morphed and been rebirthed into a new mind and life. I've lost and gained so many people and places along the way. I preached from my soap box and shared my silly soul for all to raise their eyebrows in humor or click their tongues in concern. Morphing is not easy.

I think this time I'll just quietly go into the woods and do my changing.

I'm losing my taste for YouTube. So many channels about frugality and homemaking are overdone to death! The bird has been cooked to burnt people! But everyone is looking for that new idea, that magic formula that will make all their money woes evaporate with a waive and coupon. "Clean with me!" "hashtag this and hashtag that"

"Walmart haul," "Grocery haul," "20 frugal tips," "10 things we don't buy anymore," it goes on and on. I want desperately to get away from it. However, in all honesty, I love living like this. It's a fun challenge and a good and wholesome life. But we don't feel poor. We want for nothing. The trick is learning not to want much but creature comforts. A good coffee in the morning, sun-made iced tea in the afternoon, a big, soft bed at night, and good movies to watch in the evening.

The biggest thing that makes wealth no longer necessary to me is that I live in a beautiful area surrounded by more beautiful areas, small, historic towns loaded with Victorian charm. I live in an area people save their vacation hours and money to visit and spend time walking the forest trails and dining in the old towns. People go on vacation to read in hammocks, swim, and take long, leisurely walks. This is my everyday life. Let me not take it for granted.

Chapter 5

Going Deeper Into the Wilderness

There is a scene in **Please Stand By** with Dakota Fanning where Wendy, the main character, loses most of her script when she flees from a hospital. She is on her way to Paramount Pictures to submit her script and hopefully win the $100, 000 grand prize and change her life. She is walking down an alley in tears and feeling lost and forlorn. She sits down to look over the salvaged parts of the script she once had. She reads part of it where Spock is encouraging his friend Captain Kirk. "There is only one logical direction to go: Forward," He says. She looks up to see a recycling bin under a Copy Shop sign, filled with scrap paper. She puts away the remainder of her script and wipes her eyes. After pulling out a stack of used paper from the bin, she finds a safe place to sit and rewrite the missing parts of her script. As she begins, you can see her calming down, comforted by her work—the work she loves and knows without a doubt.

I love this movie and have watched it many times. I love the beginning and this part. The parts of her routine, her scheduled life, and how immersed she was in her script writing. The movie is about a woman becoming so determined to change her life that she ultimately leaves her comfort zone and meets many obstacles on her journey. Still, they only empower her beyond anyone's belief in what she is capable of. And it turns out she is very, very capable.

But the parts I mentioned before feed that side of me that finds all this comforting. I'm not autistic (that I know of), but I'm sure I could be diagnosed with mild cases of something. I find comfort in routines and work toward a singular focus. I have chosen a few hustles, but it's not matching this Zen Utopia I'm working toward. I'm glad that I tried all the things I've tried. YouTube, blogging, and writing have been fantastic fun and creative experiences. And now, we enter a new chapter—one of more silence, more deep contemplation. I know where it is leading, but I've dragged my feet for some reason.

To slow down and release my duties of working on so many projects, here come the open plains of awkwardness and boredom as I adjust to the new daily format and begin to walk a new road that is foreign and, as with all new and foreign things, lonely and bland at first. It is an empty room except for old clutter from the previous tenant and needs a good scrubbing.

And that is when we need to sit in its emptiness and be quiet. Our guides will help us if we invite them to sit with us and take part in building a new, little world better suited for where we are. We can also use the gardening analogy. We must go outside, dig that plot up, and start replanting new fruits. Every day we go outside and weed or water to encourage growth; if we are patient, we will have an abundant harvest in the future.

I have purchased a few books by *Emerson* and *Thoreau*, a writing book by *Stephen King*, and the DVD about **Thich**

Nat Hanh Walk With Me. I bought those with my gift card from the Amazon affiliate program. $30 this time, yay! I then ordered several books from the library from *Emerson, Whitman, Thoreau...*

The old writing takes time to chew. Definitely not a speed-read sort of work like modern literature.

And so, she goes off into the wilderness to be silent and commune with the blue jay and house finch in her yard, to read hundred-year-old literature of men that also went into the wilderness. I have removed the internet from the house for seven months now.

Implementing a routine that brings comfort and structure is the best way to make a life change.

I want to run my home far more efficiently and with a monk-like devotion. I have a nice, packed little pantry that needs some straightening up and menu planning to see if I can stretch things out and save grocery money for a few weeks. I would like to do some deep cleaning because it helps me emotionally.

Our primary income is from Bali's paychecks without my writing and making videos. We lived on just Bali's income of $2600 to $2800 in the first few years of our marriage. We were just fine and comfortable, but I don't recall eating out except a night at the ol' Hometown Buffet now and then. We would go to town on Sunday with grocery envelope in hand and do our shopping for the week, then we might dine at the Hometown Buffet, not often, but how I loved that place! There was a Golden Corral that was very clean and fun too. I love having choices. The buffets repulse many, but I love them because I love to sample and dine on all sorts of things I would never have at home. I have a less-than-polished side to me. This was it for outside luxuries: no movies, no fine dining, and no new clothes. But we had so much, and our house was lovely, the farm we lived on was lush, and I learned to be content at home, tending to little people and reading stacks of books Bali retrieved from the library on his way home from work.

So, why can't I go back to that? I have been spoiled by outings and spending a lot of money since I started building a channel on YouTube and publishing books. The royalties have given us much more pocket money, and I habitually ordered on Amazon monthly, if not weekly. I had taken up grocery shopping without a budget and tried all sorts of fancies, such as vegan delights and sweets. Was I making a fortune? No, not even close. Some of those creators have purchased new homes over the years. So many of them grew their channels, and next thing you know, they are doing, "Come see our new house!". No, I just made enough to allow me to order often online and grocery shop freely.

But now I must go back to the days of a grocery envelope and stick to it. I have already cut myself off from shopping in all manner (unless I get a gift card from the affiliate program).

So, as you can see, the struggle to disentangle myself from all these bad habits that I have invested in for years is going to require a sharp blade to slice the ropes quickly, pull up the anchor, pull up the sails, and hope for a strong wind to sail far away to a simple and tranquil island where life is natural, simple and doesn't require a credit card.

Friday

I had such anxiety the other night. I suffer from these esophageal spasms. I'm unsure what it is, but a tall glass of cold water soothes it. I tossed and turned all night, drifting off now and then. I woke with just as much stress as I went to bed with. I don't know if it was unplugging from YouTube or some realizations about people we deal with.

I irritated my neighbor by asking if the hens had food. I had peeked at them the other night, and they were out of their coop, which is far, far too small for them, and the food container was knocked over and empty. I checked in the morning, and still the same, so I texted her. It turns out they let the hens loose all day and are well-tended. So, she's displeased. I apologized, but I was concerned.

Organizing play dates have been more complicated these days. I decided not to do it to myself anymore. We do fun stuff, and they can assemble with their friends when school starts again.

We will be busy the rest of the summer. My dear friend in the bay area and I have reunited. She went through a great depression and kept us all at a distance. She still suffers but is better, and she should have us around. We are a family of the best kind. She is helping with a grandchild, bringing her stress and joy. I'm turning 52 soon, and I'm finally over the baby fever. I love that the boys are more independent and long for more freedom. Not much, just little things like walking Molly in the morning without dragging both boys every time or leaving the house for an errand without bringing the whole house with me.

Other than that, I love having my boys with me all the time, and I dread the years they go off and do their thing, and I'm without them. Without them, I won't even know how to be or what to do with myself. The three of us are so bonded, and we are always together. I'll have to return to school or take up some new hobby.

But for now, I'm slowly making my way through **Walden** and contemplating a more hermited life for peace of mind and inner growth.

I adore people, but for limited amounts of time. I find most conversations harmful. There is so much crazy thinking going on out there. I'm sure there has always been plenty, but now, thanks to social media and YouTube, everyone can fly their crazy flags. All. Day. Long. And news, lord. There used to be your morning news and 5 o'clock news. Ah, but thanks to all those concerned news people, we have hundreds of news channels and groups force-feeding us news from every outlet 24/7. God Bless them for keeping us current and wracked with stress and worry.

So, that is what people talk about. They learned what they learned on some YouTube channel, Facebook, Twitter stream, or the news. Any idiot can start a YouTube channel and preach nonsense. I learned that fast in the quarantine. All the conspiracies and fearmongering by people who were some of the most neurotic and ignorant, low vibrational beings. Then money drove a lot of fear-mongering quests. Some creators learned fast that fear drives views; thus, money, money rains down. They kept it up for as long as possible. Now they try it with "wheat shortages" and inflation. According to them, we will now suffer all kinds of apocalyptic things.

The answer to mental health and well-being is if you can't unplug completely (heck, *we* can't), you choose comedy, science, literature, hobbies, history, and anything uplifting which will expand your mind in good and positive ways. I would say gardening, but the gardening channels are now spreading the doom and gloom message. Garden because of food shortages! No! Garden for emotional therapy, free (almost free) organic foods, and to feel accomplished. There's nothing like eating a meal that is mostly from your garden.

Last night, I made a pan of sauteed onions and zucchini from the garden. The garden is still not impressive. It sure was this winter, but this summer is almost there but no cigar.

Off to deep clean today. I will do my exercise routine and read, then devote the next two days to cleaning deeply and watering the garden. I am cleaning the washing machine with baking soda and vinegar. I've never cleaned it, and it smells. I did bring back the Hot Spot, but the boys are watching some great Science shows, and game time is limited to 2 hours. I ended my Amazon affiliate program and am currently deleting all my links. If I'm trying to consume less, I have to walk my talk.

I'm having an espresso from that fancy machine I found free off the street. I have opera turned up, and I'm taking a rest before the second shift. What a productive day! I'll sleep well tonight. Last night I cut the boy's hair, and I did such a good job!! Of course, after sleeping on it, they both look like wild cockatoos. Their father was jealous when he witnessed the talent. I can tell because he stared at their freshly washed and cut hair and pointed out little parts I "missed" or needed to "fix." Yeah, well, I can't help it if I got talent. I watched the hairdresser when they were boys and watched the woman on *Freakin Frugal* cut her husband's hair while talking about quitting her life-draining job. I envisioned myself cutting Arjan's hair the night before, probably one of the hundreds of things I mulled over while having my anxiety attack. I realized I needed to take the thinning shears to his hair because it's so thick that he looks like he's wearing a helmet when it grows out.

I've given myself two days to prepare for our trip to the bay area to meet my friend's grandbaby and support her.

I have been cleaning like crazy, going deep. It feels good. I will be starting the last load of cleaning rags and dog bedding in the washer. I bathed the dogs by the pear tree the other day, and I'll need to shampoo the carpet tomorrow and give it the day to dry out. The house smells really clean these days if I keep the dogs bathed and wash rugs, dog bed covers, and shampoo the large living room area rug now and then. Today I washed walls and baseboards, did four loads of laundry, and swept and mopped all the floors. I'm heading into the bathroom now. I have two boxes partly filled with purging items to donate.

I deleted most of my Pandora music channels, saving only the best. I deleted most of my YouTube channels, even my dear friend's channels. I don't want any more of the frugal stuff coming up on my feed. I can't stomach another frugal, homemaking channel. We watched fun science shows this morning.

Saturday

There is nothing like the smell of cleaning detergent and laundry soap. I got so much done yesterday, sore back and all. Today I feel great physically. A little exercise and a night of deep sleep. I'm excited to shampoo my carpet. Seeing all that dirty water and knowing that the carpet is fresh and clean is gratifying.

Sunday

It is incredible how I have been a whirling dervish with the cleaning, so inspired each day with washing walls, shampooing the main rug, and five loads of laundry, and I never tired. Then today I had a few dishes to wash and errands to run, and I felt overwhelmed. I have hit the wall. But it's all done now. I found a car wash that cleans the inside and out—what a relief. I've been cooking Aloo Gobi for Bali to eat while I'm gone and preparing the Asian sauces to take with me to cook at our friend's house in the bay area.

They live next door to *Anne Lamott*. I met her once. She was very kind. She said, "I pray for you all the abundance you could ever want." Or something like that. It was years ago, and my memory is nothing like Arjan's. Maybe all the success in life? Hum. Anyway, I'm reading her **Bird by Bird** about writing; it is fun and charming. She talks about Perfectionism and the depths that it harms us emotionally and creatively. She uses her tonsillectomy and that recovery as an example. The body will tighten around a wound to protect it; that is what perfectionism is to writing. We tighten up and avoid the pain of possible rejection or criticism. But we also avoid great artistic expression and possible life-changing work.

She also says in one section that she's just "holding the lamp so the kid can dig." It's similar to Stephen King's idea of excavating a fossil. He finds an idea, and if it interests him, he begins to write, letting the work take him to the story. With NaNoWriMo, they call it pantsing it. I have yet to decide if it's better to write with the flow and let the story tell itself or to do an outline.

My days are like this; espresso with cream and Opera playing loudly through the house, much to my children's dismay. Later it is *Thoreau* and iced tea in the hammock on the porch. In between, it is cleaning to *Cat Stevens* and *Credence Clearwater*. If there is laundry, I'm thrilled, as it is an excuse to watch parts of a movie in the middle of the day.

I wish I could nap, but it feels wrong somehow. I might be a bit more cheerful if I practiced a siesta daily.

I have some anxiety about seeing our friends tomorrow. I've planned a day of cooking in her kitchen to keep me busy and in my happy place. I haven't seen them in over two years, and it was excruciating for us to feel so rejected, although it was never personal. When people go through depression, they shut others out. Sometimes they can't be around people that are happy and healthy at the time. I know that when I'm blue, the last thing I want is cheerful dispositions dancing in my space. Happy people irritate me when I'm in that dark place. I have not experienced a dark place in so very long. Most of my depression was due to not having a family of my own. I found a happy life a couple of years before Bali showed up, and when I started building my little family, I was too busy and happy. I have my funks now and then, but it last a day, an hour, an afternoon, and I return to my happy place.

I'm packing up the ingredients and my wok. I'll make that wonderful broccoli beef recipe from **Seonkyoung Longest's** channel. I love her recipes. They are quick and easy and taste like the best Asian food restaurant you could imagine. I've tried learning Asian cooking for years without much luck, but her videos have turned that all around.

Speaking of videos. I'm enjoying this time off. I've given myself a couple of months or more. A few ladies told me I needed to turn to Jesus during this time. I'm not sure I need Jesus per se; just a small sabbatical people.

I kept having these flashbacks of my life on the fruit farm by the river. I remember being so peaceful and calm. I remember life then. I took care of two babies: one toddler and one infant. I cleaned, and not as well as I do now; my house was far bigger then. I cooked, but I kept it simple. I made so many recipes from the Dump Dinners cookbook that my husband begged me not to use the cream of mushroom anymore. I still love that cream of mushroom. I could make something out of it weekly and be happy. And back then, I read. I read and read and read. The librarian taught me how to order books online and access books from around the county and beyond. Bali would walk over to the library on his break since it was across from his store. He would bring home big bags of books, and I read under the huge, old olive tree in the backyard. I was into Amish fiction back then. It was clean literature, and I loved how they lived.

So, I keep seeing that image of my life back then and see it as an example. I've read **Essentialism** by Greg McKeown three times.

I fondly remember the next part of life, even though some were not-so-great parts. When we moved into the city, I began writing. I read everything good, bad, and popular, every genre and author, from *Stephen King* to *Nicholas Sparks* (I can't remember the authors in between, thank God for Goodreads and my list there). And I wrote like crazy. I'm not saying it was good writing. It was very dry writing. The fiction was horrible. But I loved the work. It consumed me in wonderful ways. I was a new writer with no confidence, but I was enthusiastic.

Sure, I had some issues. My family kept hurting my feelings. I was lonely with babies, no friends nearby, and my husband was always working. I spent most of the time alone doing all the homemaking and raising of children, and a man comes home late, eats, sleeps, and repeats. He had it hard too. I didn't like the neighborhood; it was old suburbia. The old city of Sacramento was charming, but I didn't like going places alone with littles. I had no friends nearby, and the neighbors weren't warm. But we had our routines of parks and library and naps, and I baked and kept our tiny house clean. The writing saved me. It gave me something to work on. It was creative and required me to dig in.

When we bought our first home, I experienced some stress and unhappiness. I didn't care for the town. I hated (this is a harsh word, but it is true here) the slummy apartments across the way and the rough street behind us. There were cops and drama every week. I grew pretty fat within the first few months of living there. I even had my back go out while playing dinosaur with Arjan and wound up splayed on the cement driveway, trying to roll myself under the shade of a tree so I wouldn't fry in the sun. I got sick one day and lay in bed under a thick blanket in triple-digit weather, and then one day, I thought I was having a stroke. I realized it might not be so extreme when I thought of taking a shower before heading off to the ER. It turned out to be this esophageal spasm that you can calm with a glass of cold water. I still have them when stressed.

Everything in me told me this was not the right place, but it was all we could afford. But then I started a channel and had my writing and blog, and I was fixing up the house and started gardening, baking, homesteading, and cooking from scratch like crazy. With the discovery of YouTube, I learned everything! I learned homesteading, better cooking, vegan cooking, baking, and how to clean deeper! I started my channel for fun and to show that you could have a good life on a small salary and stay home. I loved it at first.

But two things happened that still make me anxious to think about; first, my boys were small, and I wish I hadn't taken on so much because it stressed me out. We did a lot of fun things and spent so much time with our friends in the bay area, but I was preoccupied for sure. I still have guilt about that. I should have been focusing on them only. Then I monetized my channel, and the greed and comparisons kicked in. I wanted my channel to grow like the others. I grew envious of other channels that were thriving. It took all the joy out of it. My envy, greed, and lack of self-esteem sucked the joy out of creating.

When we moved here, I added even more things. I added the fostering and Patreon alongside writing books, blogging, and YouTube filming. What madness.

I was talking with Bali. I said, "remember when I was so sweet and calm all the time?" "Oh yes, you were so nice, never nagging." He replies. But you see, when I was sweet, I was focused on my family and housework. I kept it simple, and I read leisurely all the time. Then one day, Bali said to me, "Why do you waste your time with these silly books? Learn something, don't waste your time!" Ah, so I started studying frugality, homeschooling, homesteading, and minimalism (because frugality is the gateway drug to everything else). Then I had us move to a smaller house, then I started writing, then we bought a fixer-upper, then I started backyard homesteading and more writing, blogging, starting a channel, learning and doing and learning and more doing. Yeah, and I became a real, you know what. To be honest. I was stressed. Smart, learning, doing but stressed and so preoccupied.

I reminded him of that. "Yes, then you told me to stop reading those 'silly' books and do something more with my time to learn something." He thinks about that and starts rubbing his forehead. I continue, "Yeah, and so I did learn and got busy doing all these hustles, and now I'm not so sweet, am I? How's that working for you?" I am not a Dr. Phil fan, but I always loved that line, "How's that workin' for you?"

Yes, soul searching. That is what is happening now. Get rid of the internet, and what happens? You start thinking and pondering. I have guilt. Now my boys are 8 and 10, racing toward tweens, and then off they fly. I only have so many years to be present and set a good example. May they learn from this.

I will give it all up for them unless I can learn to balance it all. I don't know what the future holds with my channel or my books. I know that the clear message is to stop and be present. I can't tell you how often I hear it in a movie, book, or documentary, "Be present in the here and now." That is the way to peace, contentment, and fulfillment.

I already canceled my amazon affiliate program and deleted all the links from all my videos. I took off the Thank You button as well. I didn't feel good about it. People buying me coffee was sweet, but it didn't feel right. I have no more PO Box. I feel good, good, good about all that. There is a time to receive and give; right now, I need to be within and do more giving.

I'm working on getting Bali not to work so hard. The kids need him. The land needs him. I like having him around. Why does he have to work so much? He needs a life too. This overworking and money thing is a trap. You need some, but how much? We want to pay off the mortgage but let's not kill ourselves doing it.

From now on, the focus is on my beloved family I waited to have for 40 years; the home I'm so grateful to have. My dogs are getting old, and my doggie daughter needs a lot of walks and attention. The garden needs so much work. The orchard needs care. It all needs me desperately; this is my family and everything that feeds my soul and heals my heart of all the years of wandering, lost, and wounded.

Everything else is not important. I will write if it brings fun and creative energy. I'll do YouTube if I can have fun with it. It has been a blessing and gift, and I love the community. But nothing can interfere with my kids again.

My work is not the problem but my inability to pace myself. My worker bee mentality that goes on overdrive is the problem.

So, we wave goodbye from the ship's deck and leave it all. We head off to an island. Tropical, of course. There we live as simply as we can with running water and electricity. We focus on our morning coffee with some good music in the background. We read old literature, such as *Hemmingway, Whitman, Emerson, and Thoreau*. We read poetry despite not being a poetry type of person. We delve into the classics and go back in time. We keep the internet off except occasionally checking out the Hot Spot for a little internet treat. The boys and I have agreed that the library once a week is a big treat we want to keep.

I'll work in the garden with bare feet and bare hands. I keep my mental state healthy and vibrant; nothing does that, like connecting to the earth through our hands and feet.

I will keep out the crazy people and news of worldly dramas. What can we do? We can stay happy and exude that energy to others. We can lead by example. We can walk our talk. Maybe we shouldn't talk so much. Or think so much. I know what to do now. Be quiet. Nothing I have to say is so important or new.

I'm not much for meditating. It's boring. However, I find great relief when I still my mind and life flows easily. I can be silent in my head while working. I make sure that the music I hear is lovely. The books I read are harmless and thought-provoking (despite trying not to think), and the company we all keep must be the sort of people that lift us up. People that inspire or soothe, bring, or give hope and a new perspective on old issues. People and things that give us faith in all that is good prevail in the end.

Because all that is good will prevail in the end.

I'm finishing my July camp NaNoWriMo before I head off to the bay area tomorrow morning. We are thrilled to be getting out of the house and going to fancy Marin to be with our beloved family.

I want to leave you all with this story Bali has told me over the last few days. It is about his mother and how she made it being a single mother with two children in a small Indian village in Punjab, India.

Bali's father worked for a car manufacturing company in Du Bai. He was killed when a machine exploded. The company gave Bali's mother a large settlement to cover her and her two children: Bali and his sister. At the time, Bali's father had bought some land and was constructing a house. When he was killed, Bali's mother immediately stopped the second story's construction, keeping the house small and simple. She took the money from the settlement and put it all in the bank. Back then, the Indian banks paid a high interest. She took some money and bought a large lot of land to grow food and keep their cow and leased some land for growing hay for the cow. Every year she would buy 800 to 1000 lbs. of wheat and 200 lbs. of corn, and 100 lbs. of rice. She had proper storage containers that kept it all clean and dry, and they kept these packets in the flour to keep the bugs out. Bali would haul the wheat, corn, and rice on his bike, hauling 100's of lbs. home, making many trips to fill the containers. They would do that once a year. Once a month, they would take the bus to the city an hour away, and Bali's mother would take some of the interest out of their bank account to buy beans, seasoning, and whatever supplies they might need. They grew a lot of vegetables and had the cow for milk and yogurt. Bali said that farmers would ride their bikes about selling other vegetables, and she would buy whatever she wasn't growing. That is how they lived comfortably.

This is a simple story, but it makes me think about how we all shop all the time. We shop online and go grocery shopping almost daily at times. We are always running about using gas, polluting, and stressing.

This story of Bali's mother and *Daniel Suelo* and *Thoreau's* talk of economy in **Walden** makes me think hard about how little we can live with or do without, and maybe, just maybe, we would find more happiness and freedom than we imagined?!

I always thought money would buy me freedom. I could travel with my family and do this and that if I had all this money. And yes, money can be freeing and buy you many things, but often a person forgets what they want the money for, and the focus is solely on the money. How much can we make, how fast, how much can we store up, and then we want more, and it never feels like enough.

When you are flat broke, ten dollars feels like a miracle. But thousands don't feel like enough when you have a good amount of money.

Bali and I have fears and goals to quiet the fears. We want to pay off the mortgage fast. That would give such security. But at what cost for the present moment? We are working like crazy people, so we don't have to in a few years. But what if our bodies give out in that time? What if one of us gets cancer? And the boys will be off with friends in a few years and have no time for us. Why not work less now, be with the boys, enjoy life, and let the future figure itself out? Maybe a money windfall will happen and pay off our mortgage? Maybe in a few years, we will sell and move off to somewhere better and cheaper and be able to pay cash for a new nest.

I'm tired of the money trap. And a trap it has become. I've already lost a few years with my life and babies. I'm encouraging my companion to let go a little too. We will do fine with his gas station cashier earnings and my books' royalties. I have downsized our budget and feathered our nest. We can do many things and acquire a lot of things for free or very little money. We have a solid house, a sizeable yard, soft beds, an espresso pot, toys, books, art stuff, and a fantastic library, and we can walk everywhere! We have a loving family. We eat healthy foods. We can pay the bills quickly and not lose sleep.

What else does a family need?

Chapter 6

Old Money And Frugality

I've spent the morning running some errands. I had spent three days working on the house and doing more decluttering, most of all the Christmas chachka and Holiday decor. I kept the big tree, the ornaments, and all the Fall decorations, but I have to be honest: we no longer celebrate Easter or Thanksgiving. Christmas will also be different, but I don't know what it will morph into. I don't know, as Christmas has a special place in my heart. Thanksgiving will become a 'Harvest Celebration.' When you dive into the European/settlers and Native American relations over the hundreds of years, it's uncomfortable celebrating Thanksgiving as if nothing ever happened. It is as if we didn't slaughter, steal, rape, and destroy the Native Americans or what is genuinely their land. And let's not forget the 'Gift of death' from settlers, aka the chicken pox blankets, and the fact that the Indians went from a population of over 600,000 to some 60,000 by the time we were done.

I saw a bumper sticker that said, "Eat beef, the west wasn't won on salads alone." But from whom did we win this West? The Indians. And we didn't win. We betrayed, stole, and did cruel and backhanded things to wipe them out and 'steal' the West, East, South, and North. Then we destroyed it, tearing down the forest and paved over it all, polluting rivers, and shoving the remaining Indigenous tribes onto less than stellar lands as a token of our "so sorry we're cruel people" and a shrug.

So, the kids and I have decided to no longer do Thanksgiving. But hopefully, we will get to harvest more produce each year, and Fall will be a busy time for canning and dehydrating organic fruits and vegetables, but not this year again. Dang, this land is not easy to grow in. A neighbor lady down the way shook her head and looked sympathetic when I said we were trying to grow in the ground and not raised beds. "Can't do that here. The land is too difficult." She said.

Easter is not for us as we are not religious folks, and I have a very different way of thinking about Jesus. And as for the Easter bunny, the boys know that it isn't real. Easter was for finding eggs, decorating eggs, and getting special baskets when they were young. Maybe a Spring celebration instead?

Christmas. We know Kris Kringle is not real, but I'm not one to banish all fantasies. Once again, we are not religious, and over the years, I have become very turned off religion the more I study and explore and the more some Christians try to shove it down the throats of people with different views. The teachings of Jesus are good, and I love to read parts of the Bible to remind me to live simply and kindly. That's it. So, maybe a Winter celebration? We will do something but our own thing.

Obviously, we are turning all holidays into seasonal celebrations.

Thus, all the boxes of seasonal décor were donated, along with books I'll never read but kept on the shelf to make me look intelligent. I put everything on the street for the neighbors to have first dibs. The neighbors took half, and I took the other half to the Hospice Thrift down the street. They even took the small Christmas tree. Whew. It gets a little nerve-wracking to get rid of stuff. I'm more careful than ever when hauling things home now. Do we truly, truly need it? Can we use it?

I'm sitting on the porch where it's cool. I'm planting the nectarine seeds we saved from visiting our friends in the bay area. Her fruit trees had grown so big and healthy, and she had new trees. She had planted them eight years ago from seeds from the fruit of her old trees. They are now maybe 5 feet high and producing. I was inspired, so we saved the seeds from the delicious nectarines we ate from her tree. I wrapped them in a wet paper towel and put them in a zip-loc bag. Bali left some cash on my laptop, and I used to buy a bag of special seed potting soil. I love this nursery; they always give me important advice. They said to only plant organic seeds and don't put any nitrogen or manure in the soil as it will burn the seed. The seed has all it needs to get started—what a metaphor for life. I feel like I'm returning to my inner seed and finding that all I need is already there.

Our visit to Marin and being with the boy's Godparents was the best mini vacation. We lay about the pool, swimming, getting tan, cooking, and eating endlessly. My friend and I talked so much. We started a million conversations, never completing one before starting five more.

Many of the Coffee With Kate ladies say that I keep them inspired. I love that feeling. I love going somewhere and being inspired by everything around me or finding a channel I binge-watch because it fills me with new ideas and motivation. But I haven't had that in ages. I'm craving inspiration because I can't find that place, person, or channel right now.

However, this trip was much more than reuniting after years of not seeing them. We just picked up where we left off and enjoyed what felt like a vacation at some delightful resort. The boys swam all day, I cooked up a storm the first day, and they barbecued the next day. We watched good movies, and she introduced me to a fun channel called **The Niche Lady**. She thrifts all the time for her eBay business. I love thrifting but am not too motivated as we have so much, and I'm still decluttering.

I shared with my friend all the stuff I find free on the street, including groceries, and that it embarrasses Bali. She reminded me that she and my aunt used to dumpster dive all the time to decorate their homes. She took me through her house, pointing out all the paintings and furnishings she had dragged out of the garbage and off the street. She said that I would be foolish not to enjoy it if it was there.

So many things about her home and how she lives inspired me. She and Uncle D own some 80 properties or units in several counties. You could say they are wealthy or that they are in incredible debt. They are paying mortgages on all the properties. Many of the units are section 8, which is smart as you can charge the current rent prices, and the money is always in the bank because the government pays it. You can count on it. There was a time when she first started buying properties, and the recession of 2008 happened. She was very broke, as were her tenants. No one had money to pay rent or anything. She would take herself and her tenants to the soup kitchens for a hot meal. Even those that appear wealthy are a minute away from needing the food bank.

She lives in the house passed down three generations from her grandparents to her father to her. It is old and has the old charm, but parts of it could use some changing. It has the old tube and knob electric and the same plumbing. The TV room has old office-type carpet, and the kitchen has old linoleum. The furniture is decades old. Couches from her parents' lives and various pieces found on the street. She doesn't remodel or tear out this floor or that wall. She doesn't redecorate from Pier One

Imports like her neighbors. She takes good care of what she has and maintains the house with love and attention, but it stays as is. This is commendable since she lives in one of the wealthiest areas where people drive the latest car, have the latest and most popular gadgets, and redo their homes with name-brand furnishings.

Some of the fruit trees are from her grandmother. There is a lovely pool in the backyard, but when her grandparents had the house, it was a dirt backyard, and her grandmother had a kitchen garden and planted fruit trees. My friend doesn't buy new trees. She plants the seeds from the old trees. She isn't sure whether the growing trees are from her planting or the seeds from falling fruit regrow.

When she has money, it goes to travel. She loves clothes and buys all her clothes from thrift stores. She has a housekeeper that cleans her house weekly. That is her one luxury. She also hates driving and shopping, so she spends the extra money to do eCart and has everything delivered. So, she pays for others to do the things she detests, so she has time to tend to her business of running properties. She pays for others to clean, shop, and deliver goods. Other than that, she isn't a big spender. Her car is a black Mercedes that is so old the control panel looks like something out of an old Star Trek movie. I panicked when trying to find the air conditioner button. The car was a hand-me-down that cost her $2000.

She has morning routines where she walks her humble gardens and does some chores to maintain her tidy home. She likes to keep up with the laundry and empty the dishwasher. Her kitchen is always clean and tidy. She loves lotion, and I think I slathered on more in two days than in the past few months. She and her partner have their routines. They work through the day, and in the evenings, they make dinner together. Uncle D loves to grill steaks and watch Wheel of Fortune and Jeopardy. I felt like I was with my grandparents, but it was fun. They get out the economy pack of Glide floss so we can floss while watching TV. I don't know how these people on the show know the answers to the Jeopardy questions. They must study random facts 24/7 to prepare for Jeopardy's randomness. I thought I'd have some success with the "The Gullet" section since I love to eat, but the questions were far more complicated than I hoped for.

My friend has no issues with her body. She is 60 years old and not the skinny girl she used to be, yet she wears bikinis and is as confident with her body and self as anyone could dream of being. It made me comfortable, and I wore my 1930s bright blue swimsuit all day, lathering on this sunscreen that was also a bronzer. I love the fake tan I have now! I floated on the pool floats and read on the recliners. It doesn't get too hot there, and the nights are cold with the ocean breeze coming in. She has these large chimes in the upstairs balcony that make Zen-like chiming sounds all day with the gentle breeze. With the chimes and floating around the pool, I felt like I was at a retreat.

We stayed an extra day and left with delicious memories, and I was so rested. We stopped at a big farm stand. It's more like a store filled with local produce, bagged nuts, dried fruits, candies such as candied peanuts, yogurt raisins, and the best tamales!! I hadn't spent much money on the trip, and it only took half a tank in the little Toyota to get there and back, so we spent the remaining wade of cash. The boys and I filled the cart with delights and produce and purchased various tamales. I was happy to return to our beautiful forest and sweet home. So was Sam. Arjan was sad for most of the day. It's always hard to adjust back to regular ol' life.

I unpacked everything and got busy with chores. I bathed my little Molly dog. She was filthy. I gave the dogs treats all night to apologize for leaving them behind. They miss mama so much even with Bali here. I cleaned and packed the fridge with all the goods from the Farm store and gave the kitchen a thorough sweep. The pool had mosquito larvae, or so the boys claimed. I couldn't even see with glasses, but I sprinkled in two packets of chlorine and ran the pump for a few hours. I put on **The Niche Lady** to watch her peruse thrift stores and feel like I was still on vacation with my friend.

I did some cooking as well. Bali had no lunches nor any bread for toast. The trusty bread maker tossed and baked a loaf of wheat while I tried my hand at making Aloo Gobi for the second time. The first time I made it, things burnt and turned out less than stellar, so I wanted to try it again, and I had some potatoes and cauliflower that needed to be used up. This big batch turned out fantastic. Steamed up a big batch of brown rice and made handmade tortillas. There are now enough lunches in the fridge for the remaining three workdays.

Today we are finally back to our lives here. I did a load of laundry, some planting, writing, and waiting for my *Thich Nhat Hanh* documentary **Walk With Me.** That and the *Stephen King* book **On Writing**. This is the most ordering online I've done in some time.

Not long ago, Amazon didn't exist. Amazon arrived in 1994. Well, that is 28 years, half my lifetime, but what did we do before that? We went to shops and ordered from other places. I've already started ordering books from Thriftbooks and realized that the books might cost more, but I can get a bundle of them and have free shipping! So, the books on Amazon aren't that cheap once you pay the shipping on each one; they all come individually. Thriftbooks come in one package minus shipping cost.

I have had the worst luck with online ordering. I had to return a laptop from Walmart and received the worst copy of Walden from Amazon. It was missing some 300 hundred pages in its cheap print, or perhaps it was just because the print was so small. I wanted a thick copy and larger lettering to get into it with my highlighter. Yes, I want to underline and dog ear and highlight Thoreau's Walden through and through.

We have had bad luck with cheap food and fast food; eating out in general, and the many disappointments in online shopping. It has been an excellent cure for our consumerism. We appreciate homecooked more than ever, and from now on, I want to see what I'm buying before I buy it.

However, after being at a person's house who could afford anything and seeing that they are content with what they have and taking care of the old furnishings instead of replacing things, it renewed my resolve not to buy things. Except for garden stuff. That is one shopping fetish I won't get rid of. But I'll keep it local. Less driving, less

gas and pollution, more supporting the town.

Friday

I think I'm not too eager to visit again for some time. I love the excitement of going somewhere and the travel, the visit with loved ones and being in a different town if it's charming; and the ones we visit are. However, returning to our lives and trying to reacclimate is just too hard emotionally. The boys and I suffer from the "returning to the routine" funk, and we long for the people we left. We inhabited a blissful life for a couple of days without responsibilities or chores, and now we return to the laundry, cooking, vacuuming, and unending chores.

My DVD **Walk With Me** just came, and I'm watching it now as I write and sip ice water. I think we will stick close to home for a long time. I feel the energies out there in the world, and although I encounter lovely people and sweet smiles, I see some insanity running through the crowd, and the energies don't feel safe right now. We'll stay close to home, and I will create a schedule that feels good. There is one day a week when the library is tranquil. We go then. The other days have proven too busy and too many uptight souls. I will only grocery shop on certain days and times when it's early and quiet, and the stores are clean and restocked. It feels peaceful and abundant then.

I will spend my days offline. We returned the Hot Spot, and I filled a bag with movies for the week. It is the only way to separate from the world. Be not of the world. Even the Bible says it. The Tao says it. I'm sure many spiritual works suggest this for inner well-being, mental balance, and health. The Buddha left it all behind after seeing suffering and the imbalance of haves and have-nots. He isolated himself until enlightenment. Or something close to that. I haven't studied the Buddha but vaguely. I'm a Taoist type of person.

Here's the thing; social media and YouTube are set up like gambling in Las Vegas. They are engineered by people that are professional attitude or personality engineers. They study people's trends and what keeps them returning to slot machines, YouTube channels, or Facebook. They have studied how to create an addiction. Maybe they didn't think that way, but they are paid to create an app or venue that will keep the masses returning—or staying for hours. And every time we return, we stay for hours upon hours. The advertising, likes, hearts, and feeds keep the party on all day and all night. We can pontificate for years on whether we should go or stay. But only time away will reveal the truth. Only time away will release us from the hold it has on us.

An article on Linkedin by Mohand (published Aug. 8, 2018) says it perfectly: *Many social media platforms hire **'attention engineers'**, who use gambling principles to try and make these platforms as addictive as possible, with the goal of maximizing the profit that can be extracted from your attention and data. Manipulative design tactics snatch your attention in small bites throughout the day, with dopamine driving that addiction by delivering a small "high" for each notification, message or like. Our society is effectively putting highly addictive "drugs" into the hands of increasingly younger children, and schools are picking up the pieces.*

Interesting. Something to ponder.

Saturday

I've got a stack of books from the library. Poems and works by Walt Whitman and Ralph Waldo Emerson. I realized that it is Emerson I can't digest. I am very into Henry David Thoreau. I even purchased Walden from Amazon (one of the last lame purchases), and it came in this thin, tiny word mass printing. I love the book so much that I purchased a large and proper edition from Thriftbooks. I want to dive into this book and study his words. But Whitman, though he was more into the metaphysical, which I learned from doing a paper on one of his poems in Leaves of Grass in a community college English class, I find him confusing. Reading him is like figuring out directions on a paper map in heavy traffic.

Thoreau also has the old language, but if I slow down and taste the meal, I begin to understand him. He is talking about simplicity and not getting bogged down in the trap of owning things and trying to make a living. We need some way to bring in money, but there is freedom in not needing much to get by. You can live a slower life, thus spending more time on things that delight your soul, like gardening, painting, or writing.

I've been so busy filming, thinking about my channel, and making content that I looked about and saw a house that needed attention and a garden struggling. I spent two days deep cleaning before we left for Marin. Last night I watered everything, sprinkled chicken manure pellets around the plants, and watered again. I have some banana peels I've been soaking in a huge old pickle jar, and I'll put that on the tomatoes today

If I do too many hustles, it wears on me. Maybe it's because I'm turning 52 in a couple of months, but I don't know how these mothers on YouTube do it with all the kids and homesteading and filming and editing the way they do. I suspect they will burn out in so many years. Or they will look back and regret getting caught up in the channel and placing the community's needs above their children's. I know from experience that you cannot be present 100% with your family and home, create a channel, and serve the masses. It is a fine line that we creators walk.

It's 10:30, and I still haven't finished my coffee in pajamas and writing on the porch. I'll go in and do my ½ hour on the old elliptical we bought for $40 at a thrift shop and read *Anne Lamott's* book on writing. Or start reading *Stephen King's* book **On Writing** that I received yesterday. I'll take a quick soapy shower and lather on the lotion. I'll vacuum and sweep, put some time into organizing my pantry, and make some tortillas for tacos for lunch. Then I'll take the afternoon off to read and mend Sam's shirt.

Later in the day...

I'm cleaning and organizing my two pantries. One is made up of the large shelf we pulled from what is now the second bathroom, and I painted barn red from a jar of paint the neighbor gave me. It is large with three deep shelves, and I keep the everyday food items there. I work with ingredients such as coffee, pancake mix, pasta and tomato sauce, lentils, dried fruit and nuts, popcorn, my bran, wheat germ mix, and a large container of Sweet Bread Mix.

In the laundry/pantry off the kitchen, I keep cans of enchilada sauce, extra peanut butter and 25 lb. bags of beans, rice, polenta, extra bags of wheat, and items we don't use often. I also have all the dog food back there. Despite the laundry sharing the other side, it is cool and dark. The dryer has kapootzed so there is no more warming up the place by running it. I moved the wooden drying wrack next to the washer and will now hang all our clothes. Some may feel this is not doable. If you watch Asian homemaking channels, you will see that they don't have dryers. At least the ladies I watched did not seem to have one. Why? I have no idea, but it is very doable. They hang their items on a small rack inside and out on their little balconies. The dryer costs money to run and breaks down the fabric of your clothes.

I'm taking a break and would love a coffee, but I've been visited by a mild headache all day. I think it's all the busy work, exercise, sweating, and not drinking enough water. Today I've had several tumblers of ice water, and I used the oranges from the free food box, squeezed them into juice, and added Himalayan salt as a homemade electrolyte drink. Still have the headache. Perhaps an espresso?

We all jumped in the pool. I'm so happy to have that pool this year. It's big enough to swim and float about. Every time I rest on an innertube and drift off, Arjan comes to check that I haven't passed on. "I'm a very vital old lady. Just because I rest my eyes doesn't mean I'm going toward the light, for goodness sake!" I have to keep moving like a shark around here.

I have a radio in the pantry, and I turn it up and keep the back door open so we can swim and listen to the local station that caters to older folk like me. Today they are playing fun stuff. They play that New Orleans-style music and mountain music that is played at county fairs to get the geezers out there flapping their wings after a few beers in the hot sun.

It's evening, and I'll roll out a few tortillas for Bali, sit on the couch, and read. I brought home a bag full of pretty good movies. I'll watch one and give the boys my cell phone to watch whatever they like on YouTube. I don't know how they get it to work without data, but they do.

Some days I wake up and feel hesitant about the day. I can't say dread, but it does feel like the same thing every day and the same walls. Usually, I wake up excited about coffee and the day, but I've noticed that lately, I've felt a little...stifled? Bored? What? I don't know. Maybe it's coming down from having internet in the house for a little bit and traveling and being with old friends. We have that high and then fizzle out. We come down to everyday life. The good news is that our ordinary life is a good, good life. I'll get back to my contented self soon once the day is underway.

Sunday

Things are back to normal. It's overcast today and cooler, which gives us a break from the heat and stuffiness of a closed-up house. Even with air conditioning, it gets depressing being all closed up. But today, windows are wide open, and fans are going. The natural air flows through the house.

I feel like my old self. Man, oh man, that internet is a drug. We gorge on it for a few days, all the while seeing ourselves with disappointment as we lose ourselves to its ways. It is set up to keep you on there; no matter how strong you think you are, you aren't. You sit and keep pulling that handle on the slot machine, hoping for a flush of lemons or cherries (one of the creators said this, so I can't take credit for the clever metaphor). Then we take the Hot Spot back to the library, handing it over like a hot potato that scares us. We spend the next couple of days wandering about in circles around each other, lost in our lives. Thankfully, the spell lifts by the second day, and we start playing and doing the goofy things we do at home.

Today I woke up around 8: ish and rose slowly. I don't rush myself anymore. Why do that? I have no firm schedule. I have my routines, but I'm the boss, and I have no quotas to meet this quarter or any quarter unless I decide to do some strange challenge. I find I need a good 10 minutes to rise from bed and start the day. I move about like the rusted tin man, working each joint and parts of myself until the oil in my veins starts to flow, and I can move easily. Arjan has become the early bird; if I take a long time to rise, he comes into the room to check my breathing. He lays a hand on my belly to ensure it rises up and down. I told him it was best to check one's pulse. We have no hand mirrors to hold in front of the face to see if there is breath, so that's out. "I'm vital and productive, so what makes you think I'm going to kick it anytime soon?" It was a movie that brought about this fear of his. The mother died while talking with her grown son in the scene. She was ancient and in the hospital, but this scene left Arjan worried, and he has followed me everywhere closely since. He has even come into this room several times to check on me. It borders on the absurd, checking that I'm still breathing because I'm rising late. Following behind me, lurking in the shadows to make sure I don't fall and break my neck, coming around the corner when I'm quiet too long. It's like a worried mother with a new infant. I'm only 52, for goodness' sake.

I love that it's overcast and cool. I wish it would rain and give me that wonderful earthy smell when the first rains come after a hot, dusty season. That is the best part of Fall when the rains come early and wash all the dust and hot away, and the tender green grass grows quickly, making a lovely backdrop for the golden and rich red and orange hues of turning leaves. Last year was a gorgeous Fall with all the greens and colors.

I just made a simple goulash. I have no idea if that is what it is, but I like the word, which matches my dish. I sauté some ground beef, or when I'm doing my vegetarian thing, I use beyond ground. I sauté with oil, and fresh garlic, which I dug up in the garden. It's from last year and very tiny. Add Italian seasoning, salt, and some dehydrated red onion from a few years back. Bali had purchased a 20 lb. bag of red onions, and I dehydrated the ones that weren't rotting. Surprisingly, it's still flavorful. Later I add some cheap cans of Del Monte sauce and a can of diced tomatoes from the food bank box. I add some sugar and more salt. Boil up elbow macaroni. The bag grew into a big pot of pasta. Add the sauce, and there you go. We can dish up a cup here and there and eat from the pot all day. Bali had to go in and work the later shift today. There will be plenty when he gets home. I'm guessing this big, full pot is about $4, and if we had paid for the diced tomatoes and beef, maybe $7? You can barely get a sandwich for $7, and here we have a massive pot of hot, delicious pasta that we can eat all day, and I'm sure there will be plenty for tomorrow. I don't know anymore, as the boys grow like wild reeds near a stream and eat all the time now.

I prefer Bali to be here in the mornings and work a later shift. I can walk Molly in the mornings without dragging both boys with me; it has a different feel. I'm in a better mood in the mornings. I am a morning person all the way around; productive, cheerful, and great on the phone for coffee chats. By late evening I'm done. I don't want to talk or hear noise besides a bit of radio music or a movie. I turn off the power in my mind, turn to coloring or crocheting and expect to be entertained by whatever movie I've put on. It's a full day with boys talking at me, settling brotherly disputes, and working at a nice clip to clean, cook, and organize. I exercise dogs, water gardens, and comfort, listen to and explain life's stuff to two curious boys. I have catered to an old hound and a needy little Chiweenie girl and love on a middle dog that is very sensitive. I have FULL days, and the last thing I want after 7 pm is more conversation and chores. I have given my all for some 11 or 12 hours at that point.

Today has been one of those days I sit and think about how much I adore it. I woke slowly but was up by 8 am. I feel creepy if I sleep past 8 am and like a heroine of my own story if I'm up before 7 am. Something about getting up with the sun sets up the day just right. I harvested kale from the garden. This kale is from a couple of gardens past and came up on its own. It's a small but hard patch and has gifted us many smoothies this summer. We had fortifying smoothies until we were full, and then I enjoyed a cup of coffee. I have no headache today. I need to drink a lot of my ice water even though I long for iced tea. Sam makes the iced tea by leaving it in the sun all day. It reminds me of Miss B and her cheap iced tea. I can see why she loved it so much. It's so refreshing and herbily and revitalizes me in the afternoons when I begin to wilt.

I had done all the vacuuming and sweeping yesterday and finally pulled the laundry from the line. I leave it up too long, and it begins to bleach from the hot sun. I cleaned and organized the pantry shelves in the kitchen. Today I planned on working on the pantry off the kitchen. I'm organizing and condensing items such as rice and seasonings. I've been at this on and off all summer. I lined all my shelves with paper bags. I've been working through our old stores of seasoning, oats, and flour. We are finally up to date, and I bought my first bag of white flour, wheat, and sugar the other day when I found a fantastic sale. That's great about having a stocked pantry; you can wait it out for the sales.

I was mending Sam's shirt and cut the collar and cuffs off a shirt that fits me funny. I bought all these shirts online ages ago when I was a spendthrift. I don't like the fit, they make me feel big and frumpy, but I don't want to donate them as they are new. I cut off the collar and band on the sleeves, making them fit better. I wear them for cleaning and working about the house and garden. We need to wear clothes that make us feel good and comfortable.

I was cutting and sewing and suddenly remembered a heavy wooden desk Sam and I passed on the street last night when we were walking Molly. The woman came rushing out of her house when she saw us mulling around it. She encouraged me, saying it was heavy but would fit in our doorways. This old house has smaller doorways, so I have to calculate that when eyeing furniture. She got it used and free. I love when furniture gets used over and over. I told her I might be back but forgot when we got home. It is a heavy and compact wooden desk. Not so big as wide with deep drawers and a lovely honey-brown old-fashioned look. The handle was hanging on one drawer, and the weight intimidated me, but I flashed on it as I finished up the mending, and the boys were in the middle of an early 80s movie. I just popped up and hustled the boys and said, "let's get that desk before it's gone!" I grabbed the keys to the truck and called Bali, who was fussing over a crape myrtle, putting up more braces, and tying it in so it would grow strong and straight. I asked him to come and help quickly; it was right up the street, and to my delight, no one hesitated and acted like stubborn mules. Bali usually has resistance ready, "Why do you need this? You have lots of things in the house! You're just wasting time. You'll put it back on the street two months later!" But no, everyone just jumped in the truck, and we drove up the street and loaded it up. The drama came after we got home, and Bali decided to bring it in the back pantry door. The front door is large, and my bedroom is right there! He measures the little pantry door and assures me it's fine. It wasn't. The desk stuck in the doorway, so his solution is to take the hinges off the door and drag the desk through the house. I said, "How about we make it easier and take it to the front where I was waiting for you and take it through the large doorway that

is our front door and stick it right in the room, hum?"
Then he decides he'll carry it by himself down the
driveway to the front of the house and lifts it the wrong
way, and the heavy drawers fall on his ankle and foot.
Let's make things as complicated as possible.

We got it in the front door just fine and right into the
room. I spent the rest of the morning cleaning and
decorating it. Dad went to work, and Sam found the drill
and fixed the hanging drawer handle. My sweet boys are
getting so handy. I love this desk!! I almost passed it up,
but it's fantastic with its wide top. I have the radio, a large
plant, a lamp, a small fan, a stack of books, my gold
buddha, and a laptop on it! It all fits great. And this desk is
solid. I can fit a pile of things in the drawers, and it has a
pull-out piece that acts as an extra section on the desk.
This is how they used to make a desk. Solid and efficient. I
can't stand that IKEA junk. Small, slim, and flimsy. The
only bizarro thing about the desk is that the side drawers
lock, and you must open the long top drawer to get the
others to open. I'm hesitant to put anything in the
drawers in case the desk has a mood swing and won't
release my papers.

The things I find free on the street are incredible; boxes of
food, furniture, household delights, books, movies, an
espresso maker, and a pasta maker. The list goes on. Sam
loves free stuff just as much as I do. Arjan stands a
distance from us as we go through boxes on the street,
trying to look like a bystander. Bali said I was teaching the

children to panhandle. I just laughed and left my dignity outside to calm down. It's his culture. They are easily embarrassed by what others may think. I am losing that care as I get older, and let me tell you what freedom that is. Why argue?

Bali used to have issues with horse manure. When we lived in our first home, we planted a backyard garden. It was lush but produced nothing. I read a book by *Novella Carpenter, **Urban Farm***, and she was extolling the magic of horse manure. I found a horse farm with a huge pile of aged horse manure, never ending like a manure buffet. When I suggested we get a truck full, Bali was horrified. He went on about how the neighbors would complain and call the city, and our chickens would be taken away. I guess he thought horse manure was somewhat like dealing with human manure. I backed off, and in time he cooled down and realized he had been irrational, which he had, and agreed to get a truckload. After shoveling it in and out of the truck and working with it, he was made aware it was just poop made of hay, just like the cow patties his mother dried and used to start fires. The man was raised in a small village with only one TV in the whole town. He shouldn't act so shocked by things. Then he couldn't get enough of it when he watched our garden flourish and produce an abundance of peppers, dicone radish, and eggplant. We have even hauled manure up here a couple of times and will be doing more horse poop hauling come the Fall. My husband takes time to adjust to my ideas. He also used to hate thrift stores, thinking they were filthy; however, after finding fantastic name-brand shirts and jeans, he is now a huge fan of Goodwill.

And our house, now the most delightful, colorful, bohemian cottage home. It is filled and decorated with 90% free goods off the street and on Craigslist. Our freezer and shelf are filled with free foods that are just fine; clean, NOT expired. He's lucky I haven't started dumpster diving. I'm tempted all the time. If I could get away with it and not be seen or confronted by the police, I would be in there with a ladder in hand. Dumpster diving is not illegal in the US. And there was a law passed in 1996 to encourage stores, restaurants, and bakeries to donate food to the food programs. The Billy Emerson law says a store can NOT be sued over whatever they donate if it makes someone sick. So, if a store says they don't donate because they don't want to get sued, tell them there is a law to protect them. I think most stores do donate now, and with all the dumpster divers and freegans making people aware of the waste, donating is becoming a huge thing, and that is a good thing.

Chapter 7

Why Be Broke When One Can Hustle?

I could get right back to filming plenty for my channel. I could film up a storm and post a few times a week and make over $600 a month, or I could do daily short videos and make over $1,000. I've been taking another break from the channel. I may go back in a month or two. I enjoy that channel and love sharing and talking with a big, steaming cup of coffee in the early hours. Maybe that's why I'm a little funky in the mornings lately. I used to get my coffee, get the boys set up with breakfast and cartoons, and have a hearty coffee chat on camera. My ideas are fresh in the morning. Now I'm a little lost.

I need this break. I've been hustling and burning the candle at both ends for years and not as present as I felt I should have been with my family. Sure, we did lots of fun stuff, and they have a great life. Moms always home, which is more than most kids have in America. But I have guilt over not being truly present and in the moment with them. I waited 40 years to have these boys, and then I put my channel before them. Every time I shoo them out of the room because I'm recording, every time I set up that tripod, I'm choosing to serve people I don't know personally over my little boys. It makes me a little sick to think about it. I stopped doing that over a year ago. I stopped shooing them away. I just stopped recording when they came into a room or needed me. Perhaps I'm too hard on myself, but we should commit to the job 100% when we choose to have children.

When you choose to have a family, it is a choice. In today's world, you can choose this now. It's not something we have to do. So, if you choose children, choose them. Who cares if the man or the woman stays home, one of you should stay home and nurture these little souls all the way through until they leave the nest. People think a mother can go back to work when the kids go off to school, but that is when they still need a parent to be home and present front and center just as much. Kids deal with bullying at school and bad influences, and many kids return to empty homes and get into trouble. I see teenagers running wild and desperately needing a parent to care about what they are always getting into.

To raise kids who are confident, strong in mind and body, and make good decisions, parents need to coax, nurture, pay attention and help them. They need to be seen, truly seen, by the mother most of all. At least for boys. Boys have an intense bond with their mothers, and if their mothers aren't seeing, hearing, and nurturing them, they get lost and wounded in ways that affect the rest of their lives. I've seen it with my childhood friends and their relationships with their mothers. I fear that boys get hurt more profoundly and easily than we imagine. I'm talking from experience and observation of over 52 years.

When a mother works too hard and works for others, she becomes stressed and impatient.

Now that I'm not serving the corporate YouTube machine and the algorithms and just enjoying my creative self on the channel, I feel like a new person. Now that I'm not trying to crank out books to make money or keep my editor busy, I can write slowly and from the heart. I love to write now! I started this book eight months ago and will write for many more months if I feel it. I am writing for me. I don't have to do it for an editor because I'm worried she needs work or money. I don't have to get it out there to make some royalties. I don't even have to write. That alone puts the enjoyment back into it.

I'm reading good books and carrying a dictionary around these days. Remember those? I can't google things now, so I have to thumb through my paper dictionary and painfully look up all the words I don't know. But guess what? When you do it the old way, you see the spelling and don't forget the word after such work. You learn a few extra words on the way to finding the word you're looking up. I thumb through the dictionary, see all sorts of fun words, and read their meaning. I've looked up vernacular and convivial today. Old-fashioned pays off.

Just like this desk. I love this desk! It's old-fashioned. Built solid and heavy. It's compact but has a large tabletop. I almost passed on it because the top is 30 inches wide and 42 inches long. But the large surface won me over in the end. I can fit so much on here; it's spacious but fits nicely in the corner of my room. I have been writing off and on all day. I also spent some time outside sitting in the shade, reading **On Writing** *by Stephen King*, and looking up fancy words while Sam swam. He loves to show me all the tricks. I remember being little and trying to flip underwater, sit underwater, walk underwater, and jog underwater. Ah, to be little and so playful. I watch him and clap and laugh with delight. Arjan is my gentleman, and Sam is still that goofy little boy. He doesn't have much time left of that, and you bet I'm going to pay attention to every moment and be there clapping and enjoying him and all his tricks.

I have to say I love these ages the best so far. I loved the baby years and mourned as they grew out of it. I mourned as the toys in the tub became fewer, and their little bodies didn't fit well on my lap. Carrying them around is entirely out now. I had baby fever and thought I needed another, but then a funny thing happened; they matured a little and learned how to do all these things for themselves, and now life is much easier. They can make their omelets and sandwiches. They dress and bath themselves and wipe their bums. They hold doors open for me and carry my bags. Sam fixed my drawer with a power tool, and Arjan watched over him when he took a swim this morning to ensure nothing happened while I was busy with indoor chores. They are fun to talk to, do things with, and have excellent manners. Going out to eat is now pleasurable because I'm not chasing two toddlers around and taking turns with the father going to the bathroom or filling a plate at the buffet. Going to the movies is fun because they stay in their seats and don't talk through the movie. Sam would make loud comments during movies or cry out during a tense moment in the film, "here comes a jump scare!" And piss off the people seated near us. When I took them to their godparents, we didn't need to keep a worried eye on them or become frantic if one was missing. There is a deep pool and balconies on the second floor, and what stress that was when they were little. I spent seven years trailing them and always keeping a mother's hawk eye on them both. I had the energy and enthusiasm back then. Not so much now.

Nevertheless, Arjan and Sam always need me. They freak out if I talk about working outside the home, and one or the other seems to go through some separation anxiety. Sam has taken to seeking me out, standing on the porch or back stoop hollering my name if I'm gone for more than a few minutes. I've never left either child, more than a couple of hours maybe once a year, and that is with their father; they know precisely where I am and what I'm doing. I don't understand it, but Sam fears losing me. He won't let me walk Molly alone. He will rise from a deep morning slumber, hear me on the porch, and come running out in pj's to insist I take him for the walk. Arjan, as I said, checks my vitals often. All children need their mamas something fierce.

So, we are broke, and I don't worry. Thank goodness we did repairs and overhauled both cars while we had money. The dogs had all their vaccines, teeth cleaning, pulling, and blood work while we had money. The big stuff was taken care of, and all the little debts paid off. Money comes and goes. We can always make more if we need it. But I keep a grocery budget and do the freegan thing for now.

Monday

Last night, after my third bowl of goulash, I suffered from scary upper stomach pains. Now, let me clarify that my bowls were small and well spaced out, so this was not a situation brought on by overstuffing oneself. I have no idea what happened, but I was in such pain for 15 minutes or so that I thought my appendix was about to blow, and I called Bali to take me to the ER. I have never done that, but I was alarmed. It turns out the appendix is the lower right of the gut, and this was the upper middle which may be the Pancreas. I did my research once the pain subsided. Perhaps it was all the homemade white flour tortillas I'd been eating for the last couple of days, and then the pasta just sent my Pancreas over the edge. Who knows. It's not the gall bladder or appendix; gastritis is caused by heavy drinking, smoking, stress, and/or pain pills—none of which I do or have. Maybe old stress, but I feel more relaxed and mellowed out each day.

Today Bali and Sam bought some yogurt, and a farmer is selling fruit and melons by the side of the road within walking distance. I've cautiously consumed some yogurt that was plain and nonfat, quiet sour but maybe for the best right now, and some sweet fruit. I did have coffee and lived. I watched **Walk With Me** just in the back ground because I've decided to start a fully Zen-like existence in case I have residual stress, and that was what I was birthing last night.

It rained off and on today! It was overcast yesterday, and I could smell the rain. I thought about how I so look forward to the first rains and the smells, and today I had the chance to sit on the porch with my coffee and smell the lovely rain.

Friday

I brewed my espresso for a latte this morning, and I got to work. I filled two bags with books, movies, and these lovely candle sticks to donate to the thrift store. I had been saving some movies for little kids that might show up. They never do. I saved smart-looking books, so if someone were to look through my library, they would see how intellectual I am. No one cares how smart I am. I've even lost interest in my intellect. I saved the candle sticks because they were so pretty and colorful, But I haven't used them in ages and probably won't. Someone will be thrilled when they find them at the thrift. I loaded up all the small bags of rice and oats we didn't need since we had big buckets and bags. I loaded up canned foods we won't eat and bags of frozen meat—all of it. The food will go to the food bank.

Hot Spot went back today. I love having it, but the boys act like hardcore heroin addicts. They were on it all day yesterday and lost interest in anything outside the video games.

I've ordered more books that I feel I must have in my personal library. I order books from the library, and if I love them and they are the sorts of books I'll go back to repeatedly, such as spiritual books or writing books, I buy them. I had to have copies of **Happy Pocket Full Of Money,** Ann Lamott's **Bird By Bird**, **Walden,** and other writing by *Thoreau*, and *Stephen King's* **On Writing**. I love these books and want to get in there with a highlighter and dog ear them like crazy. These are study books.

Thursday

Arjan is lying on my bed, sharing his goals with me. The first goal is to swim 100 laps in the pool. A little too ambitious, "cut it back," I say. He says, "ok, 50". He has daily goals, short-term goals involving video games, and long-term goals. Goals are inspiring as long as they are things we love doing and want to improve on. Then we must be careful not to get so intense about reaching them. Stay loose, fluid, and playful, and you're more likely to succeed.

It has been a busy morning. I watered all the trees, roses, and a few parts of the garden. Some melon plants haven't even blossomed yet, and here it is, August. I get a little frustrated with what I can grow up here. On the one hand, I'm grateful for the mild Summer. After living in the valley where it was triple digits all the time, these days of 90 degrees, even high 90s, are a relief. But in the valley, we could grow like crazy. I have no luck with carrots, strawberries, or melons.

I want to take some time off gardening and work on layering the soil for a year. All the stupid fear-mongering preppers and homesteaders had me panicky, but we aren't getting anywhere fast here, and this is the third summer I haven't had anything to can. We have been working since the day we got the keys to this house. Let's grow a cover crop and let the garden go wild with it and keep adding compost and leaves, and then next fall, add sand and horse manure, more leaves, and compost. Then we dig it all in and plant the following Spring. I also need an excellent greenhouse because I need to start some plants early, and doing it in the house did not work. I did recover all the spindly tomato starts, but they are dwarfs in the garden. I also noticed that the left side of the garden grows things well. It had the rye regrow last winter, which made a big difference.

Saturday

Big library day yesterday. The morning had such a great start, with two fun conversations with the two girlfriends I talk to the most frequently on the phone. I did some chores. Sam made my bed. The house was in order when we left. Then it turned on me a little at the library. I tried to move the table in the computer room so I could re-plug the attached cord. It's one of those tables you can plug your computer into the top of it, but the bottom needs to be plugged into the wall. I tried to move a heavy table with my coffee mug unsteadily riding on top and spilled coffee everywhere. We had to run to the bathroom, get paper towels, and finish with wipes from the librarian's desk. It turns out they just had the rugs shampooed. Fortunately, the coffee didn't get to the floor, but my laptop did sit in it for a minute as I didn't move it immediately upon seeing coffee spread across the table. I just ran to the bathroom for towels. Ah, my simple brilliance amazes me.

So, no coffee made the time awkward as I felt my arm was missing. Then I forgot the earphones and the ones lent to me didn't work. I got some that worked and settled into a long day of no coffee and needing a sweater because they crank up the air there. I have simple but demanding creature comforts that I need to feel good. I need lotion, lip balm, coffee, comfortable clothes, earphones, and a goal. I thought I had a goal: to look up fun vegan recipes and inspiration, but I couldn't find any. I found YouTube to be lacking yesterday. All the videos they line up for me are so glossy and perfect. They aren't funky and interesting. They are more formulaic. I know there are still groovy little channels out there, but they are tough to find, and I usually find them only with a referral from someone that has found them.

And Sam, dear Sam. He had a dream that I had disappeared, and he hasn't been right since. We have talked about it and done our little therapy around it, but he follows me everywhere, won't let me travel far without being by my side, and won't allow walks without his going. I let him know all my whereabouts at the library; if I'm going to the bathroom or the front desk to get earphones or check out more books. He comes with me or sits at a nearby table to keep an eye on me and ensure no one takes me. I've explained that middle-aged, chubby women aren't the targets for kidnappers. We are an undervalued market. Arjan added that it would be hard to load me in a van. He was generous in saying it would take two guys. I think maybe three or four, especially if I put up a struggle. And I would. But Sam wasn't taking any chances, so he followed me around the library, sometimes sitting at a table to watch over things as I chatted with my favorite librarian.

I'm running out of movies too. We have been going there at least once a week for eight months, and we have combed through the wall of movies until we are left with strange options and bizarre movies we wouldn't otherwise watch. Lots of rewatching going on. Surprisingly, I'm still finding some good stuff. I watched **The Trip,** *with Steve Coogan and Rob Brydon.* It was funny and intelligent. The two men worked well together. Their humor and the constant back and forth could be exhausting, but they clicked. The movie was mainly about these men and their conversations while driving about the countryside and eating at various fancy restaurants. I enjoyed the banter and the scenery, the artfully done plates.

We also watched **Life Animated**, a documentary about an autistic boy and how he connected so profoundly with Disney films. His parents learned to communicate with him, and he learned about life and human emotions all through Disney films. It was fascinating. The animation and the character's reactions are so dramatic that he can decipher their feelings and reactions and understand life through their stories. This was very interesting to learn.

I tell you, I wonder if I'm not just a little, tiny bit autistic. I relate to the comfort I get from routines and use films to understand my own life. I can relate to some obsessions and how they can be focused on creative outlets. I need my home to be in order and comfortable at many levels.

I enjoy such little things. I often wonder if I'm just a simple person with some big words that make me appear intelligent. My thinking is bland at times and comical at others. My level of gratitude is high right now. I think this is a wonderful way to live. To be so easily content and find joy in little things others would take for granted.

Today has been hectic and productive. And I somehow fit the end of one movie and watched a whole other. I wouldn't recommend **Queen Bees,** but Arjan and I enjoyed watching the old ladies. Arjan used to love **The Golden Girls**. When we lived in the city's suburbs, we had this 860 sq. foot house with a postage stamp of a backyard. The house was super cute. The backyard was tiny and had no trees. The houses around us seemed smashed against our fence and just ugly, tan walls with crap stored there, except for one house next to us. They had a small yard, a huge wooden pergola, and so much lush, green viny stuff. Two gay men lived next door, and one of them was a bit of a drinker and would bring his little TV out under the canopy of the overgrown pergola and watch old sitcoms like **Threes Company**. He smoked cloves. I loved the smell of cloves. I watched **The Golden Girls** all the time, and Arjan would request them every evening. He was four years old and loved the old ladies. Still does to this day.

I loved that little house in town. Despite being 800 sq. ft., it felt spacious.

Today we own a sizeable house. A tiny 1100 sq feet in this American land of 2500 sq ft suburbs. But it feels substantial. All the rooms are separate, with a hallway and a pantry/ laundry off the kitchen, making a small house seem busy and spacious. Mirrors help open it up and light it up as well. My next mission is to find old free or cheap mirrors to hang on the opposite wall of the living room and hall to reflect the light from the large window and give the illusion of open space. Do we need more space? No. Not even when the boys grow big and tall. You need the illusion. We have a quarter acre, and every season finds us busy making little sanctuary spaces here and there. A patio and homemade pergola with the pool makes a great hang-out summer space. As the fruit and nut trees grow, we will have more shade and lovely places to place our chairs and read our books. We have the porch, and I fixed it nicely with plants and chairs and a little table to write from. We read in the hammock in the evenings or have coffee and chat on the phone in the morning from the white wicker chair, surrounded by plants, so I have privacy on the porch.

I cannot get my floors clean enough for my bare feet. I swept and mopped yesterday, and when I steamed the house, the dog hair had rewon its territory despite sweeping the day before. Then the dear boys spilled watermelon juice on the clean kitchen floor. Sam attempted to steam mop, but he looked more like he was attacking or spearing something with the mop. Then I used the Bona cloth mop. But I had to give up the good fight for the night.

Today I went after all the floors and rugs with a broom, vacuum, steamer mop, and a bottle of freshly made cleaner. I cleaned the toilet inside out and repeatedly. I must take apart the bidet weekly and scrub every part. Disgusting, but I genuinely love our bidet. I love my cleaning rags. The shower curtain was washed with all my many cloth cleaning rags made of old tea towels, wash clothes, cut-up bath towels, and the steam and Bona mop rags. I hung them on the wooden rack beside the washer. I love not having a dryer. I may not feel this way come winter.

I sit at my free oak desk, listening to classical music on the radio. The stations come in excellent at the desk. Better than anywhere in the house. I can smell the wax scent heating up in the wax lamp. The smell of Honey Suckle drifting down the hall. All this and a homemade latte to boot.

Now, I need a dinner idea. We have been eating up a storm. That's how it feels, but the foods are so good. We feast on healthy food; it tastes good and fresh. I chopped up a melon, pineapple, and three mangos with lime and tajin. There was whole wheat bread from the bread machine with vegan butter and honey (not vegan, yes, I know): lattes, and ice water. I feel like I'm at a country Inn most of the time, except I'm living here as the chef and housekeeping. But, hey, that's great because if I were to live at an Inn in a charming touristy forest town, I would have to earn my room and board. There might be a small paycheck and time off, but we must create that for ourselves, mustn't we?

I did treat myself to four more books. Dang it! I said I was done shopping for a long, long time. But I'm trying new vegan recipes, and I get so excited about vegan cooking. I used to try a lot of **Krocks In The Kitchen** recipes, which was fun. Arjan and I would watch the cooking vlogs, write down ingredients, go to the store the next day to collect these ingredients and cook all day. I can't say I'm crazy about all the Krock's recipes, but they are creative and spicy cooks. I've gotten great recipes with **Simple Sara Kitchen**; her minestrone is to gorge oneself on, and the mushroom stroganoff is another dish I can't be trusted with a large batch.

So, You're Dating a Vegan had some people that made great food. I mimicked an enchilada recipe and loved it. The plant-based, whole foods people have bland recipes. I like the down-home foods and veganizing our familiar favorites. I can make yummy lasagna, cakes, loaded burgers and burritos, chili, veggie pizza, and so on. I need to start trying out some mac and cheese recipes. I was watching **Tabitha Brown** make mac and cheese that looked very creamy. Tabitha is a huge vegan inspiration. She is fun to watch and listen to.

The vegans that stay vegans and stay healthy and happy with it, are the ones that have a lot of fun cooking and eat a lot of variety; both clean, whole foods and plenty of vegetables but also dirty at times. They enjoy junk food. That is a typical vegan. There is a channel from an athletic vegan, and she eats it all: the healthy stuff, the restaurant foods, junk foods, kale, *and* ice cream.

This was very liberating to see. This woman was thin, super fit, and glowed with health. To see her eat all the good and bad (good) stuff was a relief. So many vegans will get on your backside about "don't eat oil," "Don't eat salt or sugar," and "Don't eat that process food...so, so bad!" "Don't eat alternative meats and dairy! What are you thinking?!" "Don't have fun!" "Eat a dry potato and raw broccoli. That's how you eat for health!"

I say hell no. I want to eat all the delights I would have on a regular diet. No one says a thing if you eat a pork roast or chicken pot pie, but if you eat a "vegan" pot pie, oh boy, you are eating that awful, processed stuff. Never mind, the chicken pot pies are made with filthy and tortured factory chickens. I'd rather take my chances with a chicken made of tofu, seitan, or some strange root. And most of that alternative meat and cheese is made with vegetable proteins, wheat gluten, and basic seasonings such as salt and nutritional yeast, paprika, and such. You can read the ingredients and know what they are without looking them up in a science dictionary. Meat, on the other hand, has hormones, antibiotics, horror, pain, depression, and suffering. There's blood and puss in the milk. Sometimes fecal residue is in the meat. Yum.

Yes, so I don't listen to the hard-core plant eaters. I do it my way, and my family loves it. Sam says he doesn't want to be vegan; my kids don't have to be. They can have pasture-raised eggs and goat's milk. I buy a little real cheese and organic meats for them. But they usually want vegan meats. I do a great tofu scramble too. Each time we go back to being veganish, my cooking improves by leaps and bounds. The best way to learn vegan cuisine is to master the craft of making faux meats and then learn how to veganize everyday recipes from my cookbooks, *Allrecipes.com* and *Tasteofhome.com.* A mother said she and her daughter were vegan and veganized all the recipes from Taste Of Home cookbooks. How fun!

When we do eat meat, we get clean and pasture-raised stuff. But right now, we are going for it with the vegetarian. I already have tons of vegan seasoning and a pantry based on vegetarian cooking: beans, rice, flour, giant jars of nutritional yeast, and plain cashews. I've had years to learn this sort of shopping and cooking. It is like going home in the best way. I feel my life force return, and my cooking becomes magically delicious. Even a pot of beans with added seasoning becomes the family favorite for days. I just froze the rest to give us a break. Now I have five unidentified bags of leftovers in the freezer. I don't know why I don't take the time to write out what's in the bag. I figure, "oh, it's just a couple of things," then it's five things, and I have only a vague clue about two of the bags might be.

With vegan, you must cook ahead of time. You can't just grab a hardboiled egg and pickle or a cheese stick when ꞇry. You need to make potato salad and bread ahead of time. Make sure to have lots of easy things and fruit, popcorn, pickles, ingredients to grill up a quick vegan cheese sandwich, and such. You learn what faux cheeses and meats taste good and how to bake without eggs or use egg substitutes. You learn to make milk, cheeses, meats, steaks, and baloney.

Ah, it is a craft, vegan cooking, and baking.

So, I swore I had ordered my last online order and shopped for my last item for ages to come. But the vegan thing has required some new cookbooks for me to do it right and well. I ordered a few from Thriftbooks but was forced by pricing to order one through Amazon. I wanted to cancel my Amazon account, but thank goodness I didn't. If you delete your account, they punish you. I would have been kicked out of KDP publishing, losing all my books and work! I'm glad I read the whole document. They say, "If you choose to delete your account, this is all you will lose," and there is a long list of losses. I have a cloud reader library that would be lost as well. So, I kept the account. I don't know why I must be so dramatic about everything.

And how I love this house. Let me count the ways. Out of all the nests I've feathered and all the places I've lived, this is by far my favorite. I love looking out most of the windows and planting trees everywhere. My birthday will be here in less than two months, and I can't wait to hit the nursery. We will plant lots of bare-root fruit trees when winter is in full swing. Bali has agreed that the main garden could use a fruit tree or two. I'll plant the pluot or plum in there. It gets too much sun on one side, so I thought we should do a food forest-type system. I just ordered **The New Square Foot Gardening** book from the library.

Books from the library are a must, just as a gardening budget. I can't get too tight-fisted with the good things. Down the road, we will spend less and less on the garden and orchard as more trees make it, and we learn to grow from seeds and propagate, and the soil gets deeply amended and rich. Horse manure is free and like gold but does require a trip to the valley. Trees get big and hardy and don't require the fussing after years. I planted two nectarine seeds, and when we eat organic foods, I'll start saving and planting the seeds to see what happens. I was so inspired by my friend's peach tree (I thought it was a nectarine), which was loaded with fruit. It was planted from seed from her other peach tree. Gardening doesn't have to be so complicated and expensive.

I'm steaming some brown rice and blanching broccoli. I have no more rice wine or oyster sauce to make a stir fry. I've begun listing a few items I need for my pantry. We have three plates of fruit chopped up for snacking, and the rice and broccoli will be dinner. Sometimes it's that simple. We have days of flavorful meals, and then I need a break.

Sunday

Dental appointments tomorrow. School begins seven days later. No one can tell me when enrichment classes at the school begin. I have to power up for another long year of homeschooling, and although we have learned to do it simply and without much dispute and warfare, it is not my specialty. We will make sure Sam is up and reading this year, and I'm grateful for the Hot Spot because there is so much good stuff on YouTube for homeschooling in the way of History and Science.

Today we will organize the purge of the boy's room. I need to go through all their clothes and asses their schoolbooks and what I need for this year.

We wound up with piles of produce, and I feel like we have been gorging on it before it goes to waste. Fruits are great as you can freeze them for smoothies. That reminds me, I had weird dreams about my garden. Some of the plants were not what I thought they were, and so on.

We need to take a long break. Bali is finishing up the patio and building the pergola. The second bathroom needs to be done, and we need to replace the flooring in the old bathroom eventually. The kitchen and the pantry/laundry floor can wait. The bathroom only because that linoleum must be super gross if it was just layered like all the rest of the flooring was in this house. And the tub. We can do a cheap kit from the hardware store and repaint it.

We have been at it hardcore for years. We fixed up the first cottage we bought and then moved here, and we have been going strong for over two years. We need a slow season. I don't want to garden for a year. It will be hard because I love planting things.

I need a year off from everything but parenting and homemaking.

Cooking is simple right now. I buy some convenient foods such as bagels or big tortillas. I have all kinds of things cooked up, and we make meals from the pre-cooked.

Life is easy as it was years ago. I don't need to be online except to check email; only a few people email me with chat or recipes. As for bills, there aren't that many, and they are either autopay, so I don't have to think about it, or I do quick bill pay online with the bank. I could do it all auto and never have to think again.

I spend time resting in the recliner, watching a movie, reading a book, studying, and writing. I rest throughout the day. It's new to me to be this easy with life, not push myself to do this and that, and hustle, meet goals, and make money. I am not searching for something new to keep me busy. To move slowly and be ok with a simple day and simple task. To give up ruling the world in exchange for a broom and bean pot. That has been a wonderful exchange.

Later in the day...

I made a jar of iced coffee. Made it from the Nescafe *Clasico* instant coffee, vanilla oat milk, and lots of ice. It's strong, creamy, and icy. The kitchen looks unusually cozy with all the butter yellows and deep reds. I'm sitting at the kitchen table, writing after what feels like a full day of repeatedly cooking and cleaning the kitchen. I sweep the sand from the house often. It is tracked in from the patio and pool area. Oh, how we love that pool! It's easy to maintain, although we feel it could use a pool Roomba if such a thing exists. It needs the bottom vacuumed, but we scoop it and run the pool filter. I get small bags of chlorine for $5 at the pool store, and we bought a brush, but it doesn't fit on the stick, so Arjan has to dive underwater to scrub the sides. We'll fix it soon. The pool people said it would fit on any stick, but sometimes those people are not so helpful when they see me buying cheap bags of chlorine and discounted inflatable water pads. I'm not a big hot tub sale worth the attention. They should be glad to see me, though. I always bring cash, and they always have notes taped to the cash register asking for $1's, $5's, and $10's. I'm that gal. I work with cash envelopes, so I got what your register needs. Sell me the right brush with the right dang stick.

I like the side of the apartments we are across the street from. We are across from the big apartment entrance. There are many trees, the little outdoor post office, and the manager's office door with a cast iron and wood bend parked outside it. The pool is just beyond that, and more trees block out all the green apartments, blending into the trees they are nestled into. From this angle, it looks like a resort in the woods. Like Tahoe apartments for summer folk. But no one swims in the pool. I see umbrellas and balconies with chimes and plants. But I don't hear anyone swimming and laughing poolside. They have a barbecue area, too, and sometimes there is the smell of a barbecue, but there isn't that much activity. If we lived in those apartments, the boys and I would go down daily, swim, and lounge for a couple of hours.

I used to think this. Then we got our pool, and it's such a fun thing to do daily. Float about in the water and soak up the sun for a bit. It's excellent exercise too. I feel soothed after I've had a swim and float, then I sit outside and read and highlight my books while I dry. I dress and make myself an iced coffee and write.

People worry. I remember worrying. It's a joy kill. We live on easy street right now. We probably won't be able to retire any time soon, but retirement is a death sentence.

I feel like I'm on vacation! Why don't more people live like this? I think most people obligate themselves to side work, bringing work home, being with extended family and friends trying to keep those relations up. Many people drink heavily on the weekends. They try to catch up with laundry and cleaning, and shopping. Many people feel depressed. They watch the news and live on social media. They make their life a prison. I lived like that many years ago.

Being sober helps with happiness. Not working for anyone is enormous. Running my own home and withdrawing from many social activities that don't bring happiness is pure therapy and peace. I used to like traveling and social events when I was young. I like getting out and about, but we are talking about the grocery store and library. Or garden nursery, my other favorite hangout. I love the nursery, and I love the library and grocery shopping. I especially love doing extensive stock-up shopping at WinCo. What fun. Do you think I'm kidding? No, I'm a homemaking nerd but not a super creative one, like the kind that owns glue guns and shops weekly at the Dollar Store to craft delights for my house. *Olivia's Romantic Home* started like that. She lived in a tiny, bland apartment with her family, and she was a housewife with little income to work with. She would craft furnishings, candle holders, and decorations to doll up her house. It looked like a girl's dream dollhouse. She had a glue gun and spray paint, charming it all up. She now works out of the garage and has a huge channel.

A lot of channels lose their funky charm when they get big. Lighting improves, cameras happen, editing becomes professional, vlogs become well-rehearsed tutorials, and you no longer feel like you are watching a common sister at her craft, but you are now watching corporate YouTube filming.

I try to find that offbeat channel where the family is just a down-to-earth family living a bit off the path. Like our story, mom stays home, dad has a low-paying job, and they live on very little, but their life is filled with contentment and ease. The family has chosen a sleepy, blissful life over being nervous and stuck in commuter traffic. They live off homemade bread and downhome foods they love. Coffee is big, but drugs and alcohol have no place with them. The boys are innovative and thriving, but not in a public school. They are homeschooled a little bit free range meets Finland meets some Classic style meets unschooling.

Oh, did I describe us? So, I'm that channel I'm looking for? I am. I looked for us years ago and was inspired to start my channel, but I got lost. Then I started to figure it out, but I had no idea how I would capture what I'm living right now.

I see myself doing these funky, raw filmed montages of life here at home with some good music and some sitting and talking. Like a documentary but made simple because I'll be making them.

I wish a lazy but productive life for everyone. You can be very productive but still enjoy a slow life.

I was thinking about how obsessed our culture is with Super Sizing everything. They are obsessed with huge families. Huge shopping hauls, huge meal preps for the freezer, huge gardens, big houses, big vans and trucks, big, large, extra-large, super-sized living. I find it tiring. Me, personally. It may be my age; I don't have the energy to maintain things on a large scale. Even our quarter acre feels like a lot. The 1200 square foot garden is too much. The 1100 sq ft house is too big at times. Making three meals a day is out. The big dogs are old and can easily be exercised in the yard and spend the day napping contentedly now, but years before, they needed to be taken out all the time and run at the river or park. Molly is fulfilled after a short walk around the hood. The boys are self-sufficient in dressing, doing chores, making breakfast, and sometimes lunch if I have lots of food set up and easy to make. Life gets easier. As it should.

Bali's building the pergola. I can't wait to see the result and have that extra shade. I love the heat, but only if it is not beat directly on me. I like shade and lots of it. I think I'll rest in the recliner and finish the Tightwad Gazette. I'm on the last edition and the inspirational letters from those who went frugal and how it turned their lives around. People want a magic formula, and so here it is. Frugality is about not spending money in many areas or finding ways to need less so you don't need to make that much money or work that hard; thus, a lot of living is the end result. A lot of time to mull over life, observe life, enjoy life, and be present in daily moments that build the bonds between you and your children—more time to play with the house and play with the garden.

Monday

Diving into the *Stephen King* book **On Writing**. I never read it from the beginning, but this time I did, and it was entertaining. I'll have to order some of his older books. I have read some of his fat novels of almost over 1,000 pages. **Under The Dome**, **The Stand**. I read **The Shining** far too young, but that was a great book. When Sam learns to read well and is much older, he can read it. He is obsessed with horror, zombies, and Halloween.

I'm enjoying my coffee chats with friends. I have two friends I talk to throughout the week, sometimes daily. We have bay area friends to visit now and then. However, it's hard to leave home. I can make one three-day trip to a favorite destination once a year. We did the coast and stayed at the lodge a year ago, and then we just stayed in Marin for a couple of days this year. Why would I want to leave with my home set up to please the fussiest guest? We have a clean pool to float about in the afternoons, big soft beds to slumber at night, a good selection of movies, delicious, homecooked food, and a small library of interesting books to browse through. Not to mention the best coffee. However, you like it. I have a dreamy setup, and it's hard to try and sleep in a strange room on hard beds. People like hard beds or don't spend money on good mattresses. I love foam, myself. Hard mattresses send me to the chiropractor.

The only place I can stay and be very content is the bay area with my old friends. My family and I have spent many holidays and birthdays there. I used to live in that little town. Once with godparents and once with an artist. My mother and I spent summer visits and some holidays visiting the godparents. It is a charming little town nestled in the mountains. It used to be very blue-collar and bohemian. Then it was what my mother would call "yuppified." It became too rich for its blood. Now it's this hippy vibe. They even had a piano sitting out on the street in front of the tavern. There was a sense that people were starting to get in touch with the heart of things. People are doing things more naturally and want to slow down and have experiences.

Even my successful real estate mogul friend is driving an old, black Mercedes she got for $2,000, ordering sides of beef from local farms and getting deliveries from Misfit market.

The conversation of frugality came up regarding the YouTube community. It has been ruined by popularity. But not everyone does it the same. The more modern-day way of doing it seems to involve budget notebooks, Dollar Tree hauls, or Wal-Mart shopping. Then there is the spirited family that is zero waste and canning and growing all their foods. I have gone from extremely frugal to frivolous with extra funds. We have lived through periods where we had to be careful because we only had so much to work with. Very little to work with. We have been frugal because we had a huge goal of moving to a town we adored and getting out of a town that didn't suit us.

Now we are frugal because I don't want to work like crazy. I am perimenopausal, maybe, it seems. I am raising two highly intelligent and strong-willed boys who demand nothing less than all or most of my attention and enthusiasm. I am older, and though I have great energy much of the time, I'm slowing down and have days I need to rest. Sure, I could push myself. Drink that extra espresso every afternoon. But that makes me unpleasant, and I don't feel it's necessary anymore. You must be driven by some desired outcome or hugely inspired toward something. I am inspired only by small things these days. A super clean floor, so it feels good on my feet. A novel I'm getting into, so I rush through washing the dishes and making an iced tea so I can enjoy this treat out on the porch if it's not too hot. If it is, I go swimming with the boys, sit in my wet bathing suit under a tree in the backyard, and read while keeping an eye on my boys in the pool. I have goals to rustle up a tasty supper for us all. Big luxuries would be summed up in having a dishwasher installed. Not a lot of big dreaming going on right now. We have one significant goal: pay off the mortgage to make the future less strenuous and help the kids with their dreams as they grow up.

Fruit and nut trees grow strong, mortgages disappear, gardens become more productive, dogs pass, and kids go to college. It never ends but changes and can become more secure in some ways and more abundant in others. To have a home and own it (let's not get into the tax debate) and to grow a massive supply of organic foods can do nothing but ease the financial challenges.

Frugal has become a business. Budget planners to "keep you on track" are sold, along with packets for pricing and meal planning. Merchandise is sold in the form of T-shirts and mugs. Hundreds of links for products through affiliate programs. So many things to get on 'track' and save money. I'm guilty of it. I never sold merchandise. I almost did mugs and t-shirts because I had fun sayings people used to say should be on a shirt. Maybe it wasn't that funny what I said. Perhaps my ego told me I was funny. I did have lots and lots of affiliate links with Amazon. I used to buy everything through Amazon. I didn't sell budget and price planners or meal planners. Lord knows I can't seem motivated to do meal planning myself. I'm not good at keeping on one subject, and I am, in all honesty, not the best frugalista.

I'm a spendthrift at heart. Spendthrift is a silly name for someone that spends too much. Look at the word; Spend Thrift. I always think it means 'great with money.' But I've been reading through the Tightwad Gazette and reminded of its implications. I am a spender at heart. I love going here and there, taking long drives despite gas prices. I love eating out and not cooking or cleaning up! Heck, I'm more than excited about that. I love clothes shopping and redecorate my house all fresh and new now and then. Amy Dyczyzan talked about the three types of people. The effluent that purchased what they wanted and when they wanted. The semi-fugal types bought new, cheap cars and shopped at Walmart. Then the frugal zealots, as she called herself. She said they were close to being like the affluent folks because they got whatever they wanted but at huge discounts and often experienced a lot of Opulence (her words) or luxuries (my words).

We are the type that buys used cars in excellent condition, and we pay all cash, so there is no car payment or heavy insurance. We go to Walmart now and then, but I usually stock up on candles and wax scents there. Quality doesn't equal Walmart. We shop at WinCo or Grocery Outlet. We don't coupon because we don't use or eat what is usually couponed. We love having a stocked pantry, but it's a vague two months supply at a time with years of beans and rice. I make sure to have six months of coffee, however. I'll be at least alert and productive in challenging times. I can mend a hole somewhat, but making clothes is out. I can crotchet a blanket or scarf, but sweaters and shaped things are out. I can paint my rooms different colors and redecorate the house from free or cheap stuff found off the street, thrift stores, or Craigslist, but crafting and anything trendy is out. I get the bills paid quickly and easily. There is always money for groceries. Our wardrobes all come from Savers Thrift and various thrift stores. I have purchased clothes off Amazon and regret most of them except the stretch pants. And they were all cheap.

I do wash out baggies and Ziplocs. I keep and reuse jars, bags, paper, and plastic jugs. I work on wasting less and less. I cook almost everything from scratch. Making pizza dough, bread, crackers, and so on is normal. It is no longer special; it is a weekly chore. When we have extra money, we pay ourselves. That is how we build up our savings every time. Getting rid of non-essentials on the budget was smart. Having Bali save money and build the savings was smart. I know my weaknesses. You put the best money saver in the family to the task of building up the family savings. I don't spend. That is how I manage the money and myself. I try not to shop or spend, not at the thrift store, not online. That is the only way I can keep it under wraps, except for books. There is an exception if it's a book I need. I find them cheap on Thriftbooks or Amazon. I'm trying to stick with Thriftbooks. I've already given Amazon too many paychecks.

Tuesday

All our library dreams fell apart today. Our library had no power, and the library generator wasn't connecting. We took a walk to pass the time but still no connection. We went to the other library, which doesn't have many computers, so we thought we'd have an excuse for a Hot Spot, but they were all checked out. What we did do was find some good movies, and my writing books arrived. They are two of the three that are sold on NaNoWriMo. Sam insisted we bring home *The Shining*. We are watching it right now after some soul searching as a mother if this movie is for an eight-year-old. I asked my friend in Oregon, and we decided to let him watch it, but I was sitting with him the whole time. Sam loves horror and mystery; I think he's too young, but he found ways to watch scary things and zombie movies from an early age. Being careful of what images we store upstairs in our mind is always in my consideration. We talk about feelings, actions, and life stuff, but what we take into our mind in visuals and moments makes up the sweetness of the bread. Or the bitterness. Or fearfulness and so on.

As you can tell, I'm sitting here with Sam, but I'm now writing as the stress of the movie is too much. It's not so scary the second time (I watched it when I was young, too), but the music, lord, it's that steady stressful, ominous strings in the background of the whole movie that keeps you on edge, making sure you never relax for even a minute. I can't take that kind of stress, so I've turned to writing during the final awful, stress-filled last scene. It's a classic. I didn't know that Stanley Kubrick made this movie, but then I had never been so into film as I am lately. With no internet, for the most part, I have dived into movies, and now I go in and analyze them and suck out the meaning and message for my personal growth. Movies are stories that guide and inspire.

I made the best garden pie ever. I made salmon cakes for the boys. Just salmon, eggs, and crackers. They were not as good as Grannies, but good enough. The garden pie, aka Shepard pie but veganized and done my way, was so good. I used Beyond ground, and some other plant-made ground discounted at Grocery Outlet. I sauteed it with a bit of oil and then added two small cans of cream of mushroom and simmered it for some time to cook through. I layered this in a casserole dish and added some mixed vegetables and California mix vegetables I had sauteed a few nights ago. I love this new way of sautéing frozen vegetables. It's so flavorful. You heat up and add chicken-flavored bouillon powder, cumin, salt, and pepper. We had these with polenta one day. So, I layer that on the faux ground in cream of mushroom. Then the potatoes. I used the potato flakes, but I added soy milk, water, vegan butter, and salt. I whipped it up with the beater, and it turned fluffy. I topped it with Have A Heart Vegan shredded cheese.

My vegan cooking is so good right now. Everything I make has this wonderful flavor. Maybe it's the taste of a clean conscious.

I'm now watching **The Flamingo Kid**. This kid chooses a job parking cars at a clubhouse where affluent families come to swim and enjoy summer days. An odd clubhouse that looks more like a hotel with levels and a pool near a beach. Hum. Anyway, I was absorbed by the part where the guy, Jeffrey, is having breakfast with his family, and his father thinks he's starting a job as an assistant in an engineering office for the summer. Jeffrey tells him he wants to work at the El Flamingo. He likes parking cars. I love the energy in that scene. He was supposed to work at a miserable job in an office for the summer to earn a reputation or set it up for later after college and getting work. He chose fun and did what he liked instead. Today I find that to be a wise decision. I also observed that he ate oatmeal and a banana for breakfast while his family had eggs and bacon with biscuits. Is he vegetarian? Or just ahead of his time with healthy eating? The movie was set in 1963.

Wednesday

I finished **The Flaming Kid**. Good story about a kid figuring out the complexities of life and good choices, trust in relationships and listening to his father. I like that the kid explored life and didn't let his father dictate things. The father was a great dad but wanted his son to attend college and get an office job. Jeffrey wanted to have fun and explore his options. And he did and was raised just right enough and had just enough common sense to see the truth about things. To see the scam despite the sparkly illusion and choose the smart path.

Had a wee bit of a chat with the neighbor about raised beds, dead trees, and native plants. I derived some comfort from some of the input. He lived out in a natural clay pit of land and said after four years of amending the soil, he could dig into the ground with his hand in the summer when it usually was hard as a rock. He told me what sand to use and what would happen if I used the wrong stuff. If you use fine sand, you wind up with a fantastic brick. You get loamy soil if you use coarse sand, even decomposed granite. Just sand and compost for years, and there you go. As for raised beds, it sounds like it might be great for carrots, potatoes, and tomatoes but not necessary for all the other veggies. He never had luck with melons, except for the one time he was eating watermelon and spitting the seeds out (I suppose in the garden?), and he said he had great success with that one that grew itself. So, we need to find out what grows great here and look at the garden as what it truly is...a kitchen garden to supplement our grocery bill. We buy melons from a farmer who parks down the street and sets up a table with two types of melons. We've been eating massive amounts of melon daily. He didn't have any yellow melons today, and the watermelon isn't stacked as high. Tis the end of the season already.

I had an inspiring coffee chat with Dawn, and we discussed various ideas for her channel. She talked about her mother. Her mother was a housewife and did not work outside the home. She focused on her daily chore of running a home and raising girls. She did all the cooking, cleaning, and gardening. She ironed all the clothes and mended them. She had a daily schedule and routines of what got done on those days. Her girls went to school, and her husband did the mowing. This is simple and basic, and I loved hearing this today. It reminds me that, although our new age culture demands that the woman cook, clean, garden, and raise the kids, she is also expected to work a job outside the home or have a career. Or some side hustles, at the least. A woman is deemed lazy if she is not working outside the house part-time or doing online money-making.

Let us encourage more parents to stay home and be a little 'lazy.' This whole culture is so pro-competition and challenge-reaching, goal-making.

Even our government talks about 'competing' with this country and that country. I wonder what would happen if we just minded our own business and worked on making our country happy and green. We took care of our nature and people and became an example, not a contender. Why the need to be number one? It isn't genius. You bust your rear to be number one, and then you are, and then you fall. And if you get up there at all costs, you fall far down, down, down.

And how about we spend some time observing some countries that are having great success with living. Iceland for clean energy, France for clean water and reducing plastic, and Finland for education. And homelessness. And overall happiness amongst the citizens. Hum? Why not work with countries to improve ourselves and become an example?

Greed and corruption, competition, jealousy, and gluttony are unbearable to be around or observe.

So, I retreat to my world. It's nice here.

We ran off to the library to get the Hot Spot. It's not working that great. My Pandora keeps going down. I did have some wonderful Opera to vacuum and tidy the whole house and wipe down the kitchen.

Then another movie. I'm watching movies these days and rewatching them. I'm so into analyzing. I'm learning so much about myself through the movies I choose randomly. I'm also seeing them in a different and new light. I observe the story style, the character development, and how it's all told from beginning to end. Is there a hero's journey or just a take on life? I think it's always about the hero's journey.

Another Year, *a film by Mike Leigh,* was a meal. I initially found it a little depressing but was quickly sucked into this exploration of life for a married couple and two of their single, alcoholic friends. There was another couple with a baby, but I think they were having issues, too. I wasn't paying attention all the way through. The couple is where I am now, but the friends were me at once. It might have been me if I hadn't married and settled down. I used to drink too much and too often. I was so unhealthy and insecure. I went through decades of depression and living a lost life.

Being a housewife and mother keeps me wholesome. I am very right in this role. It is me to the core.

And now I'm learning that homemaking and raising two kids is more than enough. I don't have to DIY it all day, clean all night, and decorate every month. I don't have to be excellent with money and a soft-spoken mother who leads her boys with her kind temperament. No, you see, I'm the average garden variety with issues, but also depth and the wisdom to seek higher guidance in all matters.

I feel the healthiest in my emotions when I have a little routine. I love to drink coffee and do various things like reading or chatting on the phone. I find that on the days I do my exercise routine, I feel the best physically and mentally. I feel good if we leave the house for a little bit for groceries or to pick up something from the library. I like to spend a couple of hours through the day cleaning the whole house, but by that, I mean to run the broom or vacuum through the whole house and maybe a quick bathroom clean. It doesn't take long. I have this thing about keeping the kitchen clean and washing all the dishes and tools. This doesn't take long, and you have a lovely house for the rest of the day. I feel good if the boys and I swim in the pool in the afternoons. We love to race, and it's an excellent exercise for all of us. I love floating on the half-deflated inner tube we bought cheap at Safeway. I swim and race them, kicking and working my arms and thinking how good it is for my body and how after we play in the water and soak in the sun, we sleep well at night. I've been ready for bed by 8:30 some nights.

Thursday

Ah, I hear my Pandora playing. The Hot Spot didn't work so great yesterday, and it's awful in the late afternoon. Maybe too many people online? I am so grateful for the Hot Spot because we can enjoy it for a few days and then send it back and have a few days offline. We still choose to go to the library one day a week. I can watch YouTube there and use Grammarly. We have created nostalgia there. That is our big word these days. We all talk about what places and things we feel nostalgic about. The library and swimming in the afternoon are nostalgic.

Yesterday was such a delightful day. I got a lot done, but it was so spread out through the day, and I took the time to watch a movie, later a documentary, and did some writing and still had a clean, tidy house by the end of the day, emptied every garbage, dragged all the garbage containers to the street, chlorinated the pool after our swim, watered all the trees in the front and back, and had plenty of food laid out and candles lite in the kitchen when Bali got home.

I was thinking about all the little parts of homemaking. I feel like my life is such a vacation that I went over my duties to see if I'm earning this position. I was raised that all things required some form of suffering and hard work. But what if you work hard but enjoy it so much that it just feels like a busy day in the best way?

I made a list of my responsibilities and duties as a homemaker, and it's only half of it:

Sweeping and vacuuming the whole house. Steam mop or Bona mopping with a homemade solution for the whole house. Washing walls, light fixtures, and baseboards, windowsills. Washing windows and polishing mirrors. Dusting all furniture and changing out all the bedding, and washing linens. Doing all the laundry and hanging it out and then putting it away and going through children's clothing every season, donating the too-small clothes, putting away the season's wardrobe, and getting out the current season's wardrobe. Cleaning out the fridge and keeping it organized and filled—cleaning and organizing pantry shelves. Donating foods we won't eat. Keeping the pantry stocked and updated. Cleaning the bathroom. Taking apart the bidet and scrubbing it and the toilet top to bottom, inside and out. Scouring the shower top to bottom, scouring the sink and counter, washing the shelves, and organizing and keeping the toiletries and medicines updated and stocked. Washing all the dishes, utensils, and cooking tools a few times a day, scouring out the sink, and the top of the stove, washing the counters and tabletop and pulling out furniture and appliances to clean behind them, taking out all the garbage, recycling, and bathroom garbage. Keeping the pool clean and running the pump, scooping out stuff, chlorinating. Tending to the kitchen garden and our growing orchard and weeding, feeding, mulching, watering, and learning how to tend to pests and mold or leaf curl. Sweeping and sometimes hosing down the porch and front and back stairs. Feeding dogs twice a day and washing out their bowls, filling their water bowls. Bathing and brushing all three dogs, trimming their nails. Exercising the dogs, walking, ball throwing, playing with them throughout the day, and giving them treats. Doing some training, I learned on YouTube, so they don't bark all the time and behave better. Finding and administering natural remedies to help my older dogs feel good and sleep well. Finding natural ways to keep Molly healthy and her anal glands drained through diet and exercise (this is a big issue with some small dogs, especially Molly). Being with my kids. Listening to them for hours. Swimming with them in the afternoon and playing. Working with them in their emotions and talking through things. Homeschooling them. Creating an easy schedule during the week to do English, Writing, and Math and producing educational tools, documentaries, books, and channels they enjoy to stimulate their desire to learn more. Going for hikes on all the trails near us. Taking them to spend time with family and friends. Doing a little traveling (I haven't done much these past two years). Brewing all the coffee. Baking all the bread (bread maker gets most of the credit), making mixes, cooking from scratch. Looking up and learning new recipes. Making two meals a day and packing all Bali's lunches, baking special request cakes and dinners on everyone's birthday. Studying and researching gardening.

Homeschooling myself on everything from baking to writing. Cutting my hair and the boys' hair.

I'll think of more throughout the day. The point is that homemaking is a big job you could get paid for if you did it for someone else, and you would only have half this load. You are either the cook or the maid, *or* the nanny. You wouldn't have this long list. And I'm not done yet, but I need some breakfast and reading time. I have **Walden** in the bathroom, *Stephen King* on the elliptical, and **The Tightwad Gazette** in the living room. I'm working on several books currently.

A summers breeze moves through the house, gently caressing the faces and arms of inhabitants sitting in various positions, eating, talking amongst each other, as mother sweeps the kitchen floor. The air is warm but feels good in the cool house built of old timber and sheltered by giant redwoods on the north. A little sausage dog naps on the pillows decorating the colorful couch. The chimes tinkle lightly from the porch, and the boys laugh over a video in the bedroom. (Just me tinkering with my writing skills).

Oh, I just remembered a whole other section of my workload. The secretarial and accounting part. I manage all the money, build the savings, and pay the bills. When we wanted to buy the first house and the second house, I met with realtors, toured the counties with kids and packed PB & J's, sent in documents, signed papers, worked deals, learned from mortgage brokers, researched fixer-uppers and laws, and learned how to read blueprints and inspection reports. I write out the budget monthly and continue to find ways to conserve energy, water, and groceries. I find ways to stretch our monthly income by taking advantage of sales, markdowns, and good stuff found free. I haul things off the street to decorate and/or stock up my pantry.

I am getting so much done. I needed a few months to deep clean and declutter, but keeping up is getting easier. I have a lot of downtime now.

If I were a young married girl wanting to stay home with a child, this is how I would live and all I would need: A safe home in a safe neighborhood. It can be and should be small. The smaller the home, the less cleaning and fewer utilities and cost. All you need is one large bed and two sets of sturdy linen—lots of comforters for winter. I would want hard floors and a broom. I'd want a washer in the house, but no need for a dryer. I would run a line outside and save for a rack inside for winter. I would create a pantry inside a closet if I had to, but I would focus on stocking up so we wouldn't worry about groceries if the money was tight.

I would want to live in town to walk everywhere and learn the bus schedule. I would decorate the house by looking for garage sales and thrift stores. I would put out the word that we were a new family needing items, and if I was on Facebook, I'm sure people would be happy to purge a couch or table. I would not get credit cards of any kind. I would work from a grocery envelope or within the food stamps allotment. I would do a significant stock-up at the beginning of the month and save enough for the middle of the month and a little toward the end. I would not waste a dime on fast foods, packaged or premade foods. I would buy baking supplies, bulk rice, beans, flour, oil, sauces, and dried fruits and nuts to make all my snack foods and cereals. If you buy a 25 lb. bag of flour, you can feed the family on baked goods all month, but if you buy packaged snacks, crackers, and bread, it's all gone within days. Junk food makes us overeat. If we don't have junk around, we eat wholesome foods that fill us up and nourish our bodies. Instead of getting cable, get a Roku TV, so you have everything you desire for free.

It gets lonely when you are a housewife with a young child or two. We don't always have our families and friends around. Find ways to enjoy life for free. I love to read, and that is a big blessing. Some people don't like to read. Reading is excellent entertainment, and I get the best books from the library. You can watch movies, read, and paint. I get a lot of art supplies at the Dollar Store or Walmart. I love to listen to music and color in grown-up coloring books. I used blogging and YouTube as a way of connecting and sharing. It helped diminish the loneliness of being a mother at home. We need something that is just ours, that we love doing, and that can connect us to the outside world. When you don't have money to spare, you can't join a club, but you can join a group or volunteer.

There are so many things we can find free or cheap, but the issue can be how to get them to your house. We are very fortunate in that Bali bought a sturdy truck that has lasted years. We have hauled home lumber, sand, horse manure, trees and garden stuff, furniture, and wood. We live in town so we can walk more and drive very little. This helps preserve the vehicles and use less gas. You can haul a lot in a car or borrow a truck. Some people will deliver furniture to get rid of it. Friends that give you furniture may deliver if able.

I have used our canvas kid's wagon to drag home street finds and groceries. They're great for hauling tired little ones too.

You don't need much to have a cute house, and you can use a simple vacuum or broom and make your cleaners by keeping baking soda, jugs of white vinegar, and strong dish soap on hand. You can clothe everyone from thrift stores. I'd wait for the 50% sales and stock up. For kids, there are parks and libraries, and those two things, along with PBS cartoons in the morning, are more than enough for a good day for kids. They need a lot of play, fresh air, lots of love and fun with the parent(s), good meals, good naps, lots of being read to, and positive and upbeat music for children. They don't need much outside of that. I raised my kids very attachment style with years of nursing, co-sleeping, and cuddling, and I always carried my children in my arms. I read, read, read all the time. I was devoted and read to the boys and myself from piles of books. I played nursery rhymes and Disney music, and there were many educational toys and a giant homemade sandbox at every house. I loved PBS, and I felt it taught them a lot. I also used ABCMouse for years.

Children need lots of love and a happy home. They don't need all the "stuff." They would choose you over any iPhone. The same idea goes for us adults. We need good food, sleep, fun, exercise, lots of time with our children, good music, coffee, and books.

I would also suggest to anyone to have a little garden. Buy seeds and soil when you have a little cash, or use the food stamps to get herbs and seeds. I don't know that you can buy potting soil, but it can be found cheap. Propagate from people's healthy trees and plants. We just planted three nectarine seeds from my friend's tree. I asked the neighbor if we could have some branches off his French plum, but he thinks it's been ruined when the Black walnut was taken down. If it makes it, I'll get some branches next year and try and get them to grow. You can get and grow free trees. You can learn to save seeds. Nothing is too hard.

People worry about money when their children are babies, and it's silly because the baby will not need much for years and years. The baby is small and doesn't need a new car or SUV. The baby is small, will be for years, and won't ever need a big house. The parents think they need a new house, but families in Europe and Asia live in tiny houses and do well. They drive mopeds or bikes or public trains and do just fine. We have been brainwashed to believe in our hearts that we need the large house, the van, the two income earners, the cable, the nice clothes, and all those hauls from Target and Walmart. We need planners and new gadgets for cooking and cleaning. We need wax scents and trending wall signs to decorate our homes constantly. Wayfair and Overstock.com are front and center for online shopping. We have Amazon packages gracing our front stoop daily. We love fast food. Our kids want to shop, shop, shop too! Oh, dear. Now we all have computers and the internet, and everyone is on their phones or iPads and in their rooms, and there is credit card debt, a big mortgage, stress, and clutter in the house, the garage, and the minds of the family. The parents are working all the time and commuting hours a day. They answer calls at home and bring work home to do over the weekend between laundry and heating a Murphy's Pizza while trying to get the house clean for the week and spend some time with the family. Sometimes they have birthday parties and extended family obligations that take up the weekend, and then they return to work. Rinse and repeat. Bummer.

But this life works for a lot of people. Hurray for them if they are happy and busy and life is good. But by how overweight we are all getting and the rate of depression, mental health issues, and suicides, I feel this life has become too unnatural. I am sure we can find a way to balance the natural and the modern to create a lovely existence. And I think most people are looking at this. We are all waking up. Minimalism is a big thing. Tiny houses, RV living. Green living and food forest. People are changing, and we are getting okay with a downsized life. Thus a broom and some pans for cooking, and you are set. What is essential is your surroundings. You are set if you can live in an area you like. Contentment comes from within, but it does help to be in a nice area you feel good living in.

The other day I was talking about a movie, **Another Year**, and how it reflected my two sides. Mary was the alcoholic mess, and then we have the older couple that is grounded and happy. I don't know that I would have gone all out becoming a Mary, but I had my years, and if I hadn't straightened up, done the inner healing work and married and set up camp, I don't know that I would have stayed sober. Marriage has been safe and grounding, and I'm being taken care of for the first time in my life. I'm so busy with my routines and children that I'm happy as a ren in my heart. I love my life because it has a purpose and is charming in every way.

It's not easy to simplify. It is fun for the most part, but sometimes I fall off the wagon and act out. It's just the processing part. We process this new life, get used to it, claim it, and fall in love with it. We find hidden gems in this new way of living. And we find that our gratitude level goes up. We get excited about the little things that so many take for granted. Eating out is rare, travel is rare, and shopping is rare. When we do these things, we appreciate the moments deeply.

We start to feel better about not adding to the garbage patch in the ocean and the landfill in our town. We feel good about not losing money at these corporate stores. Right now, I feel great about not eating animals or their products. I see my garbage getting smaller. I can be someone who cares and does something to help or at least not harm. I'm raising boys to be very aware and conscientious. They will go out in the world and be good examples.

I was watching **The Shining** with Sam the other day. I questioned, letting him watch, but we both made it through, and it was more of an exploration of a classic. Films are great for teaching story telling. I'm learning to break them down into chapters, the hero's journey, and building the story arc.

Being a homemaking nerd, my favorite part was when the cook took Wendy through the pantry at the movie's beginning. I took notes, of course. He said it was enough for over a year. Then he shows her the frozen foods, all meats, and the dry goods. There wasn't a fridge. It had to be stuff to make it through five months of winter. I paused the film to take note of what was in the dry storage and get some ideas for my pantry.

Saturday

I'm looking for a miracle
I expect the impossible
I feel the intangible
And I see the invisible
The sky is the limit to what I can have
Oh Yeah, The sky is the limit to what I can have!
Just believe and receive it. God will perform it today.

Expect Your Miracle-The Clark Sisters

A lady from my channel suggested this song, and I've played it a hundred times. It is a very metaphysical Christian song, which they might not realize. Much of Christ's teachings were metaphysical but have been mangled and misinterpreted.

Bali was sharing a conversation he had with a man yesterday. The man and his wife used to work at gas stations, then went on to work at banks, found it didn't pay much, and now they do Door Dash. They work from morning to late at night. They have two older kids; one wants to go to a University to fulfill her dream. So, the father said they needed more money for this; however, they just bought two new cars, putting them in debt of over $50,000 to $60,000. They bought an SUV despite not needing it. They have four in the family. Four people will fit in a small vehicle. They probably bring in $4000 after taxes at the lowest end or around $5000. The man talked about how they didn't make enough. He asked how our family makes it on Bali's income. Bali loves to tell people he works, and I stay home. It's not accurate. I do stay home, for which I'm immeasurably grateful; however, I also work and bring in money to add to the pot.

For years I brought in around $1000 in royalties from the channel and books. I couldn't do that having a part-time job outside the home, even with a $15 an-hour wage. I would only bring home from $500 to $800 for a month of working weekends. But by writing books at home and filming content for a YouTube channel *at* home, I brought in around $800 to $1000 on average a month and over $2000 on the holidays. That is amazing.

Bali tells the man we live a simple life. That is how we do it, and that is the whole answer. We have lived under our means for years. We have had many lean years, so we are well-practiced in stretching the paychecks. We have also had years of making good money. Not what the typical Californian would think is good, but when you live on a small paycheck for years and then make a few hundred extras, it feels like wealth.

If these people can't make it on $5000 a month, what will they do when they must live on social security?

People better snap out of it. It's necessary to make it affordable. Make choices that ensure you sail through challenging times.

Enough said on that. I brought the Hot Spot home, and I can't find a thing on YouTube to entertain me. Fortunately, I found some good movies and watched

Trumbo last night. What a great movie. It's a true story about a screenwriter blacklisted with his group of writer comrades because they were communists during the cold war. It felt a little like we had that drama and division these last few years with the medical and political theater. People are quick to choose sides and turn on others out of fear of things that don't happen. Illusions. A few crazy birds start squawking upsetting things, and a hoard of people will jump on the boat and hit others with sticks if they disagree.

I love this movie because Trumbo is a screenwriter that beats the schmucks at their game and calls them out in the end. He isn't too proud or egotistic and starts writing scripts for a lousy movie company. He needs to work, and no one will hire him. He is brilliant and talented, but King Studio's (the cheap movie company that makes terrible movies) hires him to write, and write he does. He writes 18 hours a day and eventually gets work for all his friends who have been blacklisted. He fights the situation peacefully and with what he knows how to do well. Write great scripts.

How he gets so many scripts out and rewrites so many others is wild. It makes me wonder if we start writing and, say, don't have time to judge our work, constantly edit and re-edit, could we keep channeling stories infinitely? How much is talent, and how much is just pure work? How many good stories do I have, but I make them complicated or think they aren't good enough?

If you begin to put all the focus on writing stories and you go for it, do you naturally get better and have more stories begin to pour out of you? Can you open the floodgates? At this time, I feel stuck, but there was a time when I wrote prolifically. I wrote all these homemaking and frugal books and, five fictional ones, one book I rewrote completely, so it counts as six books. I wrote many books during the first two years of my writing career. I'm not saying the books were great, but they kept getting better, and writing them got easier with each book. My last was my most popular, and it was the most effortless and most fun to write. I wasn't trying to get too fancy or clever, I was starting to have fun, and I enjoyed writing that story. My stories were all very different, and I felt imaginative.

That all stopped when I dove into YouTube. My writing dwindled. I went from writing ten books (two rewrites) in less than two years to just a few books a year and all about homemaking. I wrote only one ok fictional book in the last five years. My homemaking books improved vastly, and I have mastered them. However, with all these years of blogging about homemaking, filming about it for YouTube, and writing endless books about frugality, it is all I can think about. I've obsessed for years. I read other homemakers' blogs and watched their videos. I read, watch, think about, write about, and create around it. It's been fun, and I love the topics of running a home on the cheap, but enough already.

It's time for new material in both my writing and channel content. We need to change things and try new things to inspire us.

I'm enjoying movies right now. The fun is finding the story pattern and the hero's journey in the movie, breaking it up, and identifying the parts. It's a way to teach myself how to write stories and make them good.

Sunday

Had a nice chat on the phone with a friend from Arizona. They have rain and flooding there now.

It's noon, and I just had a shower and began my day. I'll begin by baking an orange layer cake for tomorrow's birthday. Bali made the mung bean soup, and I'll make the Aloo Gobi as soon as he picks up another cauliflower and tomatoes.

He said another customer asked him how he makes it on his gas station salary. I think many people are looking at life and work in a new way, and they are tired of struggling and working jobs they don't enjoy and barely get by. This American work life takes your whole life; in the end, you are disposable. Best find your joy and invest in it. Invest in your family and build a sustainable life. Fewer bills, a small mortgage, some land, be it a small yard or an acre.

There is no mystery behind it or magic solution. I know people look at our life and wonder how we do it. I have a friend who lives on far more than we do, she's single and has a small rent, but she gets by monthly by the hair on her chin. Debt is her problem; once she takes care of it, she'll be fine. Debt is most people's issue: credit cards, car payments, and full insurance on cars. Cars are costly. I wouldn't care if we didn't have cars. We would be so slim walking everywhere. People now have outrageous mortgages and rents. Rents can't be helped, but to choose to pay a mortgage that is thousands of dollars a month is insanity. People convince themselves that they will make more money, get a better-paying job, or get that promotion, and then the mortgage will be easy. But what happens when the economy declines, things like Covid hit, a new recession, you get laid off instead of promoted, or the only jobs you can get don't pay enough? I think that greed has taken us to a whole new level, and if/when we have a crash of some sort, it will be a massive upset because we are SO out of balance.

No one can keep up the stamina required to run a business, stay employed, pay the bills, and do the extra hustles to pay the too-high rent/mortgage. People are working and hustling like crazy to stay afloat. Their cravings and greed have filled the credit cards and put them in a pool of stress to drown.

I can barely ponder it. This is a discussion that has taken place for centuries. *Lao Tzu, Thoreau, Greg McKweon*, and hundreds of sages and teachers have said that the best life is a simple, quiet life, just having the basic needs and keeping to oneself. It has been preached for thousands of years, and here we are today: more people, insanity, and greed than ever.

Let's see where it all leads. Why don't we?

My advice will always be the same. Have no debt, pay in cash, and drive a used car bought with cash that gets great gas mileage and is reliable. Buy a fixer-upper in a good area or rent a small home and save like crazy for when the housing prices plummet (and they always do). Have a yard and try and grow food.

Refrain from buying all the extras. I can attest that there is something free or cheap for every desire. Clothes obsession? Thrift stores and maybe wait for the 50% sales if you are clothes crazy. Avid reader? Library. You can get everything from the classics to the latest New York Times best seller. Movie buff? Get a cheap Roku TV to watch all the free movie channels on Roku, or if you don't have internet buy a DVD player for all the free movies you get at the library. Foodie? It may be best to have a food budget and use an envelope, but you can load up the pantry from WinCo, Grocery Outlet, or Aldis. I get all sorts of sauces and seasonings and watch YouTube cooking channels or order cookbooks from, yes, once again, the library. Café lady? Make your own coffee house in your kitchen. I can make a far better latte or mocha than any coffee house.

Live at home, watch it at home, cook at home, do it all at home. Get that cheap mortgage and start nesting.

Tuesday

Yesterday was the first day of school. This is what it looked like; a drive up to Tahoe through lovely forest, time with beloved family, a feast of vegetarian Indian dishes I made the night before, a homemade orange cake with cream cheese frosting, and a swim in the Great Lake. That was our first day back to the grind.

Today has been a little more work. We watched science videos on YouTube. There are great science and history channels on YouTube, for which I'm so grateful. Remember those days of boring science movies on old reels that everyone used as an opportunity to nap or pass notes? **Oversimplified** for history and **BeSmart** for science.

Later...

Oh boy, we got busy today. The day was a whirl of schoolwork, and piano, broken up by a short walk for Molly and some errands. We exchanged our Hot Spot for a newer model. The last one was like dial-up, only a hint faster. I had all sorts of books and the latest Venom movie. We purchased some breakfast foods and vegan foods at Grocery Outlet. In the vegan/dairy section, I exchanged vegan advice on products with another mother and daughter. They helped me pick some cream cheeses, and I shared my favorites. Vegans get excited when they meet randomly in real life. Or maybe that's just me.

It was a hot day, so we had a little cinema time with Venom and popcorn. I tried sleeping in the recliner like any true old lady would do in the afternoon, but I'm never successful with someone always sitting on me, whether a dog or child. We played in the pool for a bit, and I spent a little time sweeping sand into the cracks of the new patio.

It's almost done. It needs to be filled in with smaller bricks to finish the awkward spots and filled in with sand. Bali finished the pergola this weekend, and the frame's stain is an excellent thick red paint. He put the bamboo fencing on top for the roof. It feels like a tropical resort. I spent the morning moving outdoor furniture onto the patio under the pergola, and the neighbor heard me as he worked on the other side of the fence. He gave us a nice little beach chair that reminds me of a small director's chair.

The day's chores are still not done. I've put a pot of mung bean soup on and steamed up a pot of brown rice. I'll write with my afternoon coffee and then water the fruit trees, nut trees, and vines. I pulled up some plants in the garden. Some melons should have been ready to harvest by now, and pumpkins growing large to decorate my porch for Fall, but none are even blossoming. I now reserve water for only the plants with a future.

I know we need to do so much more to the garden soil. I wanted to just layer and add nutrients for a good year and plant a cover crop, but I'm itching to plant something now. Gardening is addictive even when it's not working out. I want melons and would eat them like crazy, but I have never had an ounce of luck. Nor have I had luck with carrots, corn, and strawberries. Potatoes. Most foods that are supposed to be easy to grow. Except for strawberries, they are fussy. It is frustrating, but the winter garden gave me some faith and inspiration to keep going, keep amending, keep planting, and maybe do some beds.

Wednesday

Garbage day and just in time. We are working on reducing our garbage, and it's not working great, but there is less plastic, and I think next week we will only have a little to offer the garbage truck. Living more naturally and making less mess is a work in progress.

I listened to **Aloneness to Oneness** on YouTube while watering the fruit and nut trees. Then I listened to another similar documentary but can't find the title to post here. I watched **Reconnect** about the Hiyauasca experience that the host of *London Reel* had. This has opened the rabbit hole of vegan documentaries and healing documentaries. These are my favorite topics; however, I find that after many of these documentaries, they haven't anything new to offer. With every cultural lifestyle, be it minimalism, plant-based eating, frugality, healing work, metaphysics, or simple living, the underlying theme is the same, the rules are the same, and the symbolism is the same. Once you learn it, the repetition allows us to rewire our brain pattern set in childhood. That is why we watch 190 different videos on one topic or read a hundred books on a new lifestyle. We are processing a new idea and integrating it into our lives, sometimes quickly, sometimes over a period of years. We take it in and try it on. We see how we feel, and if it feels good and right, we repeat until it becomes a part of us.

Staying home is an interesting lifestyle. Not everyone can do it, and I see why. Going places daily breaks up the day and gives you some social interaction. Having a job gives you purpose to get up and get ready for a full day. With a mug in hand, you clock in and start your day at the office or the shop. You have duties, routines, and responsibilities all day. You get a lunch break and a couple of other ten-minute breaks, but you are usually busy with work. Busy bees with a cheerful attitude keep a place going. Lucky is the boss that has the inspired staffer.

Home is the same game. I can't tell you how often I feel like I'm running a tiny restaurant and Lodge. When I listed my duties a few days back, I forgot to add all the therapy and nursing I also do daily and seasonally. I'm up with sick children or watching over an aging dog. The nights I lay on the couch with a pacing, nervous dog grasping his mortality. Days of settling disputes between boys and sitting with an upset child listening while they list their grievances and process their feelings. How many kung fu fights in the store isles or simulated courtroom battles over fair treatment?

You'll need skills to cover this job because it is like no other. All jobs give you one 'position.' If you choose to stay home, you have many positions—Butcher, Baker, Candlestick maker, and so on.

If you're smart, you work hard when you have the fire under you and when you feel drab, you can find yourself lounging and reading to pass the time. Sometimes, it feels so vacationy that I wonder if some guilt should be involved. Then I go over my list of duties and responsibilities and get over it. I guess it's seeing the images of these amazing homemakers spinning their wool and stuffing sausages from the pig they raised and butchered themselves that make a simple persons like myself feel like I'm lacking in areas. Not to mention the Instagram cakes and handcrafted Halloween costumes. I can't list all the deflated cakes I've iced thickly to cover up missing parts and then just decorated with dinosaurs to make them look 'fancy.' And Halloween is my least favorite holiday because of the darn costume-making, which I just don't do.

I could not keep up. Not at this age. Nor would I want to because I've given myself a wide berth of grace at this point.

Sam and I watched Venom and gorged on popcorn we bought at Grocery Outlet. They were selling enormous bags of Organic Nearly Naked Popcorn for $5.99. I have popcorn, and the fixing's here at home, but it was such a fun bag we couldn't resist. It was the size of a huge pillow. More fun, please. Less worry, thank you. I can't have us live like a miser. I'm doing well with the funds, and Bali is saving what he can. But we can't be miserable because life is too fantastic for that. Anyway, that is another topic. So, Sam and I are snuggled on the recliner and watching the movie, getting popcorn everywhere, and I feel a pang of guilt because I should be up and busy with a task. Then I step outside myself to see how content my boys are with me in the afternoon, and I shut off the mental critic.

I seem to have stumbled across some small documentaries on people who have explored and then built lives that are rich in living but void of all the modern stresses. The most content people have this in common; no commute, doing fulfilling work, do not spend time online, are out in nature as much as possible, and are not contending with addictions. The more natural and detached from worldly stuff, the happier.

It sounds like mental illness and depression are skyrocketing. Suicides are skyrocketing. It's unfortunate and very curable. The medical establishment will direct people toward therapy and perhaps pills. It's questionable how much either works for a person. Therapy can't hurt, but pills do. I feel like the solutions are just too easy and too simple. It has to be some complex mix of sedatives and intensive therapy for the mainstream to feel it's worth it. But what if unplugging and sobering up is all you need to get on the golden path? I know some people have severe chemical imbalances, but what about the average Joe suffering from a common depression?

I'm happy to see that natural alternatives are becoming a big thing. Psilocybin for healing traumas and depression is beginning to have some credibility. Marijuana is being used as medicine for everything from arthritis to seizures. People are waking up to the damage food industries and Big Pharma are doing to us and the environment. In the next five years, we will have tremendous changes in how people eat, drive, think, and live.

We are on the path to significant changes, and thank goodness. I remember a President from ages back (I won't say names not to offend anyone) saying, in so many words, that we all needed to get to shopping and working because our country was built on consumerism. I found this a frightful message. A country built on consumerism is a country built on sand. If you look ahead a few hundred years, do you genuinely think we can all consume and dispose of goods at this rate? If our oceans and lands are already trashed and polluted, and we keep up this pace or increase it threefold as "the experts" predict, it would be a horrific nightmare.

We must change now and hardcore. I thought it was so silly when they banned straws as this big move. It's a start, and that's great, but we must step it up ten levels past plastic straws. We could quickly start making natural products and grow a forest of all sorts of woods and bamboo forests to make natural products. We could stop plastic right now; everything would be packaged in natural materials, and all of it could be recycled. They say we have an aluminum shortage, but it's because we don't recycle all the aluminum and companies like new aluminum. Recycling aluminum is far cheaper and cleaner than mining it, and it's just as good as smelted and remade. A person always says it can't be done, but those same people said flying, cars, and electricity couldn't be done.

We would have water stations everywhere, and people would carry reusable bottles or purchase one. People would use cloth sacks or paper. All fast food and candy, chips, cookies, and all products would be in some form of paper. Toys and parks would be built out of wood or bamboo. Everything wood, bamboo, glass, tin, paper, whatever is biodegradable and natural. This would create so many jobs. Ocean clean-ups and massive reforesting projects for the rain forest would create more jobs and more satisfying jobs. Veganism alone would create millions of jobs. I read that in an article a bit back. A whole green and sustainable economy are waiting for us to clue in.

Thursday

I found a great video to bring anyone some faith and joy. The whole channel seems great so far; **Andrew Millison**. The video is very uplifting for those of us worrying about the ecosystems.
https://www.youtube.com/watch?v=Tpozw1CAxmU&ab_channel=AndrewMillison

And I found this gem while steam moping and listening to "writing inspiration" videos;

"Failure meant a stripping away of the inessential. I stopped pretending to myself that I was anything other than what I was and began to direct all my energy into finishing the only work that mattered to me. Had I really succeeded at anything else, I might never have found the determination to succeed in the one arena where I believed I belonged. I had been set free because my greatest fear had been realized, and I was still alive, and I still had a daughter whom I adored, and I had an old typewriter and a big idea. And so rock bottom became the solid foundation on which I rebuilt my life." ~J. K. Rowland

This is deep. It'll take some more steam-mopping to process it. But this is what I have felt for a long time. There is a time in life when you need to strip it down to the essentials and only the essentials. That includes family and good friends. We need time to focus on something we believe in on some level. Maybe we can't see it. It hasn't happened yet, so we can't reflect and tell tales. No, we are at the beginning. And we just 'know.'

For now, I'm cleaning some filthy floors. I have some laundry but no desire to be out in the heat. I think this might be the last hot week. Temperatures dip next week. The Farmer's Almanac says we have a big winter on the way.

I gorged on YouTube. Even if you watch positive and educational stuff, it can cause other things like comparing and envy or dissatisfaction with one's life. 'I wish I had a flat back yard' 'I want that food forest-type look in my backyard!' 'I would love to have so much light in the kitchen!'

So, I did find that **Andrew Millison** and I needed that. You can't watch anything about nature without the reminder we have genuinely caused a mess. The documentary's narrator always points out the despair first, and some vague hope is thrown at the crowd in the last two minutes of a ninety-minute video.

I say I want uplifting stuff, or I'm locking myself away in my bubble.

Later...

I'm having a rest with my iced tea. I've had almost three cups of coffee, which is beyond my ordinary. I got into my house cleaning today. Once the heavy work of sweeping and steaming the kitchen and bathroom, then cleaning the bathroom thoroughly, was completed, I felt light and motivated, so I decided it was past due to rearrange the living room. Rearranging whole rooms serves in many ways; deep cleaning and giving the homemaker a creative purpose for the day. I got excited by the prospect of making the living look fresh and new. It called for some brewing of the coffee and loud music. I've got this station on Pandora: the 60s', 70s', and 80s Hit Radio. I love the songs on here. Metallica's remake of Bob Segar's song, **Turn The Page,** just played. It is one of my favorite songs.

It's too hot to be outside. I'm not too fond of super-hot weather. I can go up to 90 in the shade and be fine, but it's uncomfortable. Today we cleaned inside. Next week the temps will drop, and I can get out there and get my greens planted for the fall. I love growing greens because they thrive here. It's the first taste of success I've had in the garden.

I've been watching various regenerative farming and food forest design videos. I want to build up the backyard with loads of plants, vines, and trees. When they get big and strong, they don't need that much watering, especially when you get a forest going. I see our driveway as wasted space, but Bali isn't with me on making it wild back there. He likes the driveway. He did agree to plant some fruit trees in the garden. I think an apple and a couple of plums will do great there and make it less hot in the summer for specific plants.

If you want a spotless and fresh house that cuts down on illnesses, this is what you need to do now and then; take all your pillows to the local laundry and wash them all in the huge front loaders, using detergent and some bleach. I need to do this soon. Soak all the toothbrushes in boiling water and a strong soap or bleach every couple of weeks. Pull out all appliances; washer, dryer, stove, and fridge. Scrub behind them. Take apart the vacuum and wash all the filters if it's bagless. I do this every couple of weeks. Wash the animal bowls weekly or more. Don't wear any shoes in the house.

Wash walls and baseboards monthly. Wipe down computers, phones, light switches, and remote controls with bleach weekly or more. I wash all my area rugs, bathroom rugs, cleaning rags, mop head rags, and dog bed covers with detergent and bleach. I've recently learned how to clean out my washer. I hadn't cleaned that washer in years, and the clothes weren't getting that clean smell, and there was a funky smell as the washer worked away at washing. Someone told me to hit the 'Fabric Softener' button. It says 'tub clean' under it. I added detergent, bleach, and baking soda and washed the whole machine.

Having your house deeply cleaned feels so good! To declutter it deeply, purge it hardcore and then scrub top to bottom and keep a consistent routine to keep it this clean and tidy makes me feel clear-headed.

I made a comment to Arjan about not wanting to clean all the time. I said, 'Do you think I always love cleaning?' He replied, 'you said you *loved* cleaning.' Ok, he trapped me there. I did say that, and I do love cleaning sometimes. Today was one of those days. I don't love all of it. And sometimes, it feels like downright intensive labor. But sometimes, I have the most profound thoughts on life and have these big revelations. There are times I feel creative and playful doing it. Today I had deep thoughts, emotional revelations, *and* creative bravado.

My right forearm has been itching so much lately—just that one emotional spot. If I'm stressed or working through something, I itch on my right arm; upper or lower or my chest when stressed. I wondered what the hell I could be stressed about. Today I realized that I'm afraid to write and start publishing fictional books. I'm afraid that I'll have no imagination. I'm afraid to fail and never get anywhere with it all.

I don't have to be in the same league with the heavy hitters, I can't reach for that right now, but I could produce stories and lives on the page that draw people in and make them want to stay awhile and return again and again. Can't I? Well, I wouldn't know that because I'm not getting started. I have invented a million things I must do before I can start.

So, as I steamed the bathroom floor and cleaned the room deeply, I came to terms with my fears of starting. It's new, and the future is not as comfortable or known.

And here I am, going on 52, and I am now stripping it all down. Weeding, weeding, weeding. And just learning to rest. Rest the mind.

Friday

I'm sitting at the kitchen table having a delicious smoothie. A bit smoother than the last few made from our garden kale. The kale was two years old and started tasting like it.

We had a busy day of homeschooling and grocery shopping. My fridge is now packed with salads, vegetables, and fruit. I have a big pot of Indian-style kidney beans simmering.

Let's talk about grocery envelopes for a moment.

The other day I was at Grocery Outlet. That is our store for everything except the odd items I know won't be there, such as ranch mix packets and sometimes buttermilk or goat milk. There's a list of things you won't find at this store. I do without if I can't find it at GO and wait for the glorious day we go to WinCo and load up for the season. So, I'm at GO and checking out with my favorite checker. She is an older woman, maybe in her late 60's. She's fit and healthy looking and dies her long hair a deep magenta. It looks fantastic and fun. It makes me want to dye my hair those colors when it grows out. She is obviously active and still working, and I look at a woman like that and aspire to be like her as I age. I pull out my grocery envelope to use up the remaining cash, and she and I discuss grocery envelopes. She said a grocery envelope was the only way to make it financially. She said it's hard-working at GO and resisting buying groceries all the time. I'd say! I always overspend there because GO always has new items, and this one stocks up on all kinds of health food, vegan foods, and organics. It is a very popular store and thriving because of this.

We had this quick exchange about how indispensable this envelope is to stay within the budget and get ahead financially. That little exchange with her motivated me to commit to the envelope!

Today I got online to look over my bank account. I only have one account to avoid confusion. Part of that weeding process was to simplify the bill paying and money managing process. So far, it's fine, except for what I see as I peruse the one account this morning. I see that over half the money is gone. It isn't a heart-stopping amount. We had a slight overall balance to begin with. I expected some bills to go through, and they did, but many trips to stores and corner markets are greedily devouring a large sum of it. It's no surprise. I am surprised at how often it happens; we don't recall doing it. Then hundreds of dollars are missing, and you sit there with a surprised look. I felt like we did pretty well, and I didn't register half the trips. In my head, we hadn't gone anywhere and spent little money.

Aaannnd, that is why we have an envelope. Some people have food stamps and stick to the allotted budget like their lives depend on it. Their food pantry and family depend on their being wise and cunning with this food stamp card. It's a little trickier when you have an envelope but know that if you go over for the month, you have money in the bank to back you. Or maybe this is just me. I doubt it. Articles are written on this topic. When you have the money, you itch to spend it. When a household makes more, they spend more.

There is no way to live comfortably without a rigid envelope. When it's gone, it's gone, and you must wait for the following month. Trickery and safeguarding the money purse is the only way for me to budget smartly.

Time to whip out the composition books, write up some menus, and remember some recipes. Right now, we are big into the most nutritious, cheap, easy, and tasty dinner setup; Indian soups and bean dishes, Salad with good dressings, and whole wheat tortillas. Now, I've been cheating and buying bagged salads and store-bought tortillas. However, the lettuce sometimes smells funny, even after I wash it, and we all know that making fresh, organic salads is far cheaper and healthier. Making my wheat tortillas is also far cheaper, but they never turn out as flexible. And why don't they make and sell the big wheat tortillas? I'll have to figure out how to make my own large, soft wheat tortillas.

I can make big tubs of salad, big pots of Indian beans, and stacks of tortillas for a few dollars and feed us for days. And it's not much work, just a few hours of kitchen work.

I've been thinking about Bali's mother and how she shopped and cooked. I've talked about this before. She bought wheat and corn once a year, enough to last the whole year. She grew a garden but did buy extra vegetables from local peddlers. Once a month, she would ride the bus an hour to the larger town and take out the interest on her savings. She would buy rice, beans, seasoning, and whatever else she needed for the month. She had savings from a settlement when her husband's life was shortened in a factory accident. Bali's mother had no education. She couldn't even sign her name. She was left a widow with two small children and her aging father-in-law. She could not make mistakes with money. The settlement the company gave her had to last her whole life and feed and house her small family. I asked Bali about her methods all the time, and now more than ever. She lived a simple life, and she made do. They always had plenty of nutritious food and a home.

It is Bali's job to provide for us. He goes out into the world and works to bring home a paycheck. Because he chose to be the breadwinner, I enjoy staying home with my sons and never missing a minute with them. We are so fortunate to homeschool and work on our passions. I'm fortunate to have home and time to work on writing.

My job is to create a lovely home where we can all be safe and happy. The money is debatable as to whom is in charge here. In our household, I oversaw everything: saving, managing funds, and bill paying. This is fine, but it is a big responsibility, and it is up to me to pay everything quickly, not be overdrawn at the bank, and fill the pantry and buy the extra things in one paycheck. If the monthly income is small, what can you do? You create a life that fits in that paycheck. You learn that you can still have the life you want and enjoy, but you learn to get it cheap. You learn to keep bills small and wants reasonable. We appreciate life and every little gift it gives much more when we make less money.

We enjoy life so much more with less money. Why? Because we don't gorge ourselves on everything. We don't go to the café and the theater weekly or daily and buy what we want at every twitch. Going to the theater and buying lattes, even store-bought bread, is a luxury. When we have a little money windfall, we take it into our hands with joy and gratitude. We take a few days to plan what areas it would serve us best. Most windfalls are used to pay the mortgage, buy garden seeds and trees, or work on the house. It's a game to find ways to stretch it all.

It has not created poverty consciousness. It has created a sense of luxury, leisure, and opulence in Amy Dyczyzan's words. Gratitude is the trick. And truly observing all the good that is in a small life. A small life is a considerable life. All the time we have with each other and dear friends. We all should observe life and do things we adore.

In one documentary, the narrator said that we are content once our basic needs are met. Everything we buy extra does nothing to make us happier. Many times, it makes us unhappy. The bigger house, the nicer clothes, cars, and upgraded gadgets. We don't need it. Travel would be fun with extra money. Extra money now and then can be delightful for having memorable experiences.

Alright, off to bed. The breadwinner is asleep on the couch. He loves this show on the Roku channel, **My Uncle Silas.** It's about a horny, alcoholic, old fart set in the 19th century and made to be somewhat charming with its happy little music and Victorian setting. He asked to watch it and then falls asleep, so I get stuck with the show.

I have more thoughts, but now I'm tired and ready to pull my PJs off the clothesline outside and brush my teeth.

I have planning to do, and I love to do it at night while lying in my big, soft bed. I have plans for the garden and the orchard. I have plans for my grocery envelope and menus. I have plans for my self-education on writing. I have ideas to recreate myself. But we will talk over coffee in the morning.

Saturday

I'm up before the sun having my coffee and quiet time. Candles light the kitchen and living room enough to see where a dog may lie or enable me to make my espresso pot and brew it. Knowing where all the dogs are lying about in the house is crucial. I've fallen over Babu several times while headed for the bathroom in the middle of the night. It isn't fun, and I'm not graceful. I curse as I gather myself up from being splayed out on the floor, and the dog scurries off, not knowing what happened but guessing the hallway might not have been the best place to rest for the night.

I love early mornings and watching the sunrise. The air is cool, smells of earth, and skunky. It's nature. They say an artist's most productive time is in the wee hours. I haven't discovered that yet. I love seeing Mother Earth awaken and start the day. I like seeing the neighbors leave for work and hear a busy neighborhood. I especially love that I'm not the one going to work at such hours. I sit in my pj's, having my first coffee and taking my time. I feed the dogs early and sit down to write in the recliner by the big window.

So, to continue last night's talk. I think about Bali's mother and how they lived. They lived very well off her savings. Bali said the grandfather had also received money. They were able to help others and lend money. I'm sure it was no fortune, but they didn't spend it on useless things. They had a home and land and a cow and food. Bali learned to use a sewing machine and altered his father's clothes for himself. They didn't have a car, just a bike Bali used to bring home grain and get about. They didn't buy furniture or extras. They lived as simply as you could get, and they were happy. Bali had a very good childhood.

We are getting there with simplicity. Ironically, we must work on being simple in this day and age.

There are a few ways to manage money that are extremely smart. First, pay yourself first and live on as little as you can. The second is using envelopes for whatever you don't pay online such as auto pays and online bill pay. The third is reducing grocery shopping trips. Once a month shopping is the smartest. You can stock up on produce and coffee creamer every ten days. Produce doesn't last long and goes even more quickly in our house. But to reduce the need to shop would save us so much money frivolously spent on non-essentials. Plan a big shopping day with a detailed and well-thought-out list. Work from an envelope with awareness, and do not think you have extra money elsewhere. It teaches discipline that is useful in getting ahead financially.

We could plan one day to travel to WinCo and do a major stock up, then Grocery Outlet to finish up. We shop at GO for our creamer, fruits, and veggies every ten days to two weeks. I try to get my flour from the health food store, so it's organic. WinCo is improving with vegan foods and organics but still lacking in this area. Their flours aren't non-GMO. Their huge bags of popcorn aren't either, which is a bummer. I used to buy all sorts of bulk from the coop, but they stopped that during the quarantine, and I've tried shopping with Azure, but they became so popular that it was impossible to get anything. I would put in an order, and by the time it was to be shipped here, they were out of everything but some seasonings. So, I piece it together with WinCo, Grocery Outlet, and rarely the health food store.

Oh, how I love WinCo. The bulk section is a wonderland for those who love shopping in bulk.

I earned my last gift card through Amazon Affiliates. I will miss those, but I ended the program and deleted all my links on each video. I don't want to support and encourage mindless shopping. Most of my links were for good stuff like Berkey water filters, but still, it is what I'm trying to get away from. I used to shop on Amazon so much! I have only ordered a couple of books in the last few months. I'm doing most of my shopping locally, and I have turned to Thriftbooks.com for books. I love how they send all the books simultaneously and with no shipping cost, which makes their cost about the same as Amazon.

With my last gift card of $16, I purchased a highly praised *Script Writing Bible*. It's a big, fat book and one review told me all I needed to know. She said she had her book highlighted and dog-eared throughout. She had filled stacks of composition books with ideas and work. She said this book taught her everything and more. She sounded like me. So, I ordered a used copy, and with shipping and tax, I only owed .89 cents with the help of the gift card. It will probably be my final purchase for a long time.

Today, I will stop by Dollar Tree to purchase a handful of spectacles. They used to last a bit, and now the arms come off, and the lenses fall out. I know they're a dollar, but I have an old pair that has seen a few seasons. The last few pairs didn't last the summer.

I'll have to do this before going to the library for our time. If I have no glasses, I have no reason to be at a reading institution.

My next big idea in Fall; we focus solely on the garden and orchard. I've been watching videos on a food forest, and we can create that in the back. Many of our trees have made it and are doing well. The garden is still frustrating. We have to do raised garden beds. This is over two years in, and I have harvested some small tomatoes and a couple of zucchini. If you only harvest a few zucchini, you know you have a failed garden.

In GO (this is where aha moments happen), I started talking to two fellow gardeners in the produce aisle. One grew in-ground and was having no luck this year but only due to ground squirrels. She had great luck in previous years. The other was a man who said he was 'rockin' it in his garden beds. He had to have garden beds because of a chemical in the ground. I think he said Arsenopyrite which is arsenic found around here where mining occurred. We are right by the mining spots, and a little forest near us is loaded with Arsenic. That is why they can't sell it or develop it. So, it might be time to take this to the next level and do raised beds. It will be more organized, and we can build and control the soil. I'm tired of working so hard every year to amend, dig, plant, cover crops, and haul manure from another town, only to have a smidgen of success each year.

Tuesday

The patio outside is almost done. I was adding small bricks to the void's odd spots and filling it with sand. But it's basically done, and the pergola is complete. Bali and I played house decorating last night. Put the long plastic craft table up with a checkered cloth and chairs. Bali repainted the swinging bench with the remaining red paint stain. We hauled the pots of roses, lavender, and empty pots from upfront. Several pots of propagated roses need nurturing, and the lavender is struggling. There are pots with compost and soil that have not been planted yet. Now that they are on the patio, I can nurture them better. We will use the water from the tub to water frequently, and I've already started a big jar with soaking banana peels. I started dumping my used coffee grounds in the pots as well.

Container gardening takes work. The container soil gets depleted quickly and must be added each season. Next week cools down, and I can get out there and start working on the garden and containers. The containers need compost. The compost pile needs work. The garden needs to be converted from an in-ground garden to a raised bed garden. The frame from the winter greenhouse needs to be removed. The trees need mulch.

Then deep Fall comes, and we will plant tons of trees, bushes, and plants. Oh yes, I have a vision. Many of our trees are looking good and getting strong. But each year, a few die. My answer is to plant a ton of them, so if some don't make it, so be it.

Then we have the bathroom. The floors. The outside house paint. Does it all need to be done? Yes, but we have time. I'd like to do it all like yesterday. I would hire a big crew and have them grind it out in a week. I can dream. In reality, Bali and I will do most of it by ourselves. Painfully. But then we will love the house even more because we worked so hard to make it pretty. The house will love us even more and serve us well.

Let's talk about **Jiro Dreams Of Sushi**. It's a documentary about an eighty-five-year-old sushi chef, considered the best sushi chef in the world. Jiro has won a three-star Michelin Guide rating, the first restaurant of its kind to win such a prestigious award. His sushi bar is small and can be found in a Tokyo subway station, but it is so popular that people travel far to return, and reservations are made months in advance.

Here is what Jiro says about life's work:

"Once you decide on your occupation, you must immerse yourself in your work. You need to fall in love with your work. Never complain about your job. You must dedicate your life to mastering your skill. That's the secret of success and is the key to being regarded honorably."

He has this tiny sushi bar tucked away in a subway station, yet it has had reservations for months. People that make the trip to eat his sushi. He is famous for being a master at the craft of making sushi. He's won a rating that restaurant owners kill themselves to make. It is his calling, very clearly, and he never wrestled with it. He is committed and focused. Making sushi is all he does. His restaurant doesn't serve appetizers. Just sushi.

He found what he loved and committed with all his being. In his younger years, he would leave the house at 5 am and return after 10 pm. He worked constantly.

We can commit to our homemaking. We can find any work that pleases us and commit. That singular focus brings us joy and sometimes outside accomplishments. It doesn't have to mean something to anyone but us. This new way of working and living where people have careers, families, and side hustles to make extra cash is exhausting. Some people do well with all that juggling. Or so it seems on the outside, but I bet they are missing out on something. If they are thriving at work, they may be sorely missed at home. If they want more time with their family, they have to say no to work tasks. You can't have it all, despite the legend of modern thinking. You have to choose. Choose the one thing that means everything and commit.

Since I committed to my family this year, my relationship with my sons has grown more loving and peaceful than ever. There is still some drama now and then, but small moments and we work it out right then. I'm loving and patient like I used to be when I was 100% focused on the family and home. I never freaked out about a thing because I had no stress or pressure. It would help if you didn't reenact the lousy boss or corporate culture when you work for yourself. But you do. You push yourself and compare yourself to others in the same work. You judge yourself and torture yourself with poor self-esteem or worth. Maybe that's just me.

When you do a job from the heart and soul, you fall in love with it. I love being a homemaker. Some days I wake up bored and tired of it all. That is rare. Maybe 1% of the time, I feel bored or exhausted with running the house and raising children. 99% of the time, I enjoy many parts of the work and cherish all the moments with my fast-growing boys. I know time is precious with them. I am so grateful for a million things in this way of living.

Since decluttering the house deeply and simplifying everything from my bank accounts and how I pay bills to what I cook on a regular routine, I feel rested and calm in my days. I move slowly, and the chores are done with attention. I feel like the cleaning and cooking are so easy now. It feels easy to keep the house clean, although I still must clean daily and am always tidying up. But I love tidying up. It's my favorite. Deep cleaning is no one's favorite; however, the after of a deep scrub with bubbly detergents and steaming hot water is fabulous.

I love my mornings in my adult years. In my childhood, mornings were not pleasant. My mother was mentally ill and an alcoholic, and addicted to valium. She was never right in the mornings. It was when she would wake up hung over and angry with herself. She would start finding things to hate, and the morning complaints would proceed. My bedroom door would be banged open, and she would rant with vigor. No morning was a good morning. That was my childhood. Now I wake peacefully. My children want to cuddle, and Bali is either at work or brewing coffee quietly in the kitchen. I wake with the light of day, and I can have all the time I want to drink coffee and talk with the family. My mornings are lovely. I'm grateful for that.

I'm grateful for a house to shelter us. I was grateful for the thick, foamy pad in front of the sink that feels good for my bare feet when I stand so long to wash sink after sink full of dishes and lather pots and pans. I'm grateful that Bali loves working on the house and gardening. He has become very clever and fixes, builds, and plants things and does it well.

I talked with my Oregon friend. She's coming to visit in September. We are so happy about this. She has been here already 2 or 3 times this year. And we have the godparents back. We will be meeting them up in Tahoe again this weekend. I feel very blessed with the people in my life right now.

Other great people will come into our lives, and life will change and shift. I'm sure it will be for the better. As we set our standards higher, the Universe gives us better. We are traveling to better places, spending time with more precious friends, and eating healthier and superior foods. We are careful about where we go, what we surround ourselves with, with whom we spend time, what we read, and the music we hear. We have created a delightful world. And our vibration rises because of this.

I was listening to a talk about not doing what 95% of the population does. Be the 5%. Do things off the path and differently, or you will be stuck like the rest of the population. This means living life differently. I can't digest most of the mainstream conversations in the world. It gets harder to be in the world fully after one has experienced the peace of withdrawing and getting rid of distractions.

Wednesday

I am having a big cup of coffee and sitting on the couch looking out my living room window, a view of green layers. The holly tree starts the picture and is backed by redwoods. How lucky for my eyes. And now we have that wonderful pergola and patio out back. We did some schoolwork and ate a meal out there yesterday. I sent pictures of the pergola to our friends. Bali did a great job, and it was his first pergola. Now he wants to build more. I see the gleam in his eye when he talks about putting the pergola together and pondering how a room is built.

Another bit of gratitude. I'm grateful that Bali likes to build things and carpentry, for I do not. I like nesting, not building.

So, I'm making a rather bland grocery list here. I could put so much on there, but I counter it with "can I make it at home?" and "Is this natural and healthy?" That eliminates most items right there.

Thus far, I have listed; produce, yeast for baking, bulk cereal, soy milk and creamers, dates, corn tortillas, and a few Asian sauces I need for my stir fry and Chow Mein dishes.

The way we eat right now is fantastic for our health. We don't overeat or graze all day because there are no junk foods or fun foods. The foods we have taste great but aren't easy edibles. They are flavorful bean dishes and salads, and tortillas. Last night it was an enchilada and date and nut bread. Pretty good, but not feed bag stuff. So, you have a full meal and all that nutrition when you eat. We have plain popcorn, apples, carrots, and garlic-stuffed olives as snacks. Not flavored pretzels and chips.

And it all ties in together. You eat healthily, and your budget gets healthy.

I keep watching *Jiro Dreams Of Sushi* and looking at my own mission. You must find that one main thing and commit. I have my family and home, and that is my life. And what a great life. I often feel so blessed and delighted that I can't list it here. I have moments of feeling so good around the simplest of things. A dish that turned out well, a new soap that smells good, clear skin, and a comfortable pair of flip-flops. With the pool and patio area, it feels like a vacation house. I'm thrilled about that. And to have recovered my dearest friends after two years of being separated due to severe depression. Then my Oregon friend is coming in September. I'll chat with Dawn this morning. This is so fulfilling. I have a small hand full of friends, but they are more precious than gold. They are safe, kind, deeply loving, fun, and inspiring. We laugh, share, and help each other grow and thrive.

However, I have another passion, and that is my writing. I think of Jiro, and I think of my writing.

Wednesday

I got the dates mixed up with the teacher, so we will go again tomorrow. Not a lost venture as I picked up some tissue for the bum and chlorine for the pool. It's a little past due to chlorinate. The pool looks somewhat tropical with a tinge of green. I said it looked like the Caribbean to be humorous, and so the kids would go for a swim. Today it was going toward pond-like. And that got me thinking about a stagnant body of water. The saying is that water that doesn't flow grows stagnant. Now, the way I see it with the pool, here is this large body of water chemicalized, and yet, after so many days, the chemicals wear off, and things begin to grow. Nature begins to grow, to live again. We even have those bugs that swim about. It gives me great faith in the Mother. She can heal herself quickly if we stop wrecking it and all do our part to help or step out of the way.

Today turned into an errand day and then a half library day. Once disrupted, I just went with it. We did not do a lick of schoolwork, and now I'm finishing a movie, and the boys have conned me of my cell phone again. It's late evening, and I cannot hear one more minute about gaming and guns and strategies and more gaming. I love being with my children. I love talking with them and learning about them and what they love. But this is not talking with, this is being talked *at* about a subject that bores me to tears, and I get to hear about it from waking to sleep. Again and again. Each day. 24/7. With no light at the end of the tunnel in sight. Anywhere.

I had another thought the other day. It seems some people, not many, but some have a misconception of the job of a housewife and homeschooling. Because we are at home and the schedule we follow is our own for the most part, there is the assumption we are available at all times or can accommodate anyone, anytime.

I remember Mrs. Sharon White talking about this. People would call her at home and keep her on the phone indefinitely. She asked if these people would call her at a job and take up so much time. No one with common sense would call a person at work and take up time or just drop by their office to visit.

We have the life. I won't lie. However, we also have routines and rituals. We homeschool throughout the day, and I have daily chores. Because we don't drive to a job and clock in with a timecard, just because the kids aren't dropped off at a school for a full day of classes, this doesn't mean that we have a free and open schedule.

We have the most closed schedule.

We have chosen to walk a different unbeaten path. We have chosen to do things differently and go against the norm but with the flow of the current. We have created a life that is to *our* liking, not societies or family opinions or modern say so. We learn about what we are curious about. We do work we enjoy most of the time, and it benefits the whole family and household. We build our days, our lives, and our futures to be satisfying and meet our inner needs. We crave peace and can only thrive in a safe and peaceful environment. Today with the pace of mainstream and the mental invasion of the internet and news, it is impossible to live with a peaceful and safe mindset. Removing it all and withdrawing into a self-built sanctuary can be wise.

Thursday

Here we go to the teacher's appointment again. This time we know we got the day right.

Watched **The Biggest Little Farm** this morning. I cried many times. That's what I do. I cry over anything with heart or depth. It is a must-see documentary. The farmer was a cameraman, and the wife a chef before they took on 200 acres of deserted farmland. It looked like a desert with dead dirt. They had a dream of farming the traditional way and with nature. A regenerative and biodiverse farming method, and within seven-plus years it was a healthy, lush, thriving farm. They had many obstacles, but there was always a natural solution, and the balance was found for their farm, with nature included.

The future of farming is this way. It heals the soil and makes it rich again. We need to integrate the farm animals with the orchards and the rest of the gardening. We need nature to balance out each other. Predators keep the pest minimal. Ducks eat snails, and sheep mow the orchards. Cover crops make the soil rich and absorb the rains and fill aquafers. The story was told with charm, and the cinematography was incredible. It is worth seeing and should be a requirement for all farmers to watch and see where they are going down the wrong road and what to do to have an abundant farm that will get better with time. It also accommodates nature, and nature is deserving of sanctuary. It will take care of us if we live with nature and tend to it well.

I also brought home **What The Bleep Do We Know**. I watched part of that while on the elliptical. I was reminded of Dr. Emoto's water study. He collected water from a dam and photographed it. He then placed some water in several jars, spoke words or curses or blessing from monks, played music over some jars, and then photographed the patterns the water molecules would take. The blessings and kind words made beautiful patterns. The lovely music made beautiful patterns. The jar with hateful and mean words looked polluted and scrambled, with no pattern or beauty. Words are power. Thoughts create our inner world and then move out to create our outer world. If you want to know a person, look at the state of their life, their partner, and the people who surround them.

Later...

We met with the teacher and chose some science, reading, and Geography books. Made sure the boys were in the proper classes. The school is small and divided into five groups: Dragonfly, littles, middles, olders, and scholars. The school only goes up to 8th grade. After that, we will transfer to another homeschool-based school or an apprentice program, or there is one school devoted to University preparation.

I read about the Finland school system years ago and loved it. I have been quasi-following the idea since. I had

Sam in two years of kindergarten. We homeschooled, so most of the schooling is through being outdoors in nature, fairy tales, vast amounts of me reading to them, art, music, movies, documentaries, and anything educational but done in fun and creative ways. We baked, talked, and shared our feelings to learn how to work with them and express ourselves in beneficial ways (this was for me as well). Nothing was rushed. I did a terrible job with Arjan the first year or two. The first year I remember us having meltdowns. I was still brainwashed from my years in public school. I was the one that needed major unschooling. The second year was calmer, but I was figuring out the structure and, once again, forcing this militant system. I was coming from fear. I feared I would fail them, that they would grow up unprepared for a job, college, or whatever they wanted to do but couldn't do it because I hadn't covered it all! I had this mild panic. I was also impatient. I genuinely regret the first few years. But last year, I started mellowing out and looking at myself. I didn't want to be a teacher. I didn't want to teach my boys. But I knew in my heart that homeschooling could be unique and magical and help grow strong, confident people.

And I have since learned that I *am* a good teacher after all. Not so much clever, but it is in me to teach what I know. So, I had to figure out what was driving the rigid structure and why I resisted. Fear. Plain old fear. Once I saw that and worked through it, homeschooling became pleasant and easy.

And surrender sounds like the mighty, silent warrior, but it is more like just going limp and playing dead. It isn't a glamorous ending. And now I've surrendered to the process. As in, now we focus on only one math problem at a time. One sentence at a time. One morsel of knowledge about one subject at a time. I am not shoving the whole world's history and information down their little throats overnight.

I've created more time and space for us. Therefore, I'm patient, and I have all the time to teach and guide. Now I love it. The kids are mellow about it, and I lavish them with praise, and if frustration arises, I know to step away and do a chore and have them do a simple task. If we get too frustrated, we quit for the day and resume the next day. We only commit to daily reading, writing (or English composition), math, and 10 minutes of the piano. We'll throw in a morning of science one day and history the next. Right now, we watch good videos from the science channel. We like **BeSmart** and **Smarter Everyday**. We get our history from **Oversimplified**. We have a set routine, but we are flexible; whether we finish or go in another direction, it still sets us up with good daily habits.

The boys are also learning more chores and improving on old chores. They are learning to cook and clean. This summer, they basically taught themselves how to swim. I showed them a few arm and leg moves, but they have been swimming like fish since we put in the pool.

I'm a little lazy right now, and I'm surrendering to that too. Surrender, surrender, surrender. A woman on the channel once spoke of her friend struggling with being a homemaker. The woman said she wished her friend would just surrender to it, put on a pot of coffee, and be inspired. Something like that, but the 'surrender to it and put on a pot of coffee' stayed with me forever. It means to cease and desist from being a control freak, pour that coffee and relax.

On to another topic.

Let's talk about small budgets. I always use this as an example. If someone is on disability, welfare, social security, or food stamps, they can't mess around. If they do, they are in big trouble. If you have a limited budget and you go over, where do you get the money next month to cover the overstep? I saw this unfold with a former friend of mine. This was not my friend Miss B that I share in my videos or books. This was another friend when I lived on the coast. She and I started daycares around the same time and met during a certification class. She was trying to become financially independent. At the time, she was on a lot of government assistance. She lived on so little but made it work well with a tight budget. She had it down to the penny. She and her daughter lived just fine but as simply as you can imagine. They had no car, used the library internet, and computers, and had no debt. I can't remember if she had a cell phone. I'm sure she did but the most basic.

All was well, and they lived comfortably despite living on a meager monthly amount. The trouble started with the grandmother encouraging the mother to get an electric car. It would save on gas, enable them to get around, have more freedom, and so on. Convinced the mother got a car with the grandmother's help. Then she had to get a credit card because the cost of owning a car was more than her budget could handle. The struggle began in earnest with a car and a credit card. Those two costs threw her budget out of balance and spiraled out of control. The mother and daughter had to leave the ocean town they loved, move back in with the grandmother, and go back to a town that the mother hated.

If you have only so much each month, you can't overspend. It would throw you off forever. That is sort of where we are. Not so crucial, but if I don't take things seriously and put in place foolhardy safety measures, we will be in trouble too. It can happen paycheck by paycheck. Every choice we make has an effect that can throw us off the path.

I'm finding that a grocery envelope and keeping the savings account separate from the rest of the accounts is a great start. In my head, I pretend we have far less than we do so that I make wise choices with every bit of money that comes in.

Friday

Cleaning day. I just retrieved the outdoor broom. The spider webs make the outside look like the Adams Family residence. I don't have the heart to take them down. The spiders are in there working hard, doing their thing. I respect it. And who are we to decide that we can't share a little space? They're home keeping, and I'm home keeping. The spiders and I work side by side to build our webs and feed our children. The only difference is that I have far fewer children and won't be feeding them my body.

Saturday

We are two weeks in with homeschooling, and it's getting a nice rhythm. There is some whining, and sometimes a child doesn't want to do a subject. I push a little but not past frustration. I've learned it's not worth it. Kids shut down when pushed too often, and a subject becomes a dark memory. It's best to say, "Fine, don't do Math today. Focus on English." Yesterday Sam's Math started on Geometry. He had to fit shapes into a shape and count out how many pieces it took. I suggested he get out his Magna Tiles and find the answers. He did his math and got out his Magna tiles. And his hot wheels. And his army men. And building commenced. He had reading and writing remaining, but I chose not to interrupt his play. He learns math, geometry, and engineering when he plays with the toys. I enjoy watching him play with his things, which is becoming less seldom. So, Sam didn't finish writing and reading, and Arjan didn't do much math and skipped the piano. I go with it. They are thriving and very advanced for their age in knowledge and sometimes maturity.

I'm watching **Love Is A Many Splendid Thing**. It's a classic with technicolor and old romantic charm. Sometimes the lines are bizarre, and the acting is cheesy, but I enjoy it. I love getting lost in an old film that is clean in language and scenes. I love that old-fashioned manner and talk. Men were gentlemen, and women were ladies. It's silly but nostalgic despite me not living at that age.

We had our long library day, and I watched parts of two videos on YouTube. Through my earphones, I listened to Pandora and started work on editing this mammoth book. I'm somewhat concerned since I planned on writing for a year and four more months of writing will unfold. But we haven't been perfectly unplugged. We went seven months and fell off the unplugged wagon. I'll tell you this: it is an addiction or habit that loses its power after a while, even if one does the back-and-forth thing. We get the hot spot for a few days and take it back. A week later, we are racing down the road to check another hot spot out, only to return it in three to five days. We did this for weeks. But each time we have it, I find fewer things that interest me online.

Monday

I was thinking about corporations I don't want to put my money or support into anymore: factory farming, palm oil, coconut oil, Walmart, and Amazon. I'll be honest, sometimes we can't find things except on Amazon, but I try. And candles, I find the best and cheapest candles at Walmart. I wish our Grocery Outlet carried candles. They barely have any to offer the customer. Then last night, we stopped at GO, and voila! They had a whole section of candles just like at Walmart and the same great prices! So, I had to grab a couple of fabulous jars. I want to be as local and compassionate as I can be.

I took Molly for a walk around the neighborhood with a mug of coffee and Sam in tow. She was in desperate need of a good walk. Arjan slept in, and I set Bali up with his water, coffee, and *The Biggest Little Farm.* I want to inspire him to assist me in unfolding my plans for this Fall. And I have big plans.

Every year we suffer stunted, pitiful gardens and two to three fruit tree deaths. I know it takes time, but this is frustrating me. I have been walking through the neighborhoods and observing what grows well and how it's planted in other yards. I noticed today that Rose of Sharon bushes grow great here. I spotted three yards with this delightful flower tree. I have noticed that the best gardens are in raised beds. Many locals have told me that raised beds are the way to go, or you must haul in all kinds of soil for in-ground. We have been amending like crazy for over two years with only a little luck, except this winter gave me great hope. Greens seem to grow anywhere. Artichokes do great in cool weather.

Today Bali will finish the patio, which has become a delightful place to hang out. We eat, study, read, and play under that pergola. We'll move the barbecue there tonight, and we ordered some solar lights with that warm orange glow. It was called fire-flicker something. We will see. Most solar lights have that hideous fluorescent light.

Then we commit 100% to completely redoing the garden and planting the front, side, and back yards. I want to overflow our yard with trees, plants, vines, and flowers. This will reduce water usage. The roots hold in water, and our clay soil retains moisture even more. I will learn how to make compost tea and get the number of a woman with alpaca poop. Bali agrees that we should focus all our energy for the next few months on working our little land. Pull up the dead trees and figure out where everything should be planted. We have shady sides of the yard and full sun sides, so we need to diagram where the shade lovers will go and where to plant the sun lovers.

This is important. Food prices rise, organics are outrageous, and we are wasting time just fiddling about. If we want to feed ourselves seriously, we must put a great effort initially and then tend to our orchards and gardens daily until they are strong and thriving. Once we see some success, we will be continuously inspired. In time it will get easier, and the yard will grow and grow into a lush oasis of beauty and abundant organic food.

Later…

I planted my winter greens in the empty garden patch outside the living room window. It's all clayish soil with no amendments, but greens seem to grow in anything. I will throw manure on them once they have sprouted and grown. I'll also make some compost tea. Once I figure it out. A quick Google, and I'll have it.

One dead pluot was removed, the other too big for me to tackle until the rains make the soil soggy.

Bali put bamboo and reed fencing as a roof, but it wasn't enough, so he ordered two shade clothes. One covered the pergola, and the other he stretched from the pergola to the house roof. This cuts out the afternoon blaze and creates shade over my clothesline, so I'm not exposed while hanging laundry in the morning. I love the sun and warmth but detest direct sunlight on me. Unless I'm in the water, and it's not in the triple digits. And speaking of triple digits, we had none or few up here in the mountains this summer, and here it's September in a few days, and all of a sudden, our week of 80 degrees went to 90 degrees, and the next ten days will be over 100! How bizarre the weather is this year.

I just ordered a stack of Dr. Joe Dispenza books. I've been listening to him lately. He is deep, and I need small doses. His work is transforming the personality to change the life of the person. Our personality is what we think, the things we do, and what we talk about. Change your inner world, and the outer world changes completely.

Chapter 8

Going Back Into Fall (My favorite time of year)

Middle of the night thoughts

I lay awake some nights, looking into the darkness and thinking useless thoughts about things that have passed. Things I've said that I wish I hadn't. Not big things, not anything that hurt anyone or disrupted the time/life continuum, just stupid things that made me look ignorant or nerdy. You can never take those things back. You can never turn back time and delete, edit or rewrite. That is why writing is so great. You can go back and read it, say to yourself, "well, that sure was a silly and worthless statement," and delete it and write something witty in its place. That is why silence is golden. Best to sit back and observe 'silently' until you may have something worth saying.

But that is being human. You can hold back, sit on the sidelines, not express yourself, and stay perfect. Or boring. Or you can enjoy every bit of your imperfect and flawed self. Throw it all out there and see what works and what doesn't. Be the funny guy or be the jack ass but be something.

I sometimes say downright weird or nerdy things, like I don't get out much and haven't mastered social graces. I wish I could erase many a conversation. But I also say amusing things and wise things and deep stuff. And If I kept nice and pretty and quiet, I would never say those things, I would never say the embarrassing things, but I would miss out on my good stuff. The same goes for writing. The first few books I wrote were dry and dull when I started. I'm surprised they even sold or received decent reviews. One review, in particular, helped change the whole path of my writing. A teacher used to read my books and gently suggest things through her reviews of my books. This was back when I still read my reviews. I don't anymore. She suggested I get an editor, and I did, and it helped immensely. She then said, in one review, that she wished I'd take the reader along on my journeys; take the reader shopping, thrifting, and cleaning, so they felt they were with me. I would later learn this to be 'show, don't tell' in writing. I remember chewing over that for months, wondering how I would do all that. I later started writing just that way, and my books improved tenfold.

We must embrace our faults, shortcomings, flaws, embarrassing parts, and imperfections because all those parts of us are what make us truly deep, reflective, wise, interesting, fun, silly, and stupid in marvelous ways. Those embarrassing moments make for great comedic moments you see in movies or hear comedians do their best work.

I was also thinking about my parenting. I have made so many mistakes and have such guilt. But guilt holds us back. Look back and feel it and see what makes you feel that way, and then change it all and never look back again—for example, homeschooling. Initially, I had no clue what I was doing, and Arjan and I would argue, lose my temper and threaten to send them to public school, and tears and fits would ensue. I was a terrible teacher and impatient. Arjan was stubborn. It took years to figure it out and to unschool myself and stop trying to force this old way of educating where you force all this information down the kid's throat because you're afraid they'll grow up ignorant and unskilled.

This year I feel like a natural homegrown homeschool mother. I am patient, we don't fight, and no threats have been stated. Sam is learning to read, Arjan is self-guided, the boys know more about science and history than most kids their age, and they are thriving in their piano lessons. The difference is that I'm not trying to prove anything anymore. I also downsized each lesson to a math problem, small sentence, or words. I take our lessons moment by moment—word by word. If we only do five problems that day, that is good enough. If we only figured out one math equation, that would be good enough. If Sam only read one page in Pete the Cat, great. If we only reviewed the alphabet that day, even though we have been on that for a year, it's what was needed and where we are at, and it's perfect.

So, removing the pressure and the need to be great at it, has made our homeschooling enjoyable, and the boys are thriving and excelling.

I have also noticed that they seem to leap forward quickly if we only do a little work on all subjects and then take a day off. When we work at it hours a day and every day, they don't progress very far. So, less is more. The more is less can be seen in the public school system. The kids are failing and dropping out, and the government's answer is to have more schoolwork, more homework, start them younger, more testing, no more free summers, less play time, and more and more work, work, work. And the kids are getting less and less educated, retaining less, learning less, falling to the wayside more, and being burnt out by high school.

Tuesday

Captains log: we are in the later parts of the ninth month. We had the library Hot Spot for a month, and I finally parted with it today. I returned a bag so full of books it must have weighed thirty pounds, and with it, I released our internet joy into the hands of my friend, one of the librarian ladies I enjoy chatting with often. And I am a little unsettled tonight. It leaves a void. No more Avengers on Disney plus or Stranger Things on Netflix. No checking my channel fifty times a day. Oh, what will I do?

Write and read, that is what! That darn internet takes over my mind and sucks it out. I think it's harmless because I mostly listen to Pandora, but I also watch many movies and series that are so addictive. I finished up **Stranger Things** quickly, and the last season won't come out until late 2023.

There is a saying, "Burn the ships!" from the history of Hernan Cortes, a Spanish conqueror who destroyed all but one ship out of 11 when he and his crew landed in Mexico. This way, there was no returning, no retreating from the great mission. They would have to be successful or die. No turning back. I recalled this saying this morning and did a little research. I'm not saying that Cortes was a great man, just a brilliant leader. Or was he? If his men had all died, they would have branded him as the worst and most negligent leader in history, but they succeeded and conquered, much to the demise of many people.

I could analyze this to death, and I sit at my desk by candlelight with my mind going off in various scenarios and dissecting his tactics, but let us stay focused on just one part of the history. To be concise, he destroyed his ships, ten out of eleven, so his men knew he meant business. There was no way out, no way back. It was forward and life dependent. Survival and hunger are the greatest motivators.

It was the same message I got from **Please Stand By** when the character feels forlorn and lost, she reads her remaining script, and the line is from Spock. Captain Kirk asks him what to do in their hopeless situation, and Spock replies, "There is only one logical direction to go: Forward." That stuck with me. I rewound that scene over and over.

One day I'll stop messing about and finding excuses to avoid returning to fictional writing.

I hustled this month. It took some work to get back into the work after some time off, but I've been filming and playing around with making cleaning and daily life montages with great music in the background. I made some good money this month and can afford some essentials. I will buy the computer the boys wanted in the first place and worked so hard to earn, along with a four-year warranty. Then I want to stock up on Clyde's hemp oil since it's working well and much cheaper than the chews I was buying in town. Molly's Boot the Scoot chews are necessary. I will stock up on some makeup and beauty supplies, colorful nail polish since I'm so into painting my fingernails now, and a five lb. bag of rye seed for a winter cover crop. I've also added baking pans, casserole pans, a new strand of warm Christmas lights for our faux tree, and two short fairy lights for the kitchen mirror and the bathroom mirror. I love warm lights; the bathroom twinkle lights are LED and look like hideous fluorescent lights. The strand in the kitchen is warm and sweet but with too many lights and maybe too much electricity.

You know, much of the advice to follow one's dreams is about emotion and slowly easing yourself into your new life of living your passions. Or the advice is to jump in. It can go either way. But what is often not covered is how to prepare financially; your budget and your home, and setting things up so you can afford to take a year off to do your dream. In the old film *The Secret Life Of Suzie Wong*, the main character was an architect but dreamt of being a painter. He finally saved enough money to move to Hong Kong and paint for a year. He gave himself a year to see what he could make of himself as an artist, and he would not work on anything but his craft the whole time. He rented a cheap room and lived frugally. Of course, a woman interrupted that plan, but that is beside the point I'm making here.

If you have a dream that tickles your consciousness now and then or shakes you awake in the middle of the night with dreams of a far-off life you would love to partake of; it would help if you prepared in all ways; monetarily, emotionally, and physically. It all depends on the dream. But having funds to take time off to do this dream, to throw yourself into it, is necessary. If you feel you have a chance, you need time to focus 100%, and stressing about bills will chip away at most of that focus. Having too many obligations will chip away the rest.

Save money, get rid of debt, and get big things done. We have squirreled away an emergency fund, paid off all the little debts, and took care of all the dental, dog vet visits, and major car repairs. I've been stocking up pantries and toiletries here and there. I've stocked up on dog stuff, vitamins, the first aid box, and bedding. I've purchased new pillows, extra comforters for winter, and a year or two worth of clothing for the boys. I hit thrift stores with 50% off sales and dragged stuff home from off the street. I spent my birthday this Sunday at a colossal garden nursery, loading up a trolley with fruit trees, flower and shade trees, and a bag filled with seeds for fruits, vegetables, and flowers.

Everything I do is to prepare for the future. Every wad of cash I get in my little paw is spent on home goods, garden supplies, or a big pantry stock-up.

In my case, there can be this weird thing with preparing. When will it be enough? Am I just putting off the work? I say, "oh, I need to do videos just a little longer to prepare for this and that." Or do I need to take a year to study all the books I have on writing books and scripts? Or I need to work on my inner self. And when exactly am I going to start writing?

Who cares if I suck. And am I waiting for that book or series I'll love writing? Well, we could be waiting a long time. And are we waiting for the stars and planets to align just so and for me to have an inner awakening? Oh my, that could be other lifetimes.

I need to burn the ships, take up my machete, and start trudging through the jungle, whacking away at the thick foliage to make my new path.

Wednesday

I finished a sweet black and white film, *I Remember Mama, with Irene Dunne*. It's the memories of a writer's mother, set in San Francisco. It is heartwarming; if every person had a mother like this, the world would be such a lovely place to live. It made me want to put more strength and sugar into my mothering. After finishing this feel-good movie with my coffee, I ran Sam a bubble bath at his request. It was an unusual desire for him to want a bath at eight in the morning, but our home is about finding the small delights and cozy things. I used some body wash that was sent to me as a gift, and it smelled divine! It made the bathroom smell good, and Sam still smells lovely.

The day after my birthday, I rearranged the living room completely. In the two and half years of my cleaning and redecorating, I have never tried this setup, and halfway through, I felt like it might be a mistake. However, I was too deep and kept going to the end. And I'm glad I did because it is the best setup yet. It opens up and uses the whole living room, making it brighter and more colorful, and the TV is not the focal point. More so, the piano is highlighted by the sunny picture window.

Today am finishing up the decorating and putting things in place. I moved one of the large shelving units from the boy's room to the living room, which serves a bigger purpose of holding the extra plants and books. One shelf is devoted to books and movies from the library, and one holds all the boys' schoolbooks and composition notebooks. There is also a shelf for art supplies, grown-up coloring books, and sketch pads. I made the shelves charming with buddhas, cards, candles, plants, and nick knacks I never had the heart to get rid of.

I have so many great ideas from a channel I found the other day when we still had the hot spot. The channel's name is **Randi Lynn Reed**. She is a talented artist who paints many woodland creatures in more human-like forms, such as having cottages under the ground and wearing old-fashioned clothing. I love her work. She has the most charming studio she decorates with nick knacks and her work, along with flowers and leaves Randi gathers from the woods where she spends her time getting inspiration. I watched a few of her vlogs and worked all day on the house the next morning. I rearranged my desk, so I could look out both windows in my bedroom. I'm fortunate to look out into thick green made up of tall, old trees and plants lining my porch. The flow in the whole house has improved. My next plan is to repaint the guest room and boys' rooms. They are both blue, and I'm not wild about blue. I'll try some warm pumpkins and light milk chocolates.

My cooking juju has returned after days of mac and cheese and sandwiches. We blew a wad on trips to the grocery store and eating out this month, going far beyond the grocery envelope. But interestingly enough, we stayed within the government's new guidelines for grocery budgets. It used to be $600 plus for a family of four on the frugal end and $1200 at the high end. That was three or four years ago. Today, with inflation, it is $1036.20 on the frugal end. Holy smokes! And that is just for groceries. We aren't talking dog food, medicine, toiletries, or cleaning supplies. But it is not affordable for us. That is the low end. For the moderate food budget, we have $1298.12. We might as well add up the Liberal plan. Whoa! $1564.52. And that is a party right there, what I could do with $1500. If you would love to total the new grocery budget, Google: **Official USDA Food Plans: Cost of Food at Home at Three Levels, U.S. Average, July 2022**.

I'm still sticking with our $600 envelope, and it will get easier each month as I get cleverer. One of my money-saving strategies is to make dog food instead of buying $70 worth of that stinky canned food a month. I have plenty of rice to cook up, add some cheap meat and frozen vegetables, and it should last a couple of weeks. Much healthier and cheaper. The dogs need a little something mixed in with their dry food.

Thursday

I've been up since two in the morning. It's now a semi-legal hour of four in the morning, so I got up, brewed my morning cup of coffee, and lit a couple of candles to light my navigations in the dark. Babu was there to greet me. I suppose he doesn't always sleep that well, either. I gave him a piece of the homemade wheat bread he likes and a small piece of turkey neck for Molly. She gets up with me no matter what time. She is devoted to staying by my side night and day. She lays on the bathroom rug when I pee or shower and watches me from her little bed in the kitchen, which I need to wash soon. She follows me inside and outside. She whines and barks when she finds herself on the opposite side of the door from me.

Friday

Today was a lazy day with a side of effective planning and pouring over my scratch cookbooks. I have re-found a channel I've watched on and off for a few years. *Little Village Homestead* is a sweet channel to watch and get inspired. The woman grows food in a large yard with chickens and has a small, simple home. She cans and preserves everything; her garden produce, meats, and what she gets on sale at the market. Her house is immaculate and clear of clutter. It's decorated simply. She has a fantastic pantry and root cellar stocked enough to get her and her husband through winters. In one of her videos, her husband was laid off and wouldn't be getting unemployment because he's a self-employed truck driver (I think), but she makes money on YouTube and has such a well-stocked pantry that they don't have to worry. She talks of working hard to preserve all the food and prepare for the lean times. Most of her pantry is loaded with home canning and dehydrated goods. However, she does have some store-bought sauces and packets of mixes. She has shelves of boxed foods; Hamburger Helper, Mac and Cheese, and Rice a Roni or boxed cakes that she buys on sale and said there are times we don't want to cook from scratch. Thank you! This woman focuses on the home, makes everything from scratch, and works tirelessly to grow, can, preserve, and dehydrate everything, and she feels this way that sometimes we need a boxed cake and a boxed dinner. We need breaks, and this modern age with markets allows us to lazy down a bit to recharge now and then.

I'm so impressed with her pantry. I want us to put 100% focus on the kitchen garden until I can harvest enough to can. Someday it will happen. I'll have berries for pies and jams, fruit for drying, and vegetables to can and dehydrate. I look to women like Renea to keep me inspired.

You need to work harder for an independent and humble life. If you want to work less hustling or outside the home, you must work hard in the house and yard to create abundance.

I've been watching **Little Village Homestead** and finding recipes in my **Make A Mix** and **Cheap And Good** books. Found a delicious crunchy granola bar recipe in the **Make Your Own Groceries** book. And PB & J granola bars in **Good And Cheap**. I'll go back to making my bread by hand. The boys love the Amish white bread with cheese for school lunches, and if I add honey and butter to my Whole Wheat, they love that too. I've been cheap and making bread with only wheat, oil, yeast, and water. I must go back to making things tasty. It's the only way to stay on that $600 grocery envelope. The boys fill up faster and snack less if I make healthy and hearty meals. Today was chicken-flavored rice and plain pintos seasoned with salt. The boys liked the meal. Easy and cheap and filling. I can't buy junk food, or that is all they eat, and it is gone within a day. Same with a loaf of good, sliced bread, especially sourdough, and lunch meats. They were gone within a day. So, I will go back to making it all. I'm making a grocery list now. The only way to go is to make a month-long menu. Then you can load up on ingredients wisely.

I have planned to do a big shop and do all these freezer meals. If you get burnt out on cooking and need breaks now and then, make sure to have a pantry supplied with the cream soups for casseroles and onion soup mixes, taco seasonings, ranch packets, cream sauces, canned spaghetti sauce, and those Knorr packets for flavoring soups and rice's are fantastic for quick recipes. I learned this from my **Dump Dinners**.

My energy has fully returned these past few days. I've been cooking, running the bread machine daily, and preparing for the next day of cooking by soaking beans and rummaging through the pantry. I'm reading my cookbooks and making lists. I love when I have this energy, and I can sit quietly with my books and get back into that homemaking mode.

I made $1,000 on YouTube this month, so I'm stocking up! I have anal glad chews for Molly, Hemp oils for Clyde, Rye for the garden winter cover crop, and so on. I'm back into my stocking-up mode. We don't get crazy, but if we stock up well, we don't spend much through the year, and we can save like crazy.

I've been rereading **Living On His Income** by *Mrs. Sharon White*. She talked about the 1990s when women were encouraged to work from home and do all sorts of hustles. She says, *"Mothers were exposed to more and* more teachings on earning money, and less on thrift, home keeping and motherhood. There was an explosion of schemes and genuine opportunities to make money. This desire for money took up so much of our attention that it was almost as if we didn't have as much time for holiness, prayer, keeping our marriages intact, or on devoting our entire lives to our homes and children. We had hearts that were being divided between making money and learning to live on our husband's provision."

Indeed, we can't serve two masters. We choose the home and less money or money and less home (and family time).

As *Amy Dacyczyn* has taught us with **The Complete Tightwad Gazette,** you can save more staying home if you plan and act wisely and frugally. And although I can't stomach the frugal living channels or blogs anymore, I love to peruse my books while drinking coffee and listening to my musicals on Pandora. It is the best and coziest daytime activity. I'm reminded of tips I forgot over the years; I find easy recipes and get ideas to cut costs. I am motivated to start planning, get out the whiteboard, and do menus and grocery lists. Running the house is like running a home business. You are running an Inn for your family's comfort, and it requires all the cleaning, daily freshening up, and lots of cooking and baking.

Mrs. Sharon White says the best examples of good living were learned from her grandmother and mother-in-law. They showed the most beautiful and peaceful lives. Her point was that the happiest and most content homemakers she knew focused solely on the home and family. Her grandmother and mother-in-law did not have side jobs and hustles from home or outside the home. I got this today. All these side hustles and "streams of revenue" detract from our home life and how much we immerse ourselves in our homes and families. We are distracted with making money.

Saturday

It was library day, and I spent four hours editing this book. It's good I started the editing process because it's turned into a mammoth of a book, and the year isn't over yet— three more months to finish my yearlong writing stint. I usually write a book in a few weeks and pre-edit in less than a week. Then I send it off to my editor. Now my editor is busy with life and family. Thus, I am the prominent editor. The first draft, that's me. The second draft, that's me. And the last and final proof. Sadly, that is me as well. However, I bought a year of Grammarly Premium, which is fantastic! It dissects my pages like nothing could. Blue lines, green lines, red lines. If you are a writer with Grammarly Premium, you know exactly what I'm talking about.

So, four hours of that with my earphones on listening to Classical New Age Piano on Pandora. The musicals are so cheerful and conducive for cleaning house and cooking but not great for focusing on editing a book. I get caught up in the songs and forget what I'm reading.

Back home, I cooked a few extra dishes to add to the leftover rice and beans. Some mac and cheese, roasted acorn squash, and steamed broccoli. I cooked it all up and told the boys to help themselves. They are being easy with the meal choices, do no complaining, and eat well. I felt like the boys were getting a bit picky. They head toward the tweens, and they want junk. I can't afford junk, and our bodies won't support junk.

After making a spread in the kitchen, I spent the rest of the day watching Renea from Little Village Homestead and learned a new laundry soap I may try, how to make homemade Rice a Roni in bulk, and how to make homemade sweetened condensed milk. I have most of the ingredients for all the homemade goods I've been looking up. It's time to roll up my sleeves and start prepping that pantry properly and saving big wads of cash.

The laundry soap is the most straightforward recipe I've heard of. It's just Zote soap and Borax. One Zote bar grated, four cups Borax and two buckets full of hot water. I've tried recipes with a few more ingredients, and my clothes began to turn grey and dingy, not to mention they started to smell somewhat. But I want to try this simple recipe because I love Zote. It is a miracle stain remover above anything I've ever tried, so why can't it wash my clothes well and efficiently? I would love for it to work out. I have always loved making my detergent; it saves hundreds of dollars and cuts down on buying plastic. It's something like a dollar a gallon to make.

I feel like my old self again. I have been thumbing through my TCTWG and Mrs. Sharon White, my cookbooks, and watching videos on dehydrating potatoes and making mixes such as au gratin or brownie mix. I'm watching homemade cleaner recipes. I'm inspired now, and that hasn't happened for some time. This is how I was when we bought the first house, and Granny lived with us for a season. I started taking my homemaking seriously. We gardened, had chickens, and I baked all our bread, cooked all the time, and hung the clothes on my umbrella clothesline. I was so into making everything; my cleaners, my laundry soap. I got into stocking our pantry.

Now that I have freed up more time for myself, I'm getting into my old ways, and I am happy that I am. For one, this way of living is budget friendly and not that complicated if you take it section by section. Second, it frees up more time.

Sunday

I've been working in my sunny Fall kitchen all day; Bali has been out in the garden planting a small winter garden. Two stoned DJs have been playing strange things on the radio because they're obviously high. First, it was some good, old black gospel, then they came on and started talking and laughing about who knows what, music got weird. But fun. One of the ladies tal having no time for fear-mongering. I listened t moment. I'm always happy to hear another hu......... take a stand against listening to the miserable dribble. They played the blues, and it matched our hippy day. Bali out hand hoeing his radish rows, me in my apron, the table loaded with ingredients for my scratch mixes.

It was a cozy warm Fall day. I pulled out the bin of Fall decor and did some mild decorating. I cooked up a storm; more pintos, chicken-flavored rice, and Stouffer's chicken enchiladas. I added chips, salsa, and nacho cheese to the dish. The plan was to work on editing the book, but I spent the whole day in the kitchen making mixes and cooking. I made a simple Brownie scratch mix, and then I made a batch from the mix. It was delicious. It's from the most recent and revised Make A Mix cookbook. It doesn't call for water, but that must be a mistake. It needs water. I used a little and then added some oat milk, which turned out fabulous.

I made mixes and set up my menu board. I have Breakfast Items, Side Dishes, and Main Super /where I list dinner dishes we enjoy and make often. Under that, I put Bulk Batches, where I list what I need to make in bulk and set aside to make life budget-friendly and time-saving. I will never have to buy boxes of brownies for $1.75 and going up. I have a big jar full of the mix. I don't buy crackers, pancake mix, bread, granola bars, Rice a Roni, or

...etened condensed mix. I can make the mixes myself for a fraction of the cost, and they are all so easy to make.

I've been deep cleaning and organizing my kitchen when I have the stamina. I have updated and rotated all the foods and seasoning, washed the shelves, lined them with brown paper bags, and tidied up all the shelves in the kitchen and pantry. Now I need to section each item; canned items are in one section and organized by gravies, cream of soups, vegetables, and tomato sauces. I donated a 25 lb. bag of garbanzos to the food bank in town. I can't bear one more big bag of oats or garbanzos. So, help me.

I'm watching Renea go over her full pantry on Little Village Homestead. She inspires me. I was whining with Dawn about not finding anything on YouTube to motivate me, and then I found Renea. I found her years ago, Homestead Tess did a contribution video dedicated to a few women inspiring her, and Renea and I were two women. But I'm not much like who I used to be. I haven't canned in ages, and my summer garden has been a flop for the last two and a half years. I got away from homemade stuff. If I make future videos, they must return to my homesteading world. I need to go back to the old ways when I baked all the time and made homemade laundry soap. I would simmer cinnamon and clover on the back of the stove in a little pan of water to make the house smell good. I had a great tomato patch and canned 20 quarts of spaghetti sauce, and I bought produce from Sprouts and canned and froze most of it. I used to be far more into homesteading in town. I feel myself returning to my roots, and Renea helps me get there mentally and emotionally.

So, I don't get overwhelmed and give up before I start. I'll focus on one or two things at a time. I'll focus on growing tomatoes, cucumbers for dill chips, green beans, and corn. Beans to dry next, and I'll hope for pears next year and potatoes to dehydrate. I keep trying one more thing every year, and in the next five years, I'll be canning and dehydrating like crazy.

Bali's off getting supplies to fix the second bathroom. That will be the next big project he swears he can do, and I think he can after building a lovely pergola this summer.

Monday

I'm cooking and baking my brains out! Today I mastered granola in bulk. Then crunchy granola bars that are cooling now. Two loaves of Amish white bread are cooling on the stove, and a pan of brownies is in the oven. We had easy self-serve bean, rice, and cheese burritos, but if you add chips, salsa, and nacho cheese to the bland dish, it yummies it right up there with seven and eight-star dishes.

I planned on working on the editing today. I planned that yesterday as well. It turns out that cooking ahead can take an entire day. Yesterday I bought a very expensive (and not worth it) Stouffers chicken enchilada. They sure got skimpy with the main ingredients, like chicken and sauce. The rice was expanded on, and they've upped the price a hefty $7, which did not go toward better ingredients. I thought I'd steam up some seasoned rice, boil a pot of pintos, throw the enchiladas in the oven, and work on the book. But I never left the kitchen. I made bulk scratch mixes all evening. Today I had my chiropractic appt, and not a week too soon. My neck was completely out. Sam came for the ride and helped me gather goods at Grocery Outlet. I spent $124 and filled some bags. I was surprised at how much I was able to load up.

There were two whole organic chickens, a bag with five romaine heads of lettuce, two almond milk, two pumpkin spice vegan creamers, a large block of mild cheddar and a big bag of shredded pizza mix cheeses, a Stouffers meat lasagna (even expensive at GO), buttermilk, a big jar of nacho sauce, and another bag of corn chips, and two mac and cheese. Still, all they had for cheap was the new Cheetos brand. I got it for fun (it was hideous). Oh, and canola oil and lots of butter. And two types of sausage. And two big boxes of wheat and fruit bars and two bags of organic gummy bears. Wow, I got so much! It will work well with all my pantry goods, and I should be able to cook up wonderous dishes for at least ten days to two weeks.

The granola bars are better than any Healthy Valley or that name brand. The brownies are delicious, but I'd make them gooeyer with something. Maybe condensed milk.

Amish bread is excellent for cheese sandwiches. I am now prepared for school lunches this week. Amen. I will also make some lasagnas and tuna casseroles to freeze. These Stouffers have gone up so high in price and are lacking in quality, so I feel inspired to start doing this.

I realized the boys needed easy lunches, not homecooked meals that had to be microwaved and messy, taking up playtime. They need handheld foods like sandwiches and granola bars. They need filling foods and a couple of fun items. They talk about their friends' lunches, and I get that there is some longing to have a filling and fun lunch. I can't afford store bread, lunch meats, or granola bars. Not to mention that everything has palm oil in it, and we are pretty committed to not doing the palm oil. When I bought store bread and deli meat, it lasted less than two days. The junky foods or store-bought items go so fast. The boys devour it.

Making everything from scratch means it tastes better and has no junk. Yes, sugar and salt or butter are in some things, but the ingredients are fresh and basic. The foods are far more filling because they are made of whole grains and whole foods. I can add extra wheat germs and brans to the baked items and make vegan baloney that the boys like. Making all the foods I can from scratch reduces trash (no plastic or packaging), traveling, and trips to the store. We are saving a lot of money, and we eat real food that fills us up naturally and is loaded with nutrition, so it satisfies us well. My boys enjoy the food and eat well, but they don't gorge on it or eat all day like they do with that packaged and premade food. I feel relieved. The darn school lunches were stressing me out. Now they can't complain. They will have cheese sandwiches with homemade white bread, brownies, granola bars, carrot and celery sticks, and gummy bears tomorrow. We eat mandarins like crazy in the winter, so I'll pack hot soups, minestrone or chicken dumplings, and lots of mandarins as the seasons change.

I've spent two days in the kitchen. And how satisfying and pleasant it has been. In the evenings, I sit with an espresso and watch Little Village Homestead learn a few more scratch foods to make the next day. I'm watching her lasagna making, and then I'll watch her tuna casserole. I've never used cottage cheese or ricotta, but I'll try her recipe tomorrow.

I want to get so good at making foods, sauces, and baked goods that we don't buy store-bought anything, and I can proudly cluck about how I make it all from scratch and flap my proud hen wings as I brag about it all. But we need to start baby steps. I've been making three items a day. So far, we have Bread Machine Mix, Brownie Mix, Wheat Cracker Mix, Granola, Granola Bars, and two loaves of Amish bread. I aim to keep making the mixes, so I never buy the Bisquick or Pillsbury. Then I start making the freezer and fridge items.

I feel so domestic right now that I ordered a Mexican Abuela apron off Etsy. Never ordered from Etsy before, but the aprons on Amazon are from a fraudulent Chinese company. They change their name constantly and show photos of lovely linen clothes and frock aprons for cheap, but when you get the clothing, it's a cheap material and looks made by an unskilled seamstress. I suspect they have some child labor going on. But I'll have the actual frock here soon, and I can live out my life in the kitchen, steaming, blending, stirring, and baking away.

This is October, and it is the time to prepare for a heavy writing month in November with NaNoWriMo. I will scrub and deep clean the whole house. Purge the last of the extra stuff and have plenty of mixes and freezer meals. This month is about editing this book to be done by November, so I move on to fiction.

My cooking took a 180 from boxed mac and cheese to a Make-A-Mix frenzy in the kitchen. I recently decorated my kitchen a little bit, and it's organized, thanks to work I did months ago. I love being in my kitchen right now. The sun fills it in such a warm way, having my musicals on and pots and jars everywhere as I mix, mix, mix. It's the safest and homiest place to be.

My homemaking helps my mental well-being. It helps my imagination. I work through issues, and I think up book ideas. Homemaking is my work of choice, and its benefits are a long list. And how I love this home lately. I don't watch YouTube (except **Little Village Homestead**), and I'm not subjected to commercials or outside influences. Therefore, I'm content with what I have. I'm not thinking, "oh boy, I'd love that apron or those shirts!" or "I want my living room to look like that or I need a new bed set for Fall like hers." No, I'm happy with what I have and how this home has come together after two and a half years of working on it. And I have more plans to play with this house in the future. I want to repaint the blue rooms and try a little wallpaper in the kitchen and maybe my bedroom. I need new beds for the boy's room, but there is time, and people always give away bunk beds. We will need bigger, stronger ones in a couple of years.

But I'll be content with everything else we have. We don't need new linoleum floors or a new bathtub, and we don't need new furniture.

Tuesday

Molly and I have new hobbies. She has discovered that if she lies on the back steps, she can keep an eye on the squirrels preparing for winter by burying their walnuts in my garden. Molly chased squirrels all day yesterday and left me alone. Usually, she follows me about and whines and barks until I play with her. She wants me to play with her or cuddle all day. It's a great demand, so I was thrilled with her new sport. She never catches them but hustles all day on her tiny legs. It keeps her well-occupied with a mission. My new thing is prepping food and being in my kitchen all day. She and I are two busy gals.

I learned from those squirrels. One thing is that they can propagate a new walnut forest in no time. We would have a forest in ten years if we never touched the trees that sprouted up from all the walnuts they buried. But the biggest thing was how industrial they were. They play all the time, but in between, they are burying nuts. They have all the bird seed, bird baths, and compost in our yard, and the lady across the street has tons of bird feed, pans filled with squirrel feed, and pans of water all year round. They have all their needs met, but they wisely don't count on it and still store away nuts everywhere. Last year they were so busy all day I was sure we would have a hard winter. And we did but only for a short time. I watch them to get an idea of the winter ahead and follow their lead. Squirrel things away while the weather is nice.

I read the best review for a bidet yesterday. Ours is leaking, and we looked for a new one to replace it. The title of this review as "No barnacles on this hull!" Here is the rest of the review:

I just got this today and my girlie bits love this!
First things first, I have the Neo 120. Very easy install. My cat supervised. Directions super easy to understand even for those not mechanically inclined. One nozzle, one temperature. Apparently I have excellent water pressure because on the "maiden voyage" I nearly blasted myself off the crystal ship and started laughing so hard I'm sure my apt. neighbor's heard me. And that was on the LOW setting! I had concerns about the cold water, but it's spring in NorCal and honestly, the cool water isn't so bad. In summer I'm betting it will feel like a gift from the Gods! Ladies, you will need to adjust your seating position a smidge to get all the important parts clean. For bigger voyages be sure to "bear down" to make sure you clean all the barnacles off the hull. You should have smooth sailing from here on out.

She must be a writer. She has the spirit of imagination to be so interesting and fun for just a bidet review.

Chapter 9

Finding Our Homemaking Roots

I'm so cozy when watching Renea at **Little Village Homestead** because she helps me return to my homemaking roots. I used to be very into baking and scratch cooking. I made my laundry soap and cleaners, read The Complete Tightwad Gazette front to back, and enjoyed a quiet life in the country. Renea reminds me of what I was becoming and getting back to fundamental homemaking ways. My roots. I come from many a farmer housewife. We probably all do if you think about it. Maybe 85% of us come from a great-grandmother or grandmother that was a farming homemaker. She was the mother of everything and could make a good meal out of scrapes or turn a shack into a livable home. She could fix anything and make do with sparse little. She could make anything needed in the house or kitchen without running to a supermarket. There was a day when we didn't have the luxury of a supermarket where a factory canned, dehydrated, and packaged our food. We reach for it on shelves, throw it in our cart, and when we get home, we add milk or eggs or stick it all in an oven, and voila! Dinner! Or lunch. Or breakfast.

There was a time when a homemaker set a whole day aside for laundry. From early morning to evening, washing all the clothing and bedding and hanging it out took time. Then the next day was set aside for ironing.

This is clipped from an article from yourwilliamson.com

'Wash on Monday" - A Little History of Homekeeping
JAN 27, 2020 AT 01:06 PM BY <u>ADMINJEN</u>

Laura Ingalls Wilder's book *Winter Days in the Big Woods*, the author notes the following schedule for homemakers:

- Wash on Monday
- Iron on Tuesday
- Mend on Wednesday
- Churn on Thursday
- Clean on Friday
- Bake on Saturday
- Rest on Sunday

However, in *Antiques from The Country Kitchen* by Frances Thompson, a slightly different schedule is put forth:

- Wash on Monday
- Iron on Tuesday
- Bake on Wednesday
- Brew on Thursday (later marketing/shopping)
- Churn on Friday (later housekeeping)

- Mend on Saturday
- Church on Sunday

Staple chores took all day. Some needed prepping the day before. The next day was baking and ironing to utilize the stove heat. Everything was done by hand and frugally. Most of that was not a choice. It was just how life was. I'm grateful every time I load the washer. It does all the work in under an hour. I'm grateful for lights and running water, bidets, and showers. I'm grateful for grocery stores and ovens that don't require a cord of wood.

As much as I love all the gifts of the modern era, I think it wise to go back in time and learn all we can from an old-fashioned grandmother or great-grandmother. My grandparents passed before I had time to be interested, and my mother only knew so much. She would talk more about her grandmother than her mother. She adored her grandmother. She was a robust farming housewife with plenty of boys and a big farm to run. That is all I know. My grandmother was the more modern housewife. I don't know that she gardened or had a pantry. She probably did since her homemaking began around the Great Depression. She was from a farm and quit school at a young age because she was needed at home. I'm sure my grandmother was very clever with household funds.

I made my first freezer lasagna today and used Renea's recipe. I've never used cottage cheese and ricotta before.

It is delicious. I froze one for our weekend visit to the godparents and baked the other for us as a special Friday treat. Now I need to bake some brownies, and I have the mix! How fun. I made some dish soap out of my ivory soap today as well. The soap doesn't dissolve much when it's being boiled but begins to dissolve in the solution. I had only a cup of watered-down Dawn, and my trip to WinCo may be pushed out a few days, so I looked up simple recipes. I needed something bare bones like "boil up soap pieces." That stuff works for me, not "use Dr. Bronner's, boil with vinegar and add essential oils." No. "Boil soap" Yes.

Channels like Renea's are down home and not sparkly with fancy filming and lights. You are in a humble home with a hard-working homemaker. You are learning the basics that a mother, aunt, or grandparent would have taught a child back in another era. Fortunately, we have sources such as YouTube to teach everything from making sourdough starters to cleaning deeper or gardening to canning your harvest. And when you find that one person that feels homey, you watch them do everything like you would have watched a mother, and you learn to make that lasagna and scrub behind the fridge and get out stains before they get set in the dryer.

I made a big batch of dog food the day before, and the dogs liked it. I just sauteed cheap ground beef in the bean pot and filled it with water measured out by cups. After it brewed with the meat for a bit, I added the white rice, which I still have plenty of, and the cheap California medley frozen vegetables. It made a large pot, and I froze some of it. I was glad to see the canned food done. It smells up my pantry, garbage, and the dog's breath. This is clean and doesn't have all the weird stuff.

I was reading stories from **We Survived and Thrived**, a collection of Depression Era stories edited by Ken and Janice Tate. If you need some gratitude for everyday life, this is one of the books to give that reminder, and it makes me want to learn more about homemaking. I won't be a seamstress in this lifetime, but I can improve my baking and deep cleaning. I love these stories, and I start prepping my pantry with a little more attention and taking better care of our things. One story was lovely and uplifting, with a strong message. *Changing Fortunes, by Lydia Mayfield*, tells of when she was a young wife and mother of three and raising two of her sisters' children indefinitely. She was walking to town with the children because she didn't want to use any of the gas in their old Ford but needed lids for canning. She was nervous because they already owed a tab, and she only had 4 pennies in her purse. She felt desperate, hopeless, and poor when she spied on a small rolled-up piece of paper with a rubber band. It turned out to be $3. She wrote about how she dusted off the money and carefully placed it in her purse, feeling like she had found a fortune and was transformed into a person of strength and hope. She held her head high when she stepped into the store and 'really splurged,' getting a dozen canning lids and 5 lbs. of sugar, salt, tobacco for the husband, and a .10 cent bag of candy for them all. She was thrilled and left with $1.17 in her pocket despite her shopping spree, as she described it. She wrote, *"Things never seemed so hard after that day. Maybe the economic conditions really improved a bit, or maybe it was the self-assurance and the new hope that little roll of dusty bills game me."*

Sometimes we need a little boost to get through challenging times. A little bit of money seemed like a fortune because every penny was precious back then. She just needed that money gift to renew her spirits and feel abundant, and that feeling was so strong that it lifted her up and transformed her situation.

We never want life to get this hard that a few dollars on the road become a great relief and salvation for the time being. But we need to practice wisdom in our use of money, and it wouldn't hurt us to return to a more straightforward way of living where we don't take things for granted. A life where we are grateful and content with less than what the typical American seems to require these days.

And so, I go deeply into my homemaking with new enthusiasm. I rest and do lazy things when I'm pooped out, and then my energy is renewed, and I roll up my sleeves. I could be a bit more productive, and I am when the time comes. But I read about these women getting up with the roosters and baking pies and loaves of bread before the family is up and tending to flocks of children, milking cows by hand, washing vast piles of clothes by hand in the winter, and making do with every scrap of paper and clothe. I say, "I could be a little more productive here."

I was thrifting last week. It turns out Goodwill is the place to go for Halloween costumes. They had at least five racks and some towers loaded with costumes of every kind, size, and age. I had told Sam he would have to think outside the box because his dream costume wouldn't just be handed to him. It turns out I was wrong because he found everything he wanted. He would tell you he manifested it for himself. Even Arjan, the anti-Halloween guy, found a SWAT team costume. I found quite a few treasures myself. A carved wooden statue that looks Tibetan now stands among my plants for only $15. I could not pass that up. I found Bundt cake pans and square cake pans, a cheese slicer (I hadn't seen one since childhood, very handy), a potato masher (my last one wound up in the sandbox), and some fantastic paintings and wall hangings for a few dollars. I rushed home and decorated and cooked the rest of the day. The day before, I went to the hospice down the street. They had 50% off, and I found some nice, colorful shirts, lovely new plates, and sweet little cups with flowers for only .25 cents that I'll use for my espresso machine.

I wanted some pretty plates and cups and had some pioneer woman sets in my Amazon cart for over a hundred dollars. I don't mind splurging now and then regarding our home and quality. I've learned my lessons by buying cheap stuff. I've also learned that some of the best stuff comes from the thrift store or a garage sale. So, I found my plates and cups for a few dollars at the hospice thrift, and I bought a big candle for a dollar. The thrift stores price up the candles, which is ridiculous because they want, say, six dollars for a used candle, and I could get a new, significant, scented one for that much at Walmart. I deleted my order from Amazon.

My greens are doing well in the plot in the side yard. The new trees survived the transplanting. The yard is filling up nicely, and I now enjoy looking out over the front and back yard more than ever. I filled up some blank spaces in the yard with the last tree haul. The garden looks more enchanting with the fruit trees in there. Bali and I decided to plant a few fruit trees in the garden as it gets almost too much sun in the summer, so the trees will help relieve that constant direct sunlight.

We will visit the godparents in the bay area to meet the grandbaby. The mother and baby live in the garden house with the godparents. I made two lasagnas last night, one for a visit and one for us. I was taking two, but this was a new recipe, and I couldn't wait to try it. We had lasagna and salad last night, and it was delicious. I had never used ricotta or cottage cheese before. It cut way down on the hard cheese and oil. I used very little meat as well, only a package. This is my first-time making freezer meals. In a week, I will make a huge batch of freezer meals. I have five reusable pans, one lasagna pan from the last store-bought Stouffers lasagna, two tin casserole pans in my Amazon cart, and two more bread pans. I'm looking at thrift stores, but bread and casserole pans are hard to find.

I've talked about cooking freezer meals, but I never do it. Now I'm serious about it. The last two Stouffers I purchased were chicken enchiladas and lasagna. The enchiladas upset my stomach for days. They have cut way back on the good ingredients and bulked up with rice or sauce. I used to get them for $9.99 at Grocery outlet, but they are now $20 for one. So, I can make all this cheaper, and I'll use quality ingredients. We come out healthier and more prosperous for it. I have $400 left this month for groceries, and I've made a list of ingredients I need from the store. I have a trip planned to WinCo one of these weekends then I'll set aside a couple of days to make the freezer meals and bake extra bread and granola bars. Arjan and Sam love when I cook like this. The kitchen is sunny and warm; jars and buckets are on the table, and mixing bowls filled with ingredients are on the counter. I have an espresso in the afternoon and play the radio in the pantry. Lately, our local station has been playing this old blue grass and old gospel. I feel very earthy kneading dough while listening to bluegrass.

We'll be going to the bay area on Sunday. Usually, we go up for the night or two nights, but I'm feeling so charmed with the home life that I found I only want to be gone a day. I want to get back to my big, soft bed and my dog children, wake to my stovetop espresso and my Pandora music. Arjan loves to travel and stay at other people's homes. Sam and I get homesick by nightfall. I'm eager to get back to the garden and the kitchen.

We found a money gift in our accounts this morning. I just read the story of the mother who found the $3 on the railroad tracks, and it transformed her from depressed to hopeful. I love that story. This morning I received an email with a link regarding the latest stimulus check the government is giving (because we need to print more money, right?). The gas prices have been high everywhere, especially in California, so the state gave us a check to make the difference. I check our account, and there it is. So, that is our gift, and I'll sit on this money egg for a bit and then use it for any needs and, of course, major stocking up on everything. WinCo, here I come!

Wednesday

I woke to the smell of bacon drifting down the street and into my opened window. There is something cozy about smelling fabric softener, coffee, or a hot meal when walking through the neighborhoods. You imagine a home well cared for, the inhabitants doing chores and brewing coffee for a busy day.

We had our trip to WinCo, and I still haven't put all the pantry items away. We spent $405—a bit more than last when I spent $349. The difference is that I bought a whole turkey, a large ham, two big bottles of Dawn, and a laundry basket. The meats and detergents can push up a price a bit. Besides that, I bought plenty of pantry stocking items. I spent two weeks making a list of everything I would need to complete the pantry. I thumbed through the mix cookbooks and watched Renea make freezer meals.

Yesterday I made three vegetarian lasagnas for the freezer. I even labeled them with a date and what they were! I feel like a grown-up homemaker now. I also made the Bisquick mix. I'm on a roll.

No matter how often or deeply I clean, the house never has that scrubbed clean look. It's an old house. It feels like I have a lot of rooms and nooks and crannies.

Later in the day...

I got the dishes done by 3 o'clock, and earlier I did knead bread and let it rise a couple of times, and I put a pot of black beans to simmer all day. I felt overwhelmed today. I had a shower, lotion, and dress and brewed a second coffee, but I would look about and feel so overwhelmed that I chose to sit with Sammy and watch a couple of movies. Sammy was very sick last night. He threw up a couple of times in a powerful way. We all ate the same stuff, so I'm not sure, but I pray I don't get it. We ate sliced pears and the Asian noodle soup I used to make. I use Won Ton broth bouillon, greens, and rice noodles, fortifying them in a light, warm, and brothy way. We wasted money on canned chicken soup that looked like everything Sam threw up last night. So, I made the greens and noodle soup, which was perfect.

This house needs some floor and baseboard scrubbing, and the carpet needs shampooing. That enthusiasm is somewhere within, but not today. I changed the linen on my bed and hung up the last laundry. This is all I got done and all I felt I could get done today.

Friday

It's 4 AM at last. I detest these mornings when I wake up at 2 AM and never fall asleep. I know the minute I lie down from my journey returning from the bathroom, I won't be sleeping any longer. It's a bummer. I have slept a handful of hours, and now I'll feel funky in the daytime. Dr. McDougall says we need less sleep as we age. I'm no doctor, but I can tell you I need eight hours a night to feel whole and mentally stable. Maybe 7 hours will do, but I need long, deep sleep. Maybe it's because the dogs and my bladder wake me several times a night.

A nighttime creature is out there making noises, and Molly is alert. That's all I need is her barking now.

Ok, well, let's hope she doesn't start drama. I won't let her out because I think it's a skunk. Or a raccoon. I can't deal with that right now. I want to write, Molly, until the sun comes up and I can legally move about the house. I have a cup of coffee, and by sunrise, I should be alert and ready for the day's activities, or I'll feel wilty and soggy.

Today's lineup of chores will start with rug shampooing. I can't wait. This shampooer is so light and easy to use. It was doing a great job. It acted funny last time, so we will see. I love seeing all the dirt pour out of the container, and the room smells so fresh and clean after the rug dries.

I watched a real tearjerker yesterday, **The Friend**. A writer tells the story of a man, Dane, who had become a treasured friend to him and his wife over the years. The wife has cancer, and Dane stays with them through her illness and passing. It was a long movie and started slowly. The characters are a bit blah, but as the story moves forward, the quiet strength from Dane is impressive, and the story is done in such a personal way, her death so lovingly and naturally done at home, that, well, it just makes you cry deeply. The saddest part is putting oneself in her shoes with two young girls and preparing to say goodbye to them and this life. When the wife learns she may only have six months left, she requests a sort of bucket list to the end. It is sad to realize that one day we may be out of time, and what would we do with that time? She wanted to finish a book series with her girls, reread her favorites, dye her hair blue, and sing on stage with Katy Perry.

How sweet and fragile life is; we are rushing about like rats on crack. We work, work, work and stay busy, busy, busy. To stop the slowdown is uncomfortable for most of us. The quarantine nearly killed some people just out of sheer boredom and isolation.

I think we should all act like time is limited and live like we would if we had to value our days.

I would love to be a better cook and housecleaner, but in the grand scheme, would I choose this for my last days? No, not sure what I'd do. Probably rewatch my favorite movies and sit in the forest with my family grasping the greatness of it all. And then we go home? We return to a world within worlds only to be reincarnated again? So, we are part of a great life, and we have these little experiences here on Earth and maybe on other planets. The adventure never ends.

On to other thoughts less deep. I spent $50 on cleaning supplies yesterday. I make my cleaning solutions, but I wanted to use store-bought carpet shampoo and store-bought bathroom cleaners. Vinegar and Dawn are great, but sometimes I want that actual detergent with the chemicals and smells, giving everything that scrubbed clean look and smell.

I'm preparing another two boxes for the Hospice Thrift store. The other day I felt so overwhelmed by a few chores. I had been a whirlwind of making the scratch mixes, freezer meals, daily cooking and baking, the trip to WinCo, and such. I then pooped out. I had nonperishables from our shopping trip everywhere still needing to be put away and a mound of dishes. We needed bread to start the evening meal, and laundry was piled on the couch. My floors were dirty, and the bathroom smelled. I felt so overwhelmed that I thought I would watch a movie and sit with my coffee until the drowning subsided. I started by putting on a pot of dried beans and setting up the dough. Beans and bread take hours. Starting a load of laundry sets the mood most days. Then I set about one task at a time and finished by the end of the day.

Some days it's all gravy, and other days it feels like shoveling the same pile. It's like poor Sampson rolling the rock uphill every day to repeat it again and again. No amount of decluttering or deep cleaning makes it go away. However, making these freezer meals and doing extensive shopping and cooking adventures reduces the hours spent driving, shopping, and cooking. Having less stuff tends to take care of saves hours, and if I deep clean when the energy is there, the rest of the month is a lot of tidying and minor upkeep.

My dryer went kapootz, and I chose not to replace it. What a commitment that was. I have to hang loads of damp clothes every time, even in the winter. I never have the option of getting lazy. I have, smartly, put a wooden wrack by the washer. However, I do smaller loads when hanging laundry inside. It seems a small task compared to our relatives that washed all their laundry by hand. I'm not complaining. Minor changes may seem irritating at first or lonely or monotonous. But eventually, we experience the hidden gifts. The therapy that comes out of a deep house cleaning or purging. The warmth of baking by hand in a winter kitchen. Or that moment of quiet we have when we hang clothes to dry. Homemaking has been very healing to me. Having a family has been transformative. In the corny words of Jerry McGuire (I know it was You, but I have a few people to cover here), "They complete me." And they are my boys, whom I'm sure I've had other lives with, my husband, our dogs, and all the life that now resides in our yard.

I made a lot of choices for my family, and thus far, the choices have improved the quality of our lives, so no one complains. I am no intuitive goddess with all the know-how we need. I don't always know what's suitable for the whole of us, but I can assess the negative impact of 'too much,' and there is a lot of that going around these days. We try to live like I remember families living in the 70s. People had simple homes and lives. Families had one car and small homes, and 5 o'clock news. Now we have three cars, huge empty suburban homes, and news 24/7 coming at us in all directions. I see the commercials, and I wonder how much longer the masses can live at this pace. Judging by the newest trends, many can no longer keep up and are beginning to opt-out of the race. We've heard this discussion before 'getting out of the rat race.' Every generation has this lament. And things keep getting faster and thicker with feedback and streaming info.

Many people are withdrawing somewhat. Tiny houses and minimalism are big right now. Frugal living, homesteading, gardening, and baking flourished during the quarantine. Homeschooling grew more these last two years than in the last twenty and continues to rise despite schools being open again. People are searching for a fulfilling lifestyle that is not like an all-consuming race that never ends. The Great Resignation has begun, and a new thing called Quiet Quitting. We all have to find the right pace.

For me, it was the 70s and early 80s that I felt the most nostalgic. It was a slower time with fewer interruptions. People gathered and talked. Phones hung permanently on the wall. Most homes only had one TV in the living room that sat in the corner. Movies like **Pretty In Pink**, **Some Kind Of Wonderful**, and **Breakfast Club** were my favorites, and leg warmers and flavored lip gloss. I feel like we sort of went back to that time, with the exception of the Hot Spot. We get the best of both worlds. You can mix and match time periods. Take a little from your great-grandma, a little from the present, and some from your childhood. What did you like about each decade, and do you have a thing for the past? Then incorporate it into your life. Take up canning and knitting or stay relatively modern but take up container gardening on your balcony. Maybe you do something crazy like quit your job, sell your condominium, and travel with the family. Maybe you and the family get rid of your Smart Phones, and one of you quits your job to stay home with the kids and homeschool.

It's fun to realize that we don't have to stay stuck and can change it all if we aren't happy.

I once had an uncle that ran every day. When asked why he ran every day, he replied, "then I don't have to think about it. I know that this is what I do every day." That keeps it simple. You start a good habit and do it daily without question or debate until it becomes as natural as brushing your teeth.

I'm watching **The Astronaut Farmer**. I love this moving because it is about a big dreamer who makes it happen in the end. The journey to the dream's fruition is fraught with struggles and tremendous obstacles. It makes you wonder how far is too far when pushing for your passions.

We have been without internet for a handful of days. We did get a treat yesterday when we found a Hot Spot on Bali's and my cell phones. We all plugged in greedily and devoured the serving right up. We only had 4 and 5 gigabytes, which translates to 8 or 10 hours of streaming movies. We had everything going; the boy's new computer arrived a couple of days ago, my laptop because

I wanted to edit with Grammarly Premium, then I put on Netflix to watch *The Week Of* with Adam Sandler and Chris Rock. We used up my hot spot gigabytes and then Balis by the night's end. We bound out of bed this morning with big plans. Mine was to finish a movie based on Bruce Lee and to edit this book all day with Grammarly. The boys had big plans with the new laptop. And there was no more hot spot. Ah, Sunday and all out, libraries closed, school on vacation. Nowhere to score a hot spot, and we were jonesing a bit. That's when I see the drug-like effects on us.

But the day blossomed into a lovely day with my family. We had no internet or TV except the old movies in our cupboard. I didn't feel much like reading, although I'm getting into a book on Unschooling, *The Unschooling Handbook* by *Mary Griffith*. I did read some of that with coffee this morning. Then Sam and I took miss Molly for a long walk. Sam and Arjan learned to play Solitaire. Sam asked to learn, and instead of putting him off, I stopped what I was doing and taught him right then, and he played for a long time, piquing Arjan's interest. I did very few chores slowly. I made the beds, washed a few dishes, wiped down counters and tables, took the laundry off the line, and even folded it as I took it down, saving myself future work. We ate leftover tuna casserole, sauteed frozen veggies, and the remaining ham. I froze the large ham bone for beans in the future.

Sam and I took the wagon and headed to town to find a yard sale we saw the flyer for that morning. We stopped at the corner market, bought sweet, icy slushies, and found the funky yard sale. We found a few free items on the streets and bought a few things from the yard sale. We strolled, enjoying our slushies, and Sam talked the whole way. He loves to talk. He's talking right now as I type. I've learned to type even better as a child talks at me. It's a mother/writer skill.

Bali and I got the pool covered for the season, and we ate and talked in our little sitting area under the pergola on the patio. Bali has been outside, weeding the driveway and cleaning up the patio. He loves being in the yard. He builds and plants things and works all day until it's dark. He is very proud of this land and loves working on it. He will make lots of toast and drink coffee all morning, spending time with us, and then he spends all day outside, even having his meals and afternoon coffee outside. I get it. Our yard is becoming thick and lush. All the trees we planted over my birthday week filled the garden and yards nicely. We will soon have our own forest in the next five years of planting.

My dream is to buy the small forest down the street and have enough money to have it maintained and cared for, turned into a haven for everyone on this street and the apartments. We'd have goats in there and thin out the trees, have the junk hauled off, and have colorful signs painted by children to take care of the forest, trash cans, doggie bags, and benches. We'd have little spiritual sanctuaries here and there and a large gate at the entrance with all the charm.

If I made millions, I don't know that I'd move. Maybe I would take us all to another state and town. I can see that. Or I'd fix this place up and my little forest down the street. I'd want to make the money count. Donate to projects and make my little forest the neighborhood forest. I'd love to higher all sorts of people to do all sorts of work. I can see us moving, though. We are already exploring other places, and I see another town and forest in my future. Maybe only in my mind.

Friday

The boys and I dressed up and walked to town. We decided to go out for lunch and chose a popular Mexican restaurant downtown. The patio area is a courtyard and is so charming I feel like I'm in another country. We ordered three meals from the lunch menu and sodas. The total came to over $80. I choked a little upon looking. With tip, it was almost a hundred. That is a week's worth of groceries. It was the first time in a long time that I felt buyer's remorse. I'm not cheap and like to go out and have fun, but the price for the small, bland meals was depressing. The meals were on big plates, but the food was spread out to look like more. It was just a spoon of beans and rice; they used lots of shredded lettuce to fill things up. The meals would have cost me a dollar or two each to make at home and would have tasted far better. The food didn't taste good, and I asked for bean and cheese enchiladas and only got two cheese enchiladas with barely any cheese. I don't get why they are so sparse with the beans?! What a bummer. I'm still a bit upset. I get that there is inflation, but this is too much, and at one time, $80 would have bought a fantastic meal for four people and drinks, even appetizers. Not three pathetic lunch menu meals and three sodas. We didn't even get straws, and our soup order was botched. To add insult to injury, the service sucked, and a fly kept hovering about our table! I felt cheated.

I called Bali on our walk back to confess to blowing a hundred, and he was kind. We talked about home cooking and how people go out to eat and exclaim, "What good food, what a great meal!" He says it's because so many people don't cook at home, so they don't know what truly good food taste like. I agree. Even when my cooking is off it is better than what I get out at the restaurants.

I think inflation has some effect, but the restaurants and the factory-premade meals have skyrocketed their prices and cut way back on quality and main ingredients. They are using cheap fillers like rice or lettuce to bulk things up. Even the service has gone down. I feel like there are many layers here; inflation, worker dissatisfaction, price gauging, and affordability of employees are becoming a struggle. Living costs are becoming a struggle with gas prices and housing costs.

But there is hope. If you can find affordable housing, the rest is easy. If you cook at home, you will eat like a king for a fraction of the cost of going out to eat or buying premade meals from the frozen aisle. For example, I bought a Stouffers lasagna the other day, costing me $20. They used to be $12 to $14, but the cost increased recently. The quality was not the same. Less of everything but pasta and sauce. It also gave us upset stomachs. The quality of the ingredients are also declining. I assume the food companies are getting far cheaper ingredients, which means more chemicals and pesticides, factory farming, and GMO's, and then they add more sugar and salt to mask the taste.

I bought all my ingredients at WinCo and made three freezer lasagnas. Quality ingredients and made with love. I was generous with all the ingredients, and they made big lasagnas. Total cost? $8.78 or maybe a little more, as I didn't add in the seasoning cost. This is over $11 in savings on each lasagna. These amounts add up over a week, a month, and years.

As inflation, gas, and housing rise in cost, we become more creative and have to think outside the box. And we can still have an excellent quality of life on a budget.

20th Verse

Give up learning and you will be free
From all your cares.
What is the difference between yes and no?
What is the difference between good and evil?
Must I fear what others fear?
Should I fear desolation
When there is abundance?
Should I fear darkness
When that light is shining everywhere?
In spring, some go to the park and climb the terrace,
But I alone am drifting, not knowing where I am.
Like a newborn babe before it learns to smile,
I am alone, without a place to go.
Most people have too much;
I alone seem to be missing something.
Mine is the indeed the mind of an ignoramus
In its unadulterated simplicity.
I am but a guest in this world.
While others rush about to get things done,
I accept what is offered.
I alone seem foolish,
Earning little, spending less.
Other people strive for a fame;
I avoid the limelight,
Preferring to be left alone.
Indeed, I seem like an idiot:
No mind, no worries.

I drift like a wave on the ocean.
I blow as aimless as the wind.
All men settle down in their grooves;
I alone am stubborn and remain outside.
But wherein I am most different from others is
In knowing to take sustenance from the great Mother!

~Tao Te Ching

And we are back into a beautiful Fall. It rained in September, so we have tender green grass and brilliant colors of deep orange, warm yellows, and rich reds. The days are cooler, and Halloween is this weekend. I've rolled up the beach towels, shoved them against the front and back door, and pulled out the Presto Heaters. I sit here with an old sweater that needs to be retired, but it is so comfortable I keep sowing up the holes that sprout here and there.

Aunt M is coming for the weekend, and we have been invited to the Godparent's home for Thanksgiving. I told them how we don't really do Thanksgiving or most holidays now. We celebrate Seasons and the Mother; however, if we are invited to a celebration of any kind, we are happy to oblige. I also heard from an old friend and former coworker who later became my first editor. She sent me a Blue Mountain ecard and kind words. I feel blessed by old and new friends these days. A far cry from the days of quarantine when I felt like everyone had disappeared or kept their distance out of fear. Humans were afraid of humans back then. I know this will sound crazy, but sometimes I feel nostalgic about the quarantine. It was hard on so many levels, yet there was this comfort in being home, and everyone was finding ways to cope by gardening, baking, and going within to heal and explore their very souls. Streets were calm; trails were quiet. It was also a bit creepy; towns were dead, and it felt like the zombie apocalypse the boys love to play video games. Good and bad. Thus is life. Maybe it's a twisted sort of nostalgia.

Some friends and family disappeared during that time. I didn't say it, but in my heart, I just let them go because I had no idea what the future would bring and if people would recover their senses and lose the fear that gripped them. I had to move on and build a kind world around my family and a haven within our home. Now we are content and have a sweet life without needing too many relationships. We have a few friendships that grew strong and deep during that time, and it turns out that a few choice relationships are all a person needs to feel connected and complete. We learned to be strong and independent.

But you don't need another quarantine to have that experience again. We never went back to before. I keep to myself and love my own company. I enjoy being home and having more projects than hours in the day. The boys have part-time school and social life, so that is good. That's all I care about: they have friends and a life outside the home. I don't need it or want it anymore. I had a busy life outside the home for decades. I have earned the quiet of my kitchen and long days of tasks and pondering.

Our Year Thus Far

In September 2021, I began turning off the internet modem during the day. We played and worked, and I journaled by hand in my composition books. By January 2022, we removed the internet from our house and began a little exploration of living quietly without the world's distractions. We lasted seven months. We now borrow the Hot Spot from the library. For those who don't understand what that is, it is a small modem that you plug in and get free internet in your house. We love it. Too much. But it is the modern day, and the internet can offer so many good things if you navigate carefully.

There are many unimaginable gifts when you shut down the internet and turn off the TV. You find parts of yourself lost in the clutter of the soul's closet. You take up old hobbies long forgotten. I started drawing again some forty years later. My pictures look like a kid drew them, and rightly so, I stopped drawing at age eleven, and now I'm fifty-two and taking up ink pens and pads again. I returned to reading voraciously as I used to before I parked myself in front of YouTube daily. I sat in the quiet of mornings and wept with old wounds that had a chance to come forward in the space that was now created.

Without distractions, we took up our toys, books, and pens and worked on old hobbies and games. We played chess instead of video games and read novels instead of watching the fear-mongering on the internet that has blossomed since the plague and quarantines. We found soothing and healing in the forest and peace in our little hundred-year-old house.

I have become like our society with rushing and competing. I have suffered the ailments of comparing and judgment. But by unplugging from the Matrix, I got to know myself again and see how precious a slow and humble life is. I don't need fame or fortune, I have treasures in my home and with family, and I have many gifts that I'm blessed with, such as my love of writing and reading. My children and I bonded deeply during this time, and I'm glad I journaled all this so when we forget, we will reread this and remember to shut the TV and laptops off and reconnect to each other and the Mother and Spirit. Ultimately, our Mother and Spirit feed our souls and nourish our lives.

Per my eldest son's request, we will return the Hot Spot after a glorious month of being plugged in in a couple of days. I know all the wonderment and benefits of this, but I still want to hold onto the little modem with all my claws and not let go. I'm watching movies on Amazon Prime and Weight Watcher recipes on YouTube. I have a few new channels I'm crazy about right now. The booktubers and authortube and WW channels are my favorites right now. I get on my elliptical and put in an hour of exercise while learning new recipes and watching book reviews. I've also started watching **Sweet Merry Home** to inspire my cleaning days. I watch **Allisonpaiges** and other booktubers to fill up my To Read shelf on Goodreads. Sigh. I will miss it.

However, I've prepared! I have ordered every season of **Downton Abby** from the library, and last night I watched a movie on Prime about the life of Celine Dion. Not the best movie, but I was reminded of how much I loved her songs, so I ordered three of her greatest hits CDs. My radio has a CD player, so yay for that!

I will celebrate finishing this book by making a pudding and graham cracker cake (Weight Watchers approved) and take some time off to read the stack of novels from the library (and more coming in daily, yikes!). I will have a readathon and a Celine Dionathon. Then I will start a new journey. Hopefully, I will return to my fictional writing in earnest with some Downton Abby in the background.

Oh, and I have a Christmas tree to put up soon. Oh my, lots of good stuff on the way.

My only hope for this book is to inspire and give hope. It will be wonderful if it encourages a few people to seek a better life.

Visit me at **Coffee With Kate** and share your journey with us all.

Printed in Great Britain
by Amazon

18587843R00221